THE
INTERNET
HANDBOOK
FOR
Writers,
Researchers,
AND
Journalists

2000/2001 Edition

D0878720

THE INTERNET HANDBOOK

FOR

Writers,

2000/2001 Edition

Researchers,

AND

Journalists

Mary McGuire, Linda Stilborne,
Melinda McAdams, Laurel Hyatt

THE GUILFORD PRESS

NEW YORK   LONDON

To Jack. I am forever grateful for your love and support.
— L. STILBORNE

For N'Gai, Noah, Scoot, and Tracy.
— M. MCADAMS

Published in the United States by The Guilford Press
A Division of Guilford Publications Inc.
72 Spring Street, New York, NY 10012
www.guilford.com

First published in Canada by Trifolium Books, Inc.
Copyright © 2000 Trifolium Books Inc.

Last digit is print number: 9 8 7 6 5 4 3 2 1

Library of Congress Cataloging-in-Publication Data

The internet handbook for writers, researchers, and journalists / Mary McGuire ... [et al.].—
2000/2001 ed.
p. cm.
Includes bibliographical references and index.
ISBN 1-57230-550-9
1. Computer network resources. 2. Authorship—Computer network resources. I. McGuire, Mary, 1956–

ZA4201 .I566 2000
025.04—dc21   99-056397

Editing/production coordination: Francine Geraci
Cover and text design/layout: Jack Steiner Graphic Design

Printed in Canada

Acknowledgments

The authors and publisher would like to thank the Unisys Corporation for granting permission to include in our book its excellent Glossary, "Information Superhighway Driver's Manual: Key Terms and Concepts That Will Put You in the Passing Lane." Special thanks to James B. Senior and Michael Heck of Unisys Corporation for providing us with all the material we needed on such a timely basis, and to Jim Chiponis for his delightful cartoons.

stay on top of what's on the net...on the net

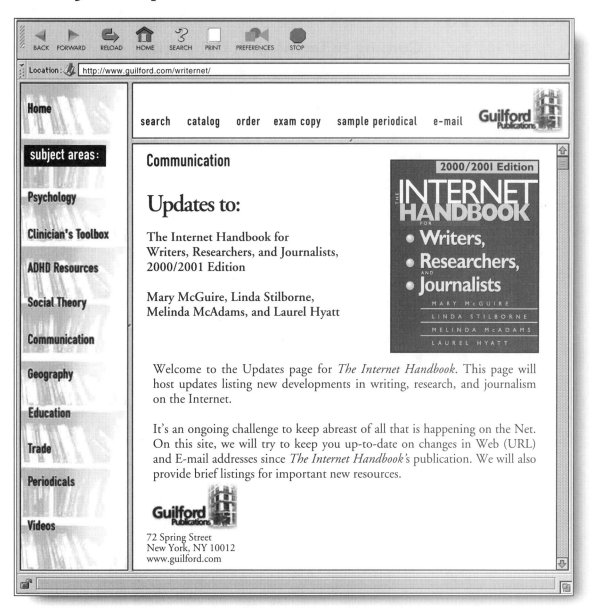

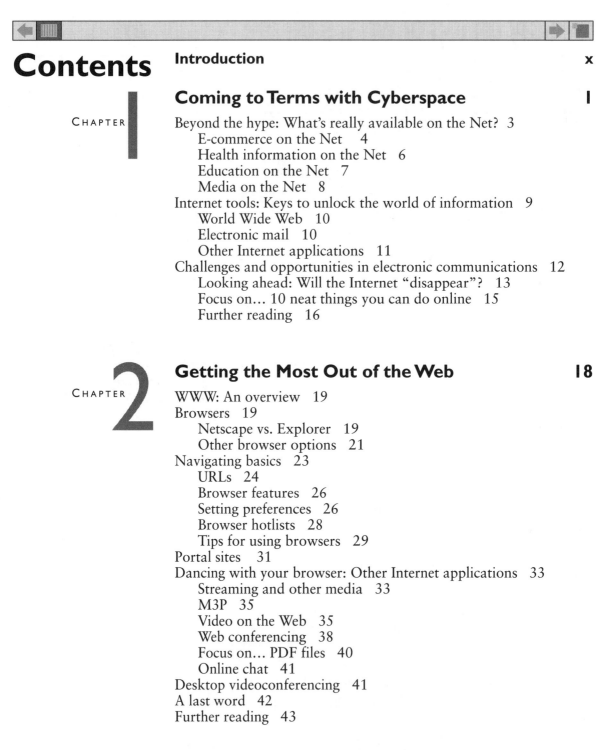

Contents

Introduction

The Internet has dramatically changed the lives of writers, researchers, and journalists. In the three years since the first edition of this book was published, the Net has gone from being a useful tool to one that is now essential for media professionals — more powerful than the telephone and the word processor put together.

The Internet Handbook for Writers, Researchers, and Journalists, 2000/2001 Edition, is for people who want to use the Internet with skill and ease.

In simplest terms, information professionals find things out, check them out, and tell others about them in clear and compelling ways. The Internet has changed how we do all three of those things — and it will undoubtedly continue to do so as it grows and matures.

Skillfully used, the Internet gives writers, researchers, and reporters access to a much wider range of information and expert sources much more quickly than any other medium. Instead of going to the library to find the latest government policy on health care, you can stay at your desk and bring it up on your own computer screen with just a few keystrokes. Instead of scouring local newspapers for stories on a topic you are researching, you can search hundreds of newspapers from around the world in just seconds by visiting the right Web sites. Instead of spending all day on the phone trying to find the leading experts on right-wing militia groups in the United States, you can post a query to the proper mailing list and gets lots of useful leads from people with first-hand knowledge of the issue. Instead of playing telephone tag with someone who has information you need, you can use e-mail to communicate more efficiently. The Internet also provides an abundance of new opportunities to publish your work for a worldwide audience.

This edition of *The Internet Handbook for Writers, Researchers, and Journalists* has been completely updated and revised. Like the previous edition, it is designed to help you, as an information professional, to understand the Internet and use it efficiently and effectively to find the information, services, and experts you need, when you need them. This revised edition includes up-to-date information and advice on:

- using the newest versions of e-mail and browser software
- choosing from the newer multimedia applications, such as streaming media, Web conferencing, and desktop videoconferencing

- developing online search strategies for the best, and fastest, results
- navigating the latest, most powerful search tools
- managing information overload
- writing for an online audience
- creating your own Web pages (something you won't find in most other guides to the Internet).

The Internet Handbook for Writers, Researchers, and Journalists, 2000/2001 Edition, is written especially for people who are relatively new to the Internet or for current users who simply want to use it more efficiently and effectively. It is written in plain English on the assumption that writers, researchers, and journalists don't have the time or inclination to become computer geeks.

Chapters 1 and 2 give you the information you need start exploring the Internet using the two most important applications — electronic mail and the Web browser. If you've already made it that far, Chapter 3 will help you develop and refine your search strategies and techniques, using all the latest search tools.

The chapters that follow give an overview of the most helpful Internet resources for writers, researchers, and journalists: the "undiscovered Web" of database, library, government, and media sources (Chapter 4); a comparison of popular e-mail programs, together with online sources for locating experts, newsgroups, and mailing lists (Chapter 5). Chapter 6 tells you how to meet the two biggest challenges of online research: (a) not becoming overwhelmed by all the information and (b) sifting the wheat from the chaff. Chapter 7 contains the basics of mastering HTML, tips for writing effectively for online readers, and other invaluable information for publishing on the Web.

Throughout the book, you'll find these other useful features:

FYI. Helpful hints and practical suggestions for learning about the Net and making the most of your time online.

tech.ease. Technical points that are not essential, yet are useful to know about.

Focus On... A look at special Internet applications and technologies, showing how to get the most from them quickly and easily.

INFOnuggets. Facts and figures that illustrate current trends and offer insights into Internet life.

Resources on the Web. Our unique, expanded Appendix of Web sites puts hundreds of professional and general-interest Internet resources at your fingertips.

Appendices. Here you'll find quick references for citing online sources and dealing with copyright issues. Included is the Associated Press (1997) policy for electronic news gathering.

Glossary. For quick reference, check the handy glossary of Internet terms in the back of the book.

The Internet Handbook for Writers, Researchers, and Journalists, 2000/2001 Edition, is chock-full of useful advice for anyone who wants to know how to locate the best resources of the world's largest library without leaving home. We hope this book and these resources help you to become an even better writer, researcher, editor, journalist, or student than you already are.

Coming to Terms with Cyberspace

CHAPTER

❝[My problem with] the Internet is that it's about facts and figures and information. But without the flesh and blood and the breathing that goes on, who am I talking to? What do they look like? Is it a multitude? Are there 25 people there? … That part — the human touch, that's what's missing.**❞**

— From "An Interview with Studs Terkel," *Mother Jones*,
September/October 1995, p. 22.
http://bsd.mojones.com/mother_jones/SO95/eastman.html

Studs Terkel's feelings still ring true for many people — despite the many new sophisticated applications that are now available on the Net.

The Internet still isn't everyone's favorite hangout. A recent study indicated that a growing segment of the population who have tried the Internet have discontinued use. In 1999, 27.7 million adults said goodbye to the Net, and only about a third of these past users expect to go online again any time soon ("CyberDialogue study shows U.S. Internet audience growth slowing," *CyberDialogue,* November 1999, www.cyberdialogue.com/index_4.html). It's not surprising that some people have become a bit disenchanted with the Net, though most of us are still reserving judgment. We just want to know more about it.

Most of us already know that the Internet is a great new medium for information and communication. But even experienced cybernauts are often torn between appreciation for the many positive things about the Internet and frustration over the negatives.

Here are some of the things we *like* to do on the Net:

- visit virtual museums
- buy books
- hear about jobs
- do research
- network with other professionals
- get news from around the world tailored to our interests
- take courses through distance education
- consult with educators, academics, health professionals, and other experts
- find health information

- rediscover old friends and make new ones
- find out about restaurants, vacation destinations, and other travel information
- check schedules for buses, trains, and airplanes
- get the latest government information
- let the government know what we think.

And here are some things we *dislike* about the Internet:

- reading text on a screen
- pop-up ads
- graphics that take forever to load
- Web addresses that are constantly changing
- finding 300 messages in our e-mail box
- finding that 200 of those messages are much longer than they need to be (some folks have not yet grasped the difference between e-mail and letters!)
- dealing with people in "not-real time"
- having to distinguish between "real time" and some other kind of time
- flaming and other forms of electronic nastiness
- the sense that, because things change so quickly on the Internet, we have to struggle to keep up just so we won't be left behind.

If you are currently using the Internet, you can probably add to both these lists.

Those who have spent time on the Internet often feel overwhelmed by its vastness. Even though it has been around for a number of years (the millennium marked its thirty-first anniversary), the Internet is still evolving. It is multifaceted and complex, and although it has changed radically in the last few years, it remains a vast, uncharted frontier. It's great fun to explore, but there are also bound to be challenges — and even a few unpleasant surprises — along with the thrills.

Despite that, there are solid reasons for spending time learning more about how to use the Net. If you are a professional researcher, a writer, a journalist, an editor, or a student, you can't afford not to use the Internet efficiently.

INFOnugget

Q. Who invented the Web, anyway?

A. Tim Berners-Lee. In 1989 Berners-Lee was working at CERN, a high-energy physics lab in Switzerland, when he got the idea for a system that would link scientific documents via the Internet, making them available to researchers worldwide. By the end of 1990, the Web consisted of one server at the CERN lab in Switzerland and one file, the CERN phone book. Today, the number of files is approaching 30 million and there are more than 200,000 servers. Berners-Lee currently heads the World Wide Web Consortium in Cambridge, Massachusetts.

In the end, two things will help to overcome some of the difficulties that people sometimes encounter with the Internet — one is the technology itself, which is constantly improving; the other is a willingness to devote some time to learning. The Internet makes available a great mix of information, services, and tools. It makes sense that exploring and learning to use these should require an investment of time up front.

> "More and more journals are reviewed and published electronically, giving faster turnaround and quicker feedback. I can reach a researcher directly, and perhaps get an answer within an hour. ... Networks are terrific.
>
> "On the other hand, I've watched researchers waste morning after morning, reading irrelevant net news, plowing through e-mail and fine tuning their screen savers."
>
> — *Clifford Stoll*, Silicon Snake Oil: Second Thoughts on the Information Highway. *New York: Doubleday, 1995, p. 91.*

The Internet Handbook for Writers, Researchers, and Journalists will show you how to use the Internet efficiently as a research tool. It's not necessary to understand everything about the Internet, but it is important to be able to select and make use of the kinds of features and resources that will be of most value to *you*.

The first step is to get an overview of what's available on the Net. The second is to start learning about the tools that will get you where you want to go.

CHAPTER HIGHLIGHTS

- ■ **Beyond the hype: What's really available on the Net?**
- ■ **Internet tools: Keys to unlock the world of information**
- ■ **Challenges and opportunities in electronic communications**
- ■ **Looking ahead: Will the Internet "disappear"?**

Beyond the hype: What's really available on the Net?

The Internet is an extensive system of interlinked yet independent computer networks. In less than two decades, the Internet has evolved from a highly specialized communications network used mostly for military and academic purposes into a massive electronic bazaar. Today, the Internet includes:

- academic and government computers
- computers from research institutions
- commercial agencies and financial institutions
- computerized library catalogs and information databases
- community-based computers (sometimes called *freenets*)

Technogeek

- diverse small, local computers (called *bulletin boards*) where technogeeks are known to hang out
- network service providers (such as America Online).

Anyone who has an account on one of these computers can send electronic mail throughout the network and access resources from thousands of other computers on the network. Virtually any corner of the globe is now as close as your own backyard.

Because of the free-wheeling culture of the Internet and its overall lack of structure and external controls, it can be challenging to determine where the real value is. However, those who take time to learn about it soon discover that the Internet is a microcosm of our society.

The following "snapshots" of daily activities on the Internet reveal a cyberworld that is as dynamic, varied, and controversial as the world reflected in print or broadcast news. They also suggest the richness of the Internet as a source of information for students and researchers, as well as its potential as a tool for writers and journalists with its wealth of contacts, story ideas, and background information.

E-commerce on the Net

Many experts see e-commerce as the fastest-growing area of the Internet and expect that within a few years, the Net will transform the traditional marketplace.

Your local bagel shop may not be online, but hundreds of thousands of other businesses are. Yahoo!, a popular Internet portal site, lists more than 527,036 companies on the Internet, and this list includes only the most prominent. While books, music, computer products, toys, high-end gifts, gourmet foods, and travel bargains are a few of the hottest-selling items on the electronic marketplace, you can also find more esoteric items, such as bear repellent, brooms, and ear candles. There are legal firms, advertising agencies, car dealerships, financial institutions, publishers, and bookstores. (And, yes, there are even a few bagel shops: Bagel Oasis in New York will ship bagels to your home or office.)

Amazon.com (pronounced "Amazon-dot-com"), one of a number of virtual bookstores on the Net, is an example of a particularly successful online business. It's located — sort of — in Seattle, Washington, but its services are available almost anywhere around the globe. Amazon claims to offer more than five times as many titles as its nearest (non-cyber) competitor, so it is not surprising that one patron managed to locate two books that he had been seeking for five years, while another successfully tracked down a book from the 1970s (which arrived with its original price tag still in place!). Amazon has expanded its online product, and recently formed a partnership with Sotheby's, the famous upscale auction

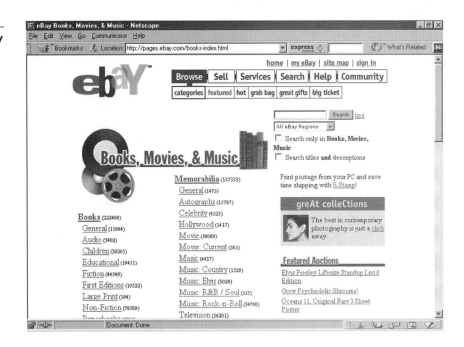

house. Now at Amazon — in addition to books, videos, software, and CDs — you might be able to pick up a late eighteenth-century Italian painted armchair or a nifty pair of Chinese Wucai jars.

The Internet has reached a critical mass in terms of the number of people connecting from home, and it has now become a viable and rapidly expanding arena for buying and selling. The year 1999 saw a doubling of the number of Internet users (from 35% to 70%) who have purchased products or services online or who plan to do so soon. Online auctions, such as eBay and Bid.com, represent almost 30% of all online transactions. One analyst predicts that the value of goods and services sold through Internet auctions will be close to $129 billion by the year 2002.

On the Internet, researchers and journalists can also tap into the latest economic, business, or stock market news. They can talk to small business owners or sample discussion groups on controversial topics, such as the advantages and disadvantages of a flat tax or the future of work. There are many resources providing information on setting up a small business or on telecommuting — two hot business trends.

Health information on the Net

The Internet is a terrific source for the latest medical news, and for sharing medical opinions and research. There are an estimated 500 health-related discussion groups on the Internet, and many more health resources on the World Wide Web.

Premier health agencies such as the Mayo Clinic, the U.S. Centers for Disease Control, and Health Canada provide research information online. Journalists can find out about exciting new areas of research, such as DNA vaccines, or they can consult medical specialists to verify information about bone marrow transplants. Researchers are able to access study results and health information databases.

Audiophiles may prefer to keep abreast of the latest developments in medicine by tuning into **The Health Show (National Productions, www.wamc.org/natprod.html)** or listening to a lecture broadcast from the George Washington University Medical Center.

Alternative health information can also be found in abundance on the Net. In fact, practitioners involved in alternative approaches to health care have benefited greatly from being able to use the Internet as a resource for sharing information and lobbying for their discipline. The Internet makes available information about acupuncture, chiropractors, herbs, vitamins, iridology, gemstone therapy, and even a traditional favorite — leeches.

Increasingly, scientists and researchers use the Internet to share information and ideas. A project from the National Library of Medicine has produced a spectacular resource consisting of 21,000 pictures of the human body. The **Visible Human Project (www.nlm.nih.gov/research/visible/visible_human.html)** provides a complete, anatomically detailed, three-dimensional representation of the human body. The project is, among other things, a prototype for the development and dissemination of a medical image library.

At MIT, experiments are underway using computer-assisted surgery (the computers are located a short distance away from the operating table). With the anticipated explosive growth in fiber-optic telecommunications, in which data is transmitted at astonishing speeds through an incredibly thin stream of light, remote surgery will soon be possible over a significant distance. The Internet is truly a gateway to understanding the latest developments in science and medicine. It is also at the heart of new scientific breakthroughs.

Education on the Net

While there are hundreds of useful resources for teachers and nearly 6,000 elementary and secondary schools posting information on the Internet, the power of this technology is particularly evident in two areas of alternative education: distance education and home schooling. In 1998, the American Council on Education estimated that 85% of "traditional" colleges and universities either offered, or would soon offer, distance-accessible courses. At **NewPromise.com** (**www.caso.com/home/home.phtml**) you can search for accredited online courses, apply for financial aid, buy textbooks, and kick-start your career.

> "The sleek towers and domed halls of Singapore's Temasek Polytechnic offer the services students dream of — state-of-the-art libraries and data bases, easy course registration, tutorials, study guides, financial advice for tuition and more — all without hours or energy wasted waiting in line. If seeing is believing, why not wander over to the students' center for a quick visit? A few keystrokes on the Internet and you are there."
>
> — *Amy Otchet, "WWW.$$$@ONLINE.EDUCATION,"* UNESCO Courier, *October 1998.*

Hungry Minds (**www.hungryminds.com/**) has taken a slightly unorthodox approach in initiating People's U. Here you can take

Blackboard.com is an online learning service that allows educators quick and easy setup and delivery of courses online. Blackboard's course sites allow instructors to post learning materials, hold class discussions, and even issue tests online. You can try out the service for free, or sign up for a course at: **www.blackboard.com/**

FIGURE 1-2
People's U.

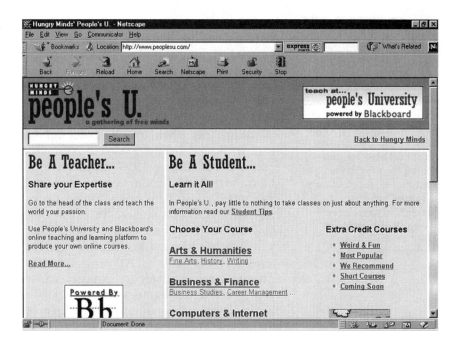

classes on just about anything for just about nothing, and anyone with an area of expertise and an interest in online education is welcome to teach a course.

SmartPlanet.com (**www.smartplanet.com/sphome.asp**) and InternetCollege.com (**www.internetcollege.com/**) are also good sources for finding out about free or inexpensive courses.

Electronic campuses are open twenty-four hours a day, seven days a week, and online courses are available in almost everything: Advanced Composition, Macroeconomics, African Elephants, Urban Shamanism.

Students from around the world can enroll in online courses. Some may use them to supplement courses from local institutions, while professionals pursuing life-long learning opportunities value the flexibility of distance learning. There are even a number of primary and secondary schools now offering high school courses over the Internet.

Similarly, the Internet has become a major resource for home schoolers, who can connect to courses, online tutors, and learning services. Once isolated in their own communities, such students can now participate in live online discussion groups, projects, and activities with other kids being schooled at home.

If you are a journalist or a social science researcher, you will be intrigued by the broad social changes signaled by this kind of growth. Undoubtedly, the Internet will fuel even greater growth in alternative and distance learning in the years ahead.

Media on the Net

No area has been more profoundly affected by the Internet than the media. Traditional print and broadcast sources are now reinventing themselves online. Change is further fueled as existing print and broadcast agencies merge, and media conglomerates compete with telephone companies for dominance on the information highway.

Radio has been on the Internet since 1993. The first-ever Internet video broadcast of a rock concert featured the Rolling Stones in November 1994. In just a few years, audio and video on the Internet have become commonplace. In 1999, an estimated 170 million video streams were served up over the Internet, with Paul McCartney at The Cavern in Liverpool attracting 5,000,000 Web viewers.

There are several hundred newspapers on the Net, as well as news services such as AP and Reuters. News is available on the Internet from over eighty countries in the world. **NewsDirectory. com** (**www.newsdirectory.com/**) lists over 8,200 print publications that now maintain an active presence on the Web. This total does not include the hundreds of publications that exist only online.

FIGURE 1-3

Salon is a popular online magazine.

To sample the online press, try these popular online magazines:

Hotwired
http://hotwired.lycos.com/

The Onion
www.theonion.com/

Salon
www.salon.com/

Slate Magazine
www.slate.com/

The online versions of many publications (also called *cybergeists*) usually give you a sampling of their latest issue and sometimes offer complete back issues. These publications also provide online links that relate to current features, invite dialogue, offer online interviews with authors or guest "speakers," and in some cases facilitate discussion groups related to topics of interest to readers.

Increasingly, publications on the Internet are developing multimedia formats that integrate text, sound, graphics, and animation. Journalists can use the Net to access stock photos, and photojournalists can transmit their photos almost instantaneously using electronic communications. One journalist explains that these days, an editor can receive a picture from a photographer in the field, view it, and in the next instant request a different angle for a photo shoot that's taking place halfway around the world.

Internet tools: Keys to unlock the world of information

Journalists and researchers need to know more about the Internet than simply how to find information and contacts. They also need to know about the social and economic trends and changes represented in the day's events. They need to understand the role that the Internet increasingly plays in giving them access to databases for background information and as an important source for verifying facts.

Students, too, are expected to develop an up-to-date awareness of many different fields as they pursue a diploma or a degree. Many on-campus classes are now complemented by online Internet discussions, while more and more students also use the Internet to work on team projects.

The Internet is becoming a virtual work environment. Freelance writers and editors will find many new opportunities by learning about telecommunications technologies and incorporating new media into their work lives. The editor of one widely distributed high-tech weekly is able to work from the tranquillity of her home by the seaside in Nova Scotia — far removed from the hectic offices of the agency that sends her a regular paycheck.

Media professionals also have a substantial contribution to make in helping to shape the online world. Journalists in particular will appreciate becoming actively involved in the creation of a new medium that has the potential to reach millions of people around the globe.

Keeping up with technology makes this possible. As with any learning venture, success depends on mastering the basics. The two biggest applications of Internet technology are still the World Wide Web and electronic mail — but like everything on the Net, these established applications continue to change.

World Wide Web

The World Wide Web is a vast collection of text, graphics, sound, and increasingly, video files. With special software called a Web browser you can view the material on the Web by pointing the cursor and clicking your mouse button. Among the millions of Web pages you will find up-to-the minute news stories, online museum exhibits (where you can view panoramic images and walk through three-dimensional exhibits), art gallery displays, government information and services, distance learning courses, weather maps, huge databases, online auctions, online banking, and interactive computer games, to name just a few possibilities. You can also use a Web browser as a communications tool — for example, to send electronic mail or to participate in online discussions.

Technologies such as Web conferencing (in which messages are posted to the Web for ongoing discussions) are cropping up everywhere. And a programming language called Java, which delivers interactive applications to your desktop, has greatly enhanced the once relatively static presentation of text and graphics on the Web.

Electronic mail

Electronic mail rivals the Web as the most common Internet application; some consider it the most powerful application on the Net. E-mail lets you communicate with anyone who has an Internet address. It allows you to send and receive individual messages, subscribe to electronic newsletters and information updates, and participate in group discussions. Many people with limited Internet access rely on electronic mail to obtain online publications, software, and even information from Web pages. With the advent of "smart phones," which let you access e-mail messages without a computer, the use of e-mail will become even more commonplace.

E-mail attachments let you send and receive files. Submitting your résumé as an e-mail attachment is now a common way to apply for jobs. With the newest software, e-mail is now also a way to send colorful Web pages and distribute audio and video clips.

For journalists, electronic mail can be a method for making contacts with experts, conducting interviews, and networking with colleagues. Many researchers use electronic mail contacts to conduct surveys or focus groups and to locate information sources.

Through electronic mail, researchers, writers, and students can also join worldwide discussion groups. There are close to 40,000 different discussion groups on the Internet. Participants use them to keep abreast of professional news, to gain background on particular topics, and to pursue personal interests. Journalists might join JOURNET, a discussion group for journalism educators, or CARR-L, which discusses the use of computers in journalism. YAFICT-L offers writing tips, market possibilities, workshops, and personal support for writers of young adult fiction. An Internet mailing address gives you access to discussion groups in business, politics, arts, health, humanities, science, nature, and recreation. Today, Internet newsgroups and listservers are valuable communications tools. (We discuss newsgroups and listservers in detail in Chapter 5.)

Other Internet applications

Although the Web and electronic mail are currently the two most important technologies on the Internet, there are other Internet tools as well. Most of these are accessible using just your Web browser, although some require more specialized software. (Web browsers and related applications are described in Chapter 2.)

Online chat and conferencing. It is possible to participate in real-time text communications on the Internet by using a "chat" environment such as Yahoo Chat or ChatAbout from About.com. These give you access to *chat rooms*, where users engage in social conversation or take part in scheduled events, such as online discussions with politicians or best-selling authors. You can join in, or just "lurk" (observe) as participants use their keyboards to talk about the latest equipment for backpacking or to brush up on their Italian.

Audio and video technologies. The Internet offers other increasingly sophisticated communications possibilities. Using the audio

You can start your own e-mail newsletter or discussion list at **Topica (www.topica. com/)**. Lists can be private or public. This service, which is currently free, even maintains an archive of list-servers.

INFOnugget

Forrester Research predicts that by 2003 there will be 27.4 million homes in North America with high-speed Internet connections. This is roughly two-thirds of the current number of dial-up accounts.

features of an instant messaging service or the latest voice-over-Internet technologies such as Dialpad or Visitalk, which allow you to dial free long-distance calls through the Internet, the computer is emerging as a replacement for traditional telephone service.

With newer, very high-speed modems now available and the latest desktop delivery techniques, audio and video broadcasts over the Web are almost commonplace. Today you can access Net "TV channels" featuring adventures, westerns, nature programs, sports, lifestyles programming, and a host of other genres. There are also talking books and readings of poetry and short stories. The **Seeing Ear Theater** (www.scifi.com/set/readings/) offers readings of science fiction stories, some with synchronized illustrations, photos, and animation. Audio and video programming on the Internet is available from a number countries around the world. (Audio and video on the Net are described in Chapter 2.)

One of the most exciting developments is that opportunities for broadcasting to the world are increasingly available to individuals — not just networks and large corporations. **Freespeech** (www.freespeech.org/) is an audio/video Webcasting site for activist groups whose political critiques are sometimes ignored by the mainstream media. Similarly, **studioNEXT** (www.studionext.com/) sees the future of entertainment in showcasing independently made short films, animations, videos, and games.

Desktop videoconferencing over the Internet is another emerging application for business and education. Participants can see and hear one another, and even share computer applications.

Challenges and opportunities in electronic communications

The Internet holds exciting possibilities for news gathering and other mass media. It also poses a number of challenges.

Although the Net offers a wealth of information, much of it is of questionable value. Most of us like our information served up in carefully selected, easily digestible bites. We don't necessarily want to know when *Pokémon* broadcasts in Tokyo, or which San Diego grocery stores deliver. While it's thrilling to be able to send messages to people all over the world via the Internet, it is less of a thrill to have hundreds of people we don't know sending messages to us.

A big challenge for writers and journalists is how to attract and sustain an audience. Someone has estimated that the average amount of time spent on a Web page is about fifteen seconds — not much time in which to build readership. How do you write a story that will capture the attention of even a fraction of the millions of people who use the Internet? And how will anyone find an article you've written in a technology-mediated universe that must be navigated by computerized search engines, and where your piece may well be served up along with hundreds of others on the same topic?

> "…I haven't really seen a lot that's cool on the Internet. There's an awful lot of distracting stuff. There's not a Web page you can go to these days that is not constantly flashing something off in a corner of your eyes and trying to draw your attention away from what you're trying to do."
>
> — *Ray Tomlinson (inventor of e-mail)*, ZineZone *interview, www.zinezone.com/zones/digital/internet/tomlinson/*

But the Internet also represents new markets for many writers. Journalists in small communities and those working for smaller publications can draw on a much broader range of sources than were previously readily available. Electronic communications provide unique opportunities for interviews, and story ideas abound.

For researchers, the Internet poses some new challenges as well, such as mastering the many different ways to search the Web and keeping abreast of what's available. While this takes time and effort, most researchers will benefit from the mushrooming of resources that are accessible online.

The most important factor in mastering the electronic universe is learning to use the Internet well. It's a cinch to call up your Web browser and start surfing, but it takes time and a deeper understanding of what the Internet is all about to use it effectively.

Looking ahead: Will the Internet "disappear"?

We have talked about some of the good things on the Internet, and acknowledged a few of the drawbacks. But what does the future hold?

Clearly, the technology will continue to develop so that people will be able to do more and more things on the Internet — watch movies, play 3D chess, book a business trip, order take-out food. We believe that the two most important applications for the Internet will continue to be information exchange and global communications. Both areas offer phenomenal opportunities for Internet-savvy reporters and information professionals — opportunities that we've only just begun to explore.

We anticipate that there will be even more demand for writers and researchers to participate in developing services on the Internet. Interestingly, much of the future demand for writers and content experts will come not from the traditional publishing community (though publishers too are finding a place on the Web), but from other kinds of companies with products to sell. Whereas traditional print publications control content but need commercial advertisers to cover printing costs, advertising online needs useful, informative articles to attract readership. Commercial sponsors are therefore becoming more involved in developing online publications and information sources. For example, Toyota sponsors six different electronic magazines; L.L. Bean provides access to a database of national parks; and Molson, the Canadian beer company, provides listings for upcoming concerts across Canada.

The Internet remains in many ways unpredictable. Who would have guessed, just a few years ago, that electronic mail would edge out the post office ("snail mail") as the primary vehicle for business communication — or that if you missed the broadcast of a sporting event on TV you could easily catch it later on the Web. Figuring out just where the opportunities will be is one of the things that makes the Internet interesting and fun.

As the technology continues to develop, the Internet promises radical changes in the way we communicate, at work and at play. Freeman Dyson, a Princeton University physicist and futurist, sug-gests that the Net is the transforming technology of our time. With the proliferation of Web-TV (for Internet access via your television), wireless communications, and "information appliances" for access-ing the Internet away from your desktop computer (such as palm-sized computers, e-mail phones, and portable devices for playing music files), the Internet is rapidly becoming so much a part of our lives that we will probably one day cease to be aware of its impact. Like electricity, running water, and indoor toilets, the Internet will become such an integral part of our lives that it will "virtually" dis-appear from public consciousness.

For the time being, however, the Net is still developing, still grabbing the headlines, and still continuing to amaze us. Over the next few years, the best opportunities will go to those who become most skilled at using and developing material for this new medium.

10 neat things you can do online

The Internet is fast becoming as handy as a Swiss army knife. Here are ten neat and newsy things you can do online.

1. **Read news... and more news**
   The *Miami Herald,* the *New York Times,* the *Globe and Mail,* Reuters News, and *USA Today* — they're all on the Internet. The great thing about news on the Net is that you can find out about events that may not be covered in your local daily and explore them in greater depth. You can find a list of newspapers on the Web at:

   NewsDirectory.com (www.newsd.com/)

   or sample the latest headlines from over 1500 sources at:

   Moreover.com (www.moreover.com/).

2. **Set up a customized news service**
   On the Net, you can even create a customized version of the news at places like EntryPoint, Crayon, Yahoo!, or Excite. Some people like being able to focus on really "important" topics like the stock market or sports. Others dislike customized news services, claiming they miss the fun of reading an eclectic mix of stories. (Whatever happened to that story about the whales in Minnesota?) Find out for yourself what you think about customized news. You can try one of the original personalized news services at:

   Crayon (www.crayon.net/)

3. **Buy stuff... and more stuff**
   There's not too much in the way of consumer goods that you can't find for sale somewhere on the Net — from used furniture to cut-rate air fares. If you continue to prefer the social aspects of a trek to your local shopping mall, you can still find product reviews, price comparisons, and coupons on the Net. **Consumer World** is the place to start at:

   www.consumerworld.com/

4. **Download software**
   The Internet is the quintessential software supermarket. Free software, shareware, and demo versions of software can be installed and ready to go on your computer with a few clicks of your mouse. Try Brainstorming 101, Ideas for Excellence, The Right Résumé, or Track AboutTime for tracking projects, time, and billing. You will find these and other software goodies at:

   C|Net's **Download.com (http://download.cnet.com/)**

5. **Feed the world**
   The Hunger Site was developed as a response to world hunger. When you visit it and click on the "Donate Free Food" button, the site's daily corporate sponsors send an actual donation to the United Nations World Food Program. In its first six months of operation, the Hunger Site secured 1,585 metric tons of food for developing nations. You can participate by visiting **The Hunger Site** at:

   www.thehungersite.com/

6. **Make a phone call**
   Using the Internet to phone long distance is a bit like using a scratchy cell phone, but it's free, so who's complaining? To find out more, visit:

   Dialpad.com (www.dialpad.com/) or **HotTelephone (www.hottelephone.com/)**

7. **Receive a fax**

   You can receive free faxes and telephone voice messages over the Internet. Faxes are converted into graphics files and sent via e-mail as attachments. Unfortunately, with the free fax service, the sender will need to access a long-distance number to send you a fax, but for a monthly fee you can sign up for a number in your choice of eighty different cities. A fax-sending service is also available for a small fee. You can check out this service at:

   JFax.com (www.jfax.com/)

8. **Surf the radio**

   Tune in to any one of the more than 240+ audio channels available on the Net. The selection includes country, rock, new age, and news played on stations from Iceland to New Zealand. If your tastes aren't satisfied by selections from NPR, the CBC, or the BBC, you can swing over to Texas Rebel Radio, the top-rated station among Internet radio junkies. Find radio stations and live broadcasts using the **Real Guide** at:

   http://realguide.real.com/

9. **Publish a zine**

   "Zine" is short for "magazine" or "fanzine," and the term *e-zine* is used to describe the low-budget, low-key, and often little-known publications that are everywhere on the Internet. E-zines are often someone's labor of love. With imagination and a list-hosting service, you too can publish an e-zine. Access some popular e-zines and find out how to publish your own at:

   Zinebook.com (www.zinebook.com/index. html)

10. **Cheat**

    A team of computer scientists at Duke University has created a computer program capable of solving crossword puzzles. The program, called Proverb: The Probabilistic Cruciverbalist, averages 98% letters correct on puzzles from *USA Today,* the *Los Angeles Times,* and the *New York Times,* requiring approximately fifteen minutes per puzzle. Now, you can take advantage of this ingenious use of technology and search for the answers to crossword clues at:

    OneAcross (http://oneacross.com/)

Further reading

Berners-Lee, Tim. *Weaving the Web: The Original Design and Ultimate Destiny of the World Wide Web by its Inventor.* San Francisco: Harper, 1999.

Brown, Chip. "Fear.com: On the Web Because They Have to Be, Newspapers Try to Figure Out What to Do There." http://ajr.newslink.org/special/part12.html

Drucker, Peter. "Beyond the Information Revolution." *Atlantic Monthly,* October 1999. www.theatlantic.com/issues/99oct/9910drucker.htm

Harris, Charlie. "Using the Internet for Research: FAQ." www.purefiction.com/pages/res1.htm

Kahney, Leander. "E-Books: The Next Killer App." *Wired Magazine,* September 1999.
www.wired.com/news/technology/0,1282,21550,00.html

Morris, Kenneth M. *The User's Guide to the Information Age.* New York: McGraw-Hill, 1999.

"Newspapers and the Internet: Caught in the Web." *The Economist,* July 17, 1999.
www.britannica.com/bcom/magazine/article/0,5744,88044,00.html

"We're All Nerds Now." *Columbia Journalism Review,* March/April 1999.
www.cjr.org/year/99/2/nerds.asp

Getting the Most Out of the Web

"[The Web] is ... amazingly complicated despite the seductive simplicity of its easy-to-use hypertext human interface. One wag compared WWW navigation to trying to get from one part of a city to another by moving through a series of tunnels connecting the basements of the city's buildings.**"**
— THOMAS COPLEY, MAKE THE LINKS WORKSHOP

The Web is seductive. Once you've connected for the first time, the temptation is to start "surfing" the universe. This is not difficult to do; most Web browsers are designed to help you find your way around. Netscape, for example, gives simple, point-and-click access to the Web. Using Netscape's Search button quickly brings up a search window and a tempting list of places to go: Shopping, Travel, Games, and so on. Highlighted links to other Web pages and browser navigation features make it a snap to continue gliding around, sampling everything from the Toronto Maple Leafs hockey team to Hillary's Hair (a site that features hairstyles worn by Hillary Clinton). The only hazard here is the fallout that might result from neglecting your family, your job, your sleep, and other aspects of the "real" world competing for your attention.

As tempting as it is to continue randomly sampling the wealth of goodies on the Net, sooner or later you will want to move on and learn how to use the Web efficiently as a research tool. If you have already been online for a while, you've doubtless been frustrated at times by the difficulty of locating information quickly. As a new (or not-so-new) Web user, you'll want to find the best sites for your area of interest, know how to return to important resources, go directly to a resource that a colleague has recommended, and make use of links to download files rather than display Web pages.

This chapter covers the mechanics of Web browsers and the World Wide Web (WWW).

CHAPTER HIGHLIGHTS

- **WWW: An overview**
- **Browsers**
- **Navigating basics**
- **Portal sites**
- **Dancing with your browser: Other Internet applications**

WWW: An overview

The World Wide Web provides easy access over the Internet to a variety of media. Web pages can display text, pictures, sound, video, and animated graphics.

One common feature of Web pages is *hypertext links* (or *hyperlinks*). These are spots on which you can click to move from one page to the next. Clicking on a link brings up a screen (or more) of information related to that link.

A simple example of a hypertext link would be a highlighted word within a document onscreen. You can click on that word to find its definition. Or, you might be viewing a document about health and nutrition, and discover a link to another document that provides in-depth information about vitamins.

Hypermedia is another term you will encounter on the Web. It is similar to hypertext in that both denote the ability to access further information from a document. But hypermedia makes it possible to access other kinds of media besides text, such as pictures or sound files.

Increasingly, Web pages are interactive in design. Web-based forms invite visitors to provide information by filling in blank fields displayed on the screen. The site's computer customizes its responses based on how you have filled in the fields. You can ask the computer to send you an electronic mail reminder for an important date, or to create a personalized edition of today's news tailored to your needs or interests.

Multimedia formats (combining graphics, sound, and animation) are delivered over the Web via special helper software called *plug-ins*. These are programs specifically designed to work with particular kinds of files, such as movie files or audio files. Web pages can also "talk to" software on your desktop, and your desktop software can be used to download information from a Web page.

Browsers

Netscape vs. Explorer

The client software used to access the World Wide Web is called a *browser*. New and improved Web browsers are always on the horizon. The two most popular are **Netscape** (available from **www.netscape.com/**) and **Internet Explorer** (available from **www.microsoft.com/ie/**), and versions of these browsers are constantly updated. Your access provider may have supplied you with a browser, or told you where to obtain the latest versions of these popular Web browsers. If you are using the Windows 95 or Windows 98 operating system, Internet Explorer may already be installed on your desktop. Internet Explorer or Netscape Navigator are now commonly bundled in with the purchase of a new PC system.

FIGURE 2-1

Clicking on highlighted
hyperlinks brings up a
new page (below).

tech.ease

In this chapter, we will provide
examples from **Netscape
Communicator 4.61** and
Internet Explorer 5.0. If you
are using an earlier version of
either of these programs, the
details regarding menu options
and features may not be the
same.

Both Netscape and Explorer offer many of the same features,
and versions are available for both Macintosh and Windows operating systems. Both provide a toolbar for easy navigation and
accept plug-ins for accessing many different types of files. With

FIG 2-2

Netscape toolbar

FIG 2-3

Internet Explorer toolbar

either browser you will be able to track sites you've visited in the current session, save and print documents, and save references to sites you want to visit again. If you have configured your browser with information on how to locate news and mail on your Internet service provider's computer, you can read and post messages to Internet discussion groups (called newsgroups), and receive and send electronic mail.

The latest versions of these browsers also include sophisticated features such as the ability to chat and exchange files in real time, and to create Web pages. If you are using an older version of Netscape or Explorer, you may wish to download the latest version. However, the newer versions require a lot of disk space and computer memory, which may not be available if you have an older computer.

Because Netscape and Explorer offer very similar features, the choice between them is mostly a matter of personal preference. When you first start out, it's easiest to stick with the browser that is supplied or recommended by your Internet service provider (ISP), but don't be afraid to download and try out another browser.

Other browser options

While Netscape and Internet Explorer are the browsers of choice for an overwhelming number of users, they may not be ideally suited to your needs. Many Macintosh users prefer a browser called **Cyberdog** (www.cyberdog.org/) or a newer Mac browser called **iCab** (www.icab.de/B).

Tango (www.alis.com/) is a browser that has been designed to handle multiple languages and non-English character sets. The **Lycos** browser (http://lycos.neoplanet.com/) features a high level of user customization.

Another browser called **Opera** (www.opera.com/) is a practical alternative to either Netscape or Internet Explorer. Opera is not yet well known, but it's gaining popularity because it's easy to use and very efficient. Its basic features include:

- quick-loading pages
- ability to access and view multiple Web pages simultaneously in individual windows

---

tech.ease

While it is not essential to have the very latest browser on your computer, if you do have an older browser, you may not be able to display Web pages that use newer features. Keeping up with the latest technologies is like trying to focus on a moving target. If you are regularly having difficulty loading Web pages into your browser, it's time to upgrade.

A good source for keeping up to date on Macintosh technology and the Internet is the long-standing electronic magazine **TidBits**. You can subscribe to receive weekly issues of TidBits via electronic mail, or you can access their Web site and search back issues at:
www.tidbits.com/

If you are a Mac user, you will also want to check out one of the best Macintosh information sources on the Net — **The Ultimate Macintosh** at:
www.flashpaper.com/umac

FIGURE 2-4

The Opera browser can
view multiple Web pages
simultaneously.

- ability to save pages from one session to the next
- limited requirement for computer disk space
- several convenient design features, such as a zoom function and the ability to change the color of a background or text font (handy for when you encounter one of those unreadable black pages done by geeks who live in dungeons).

It's almost impossible to talk about Opera without making some reference to David and Goliath. While it's not likely that Opera will seriously threaten either Netscape or Explorer, many of its features could be valuable for people with older computers or slow connections. Opera is also a good choice for serious researchers, since it provides basic, practical features (whereas the browser giants tend to focus on features with broad marketplace appeal, such as quick access to online shopping and music). Currently, Opera is designed for Windows, but versions are being developed for other operating systems. The registration fee for Opera is $35 U.S., but you can download and use the software for thirty days for free.

The latest versions of most Web browsers attempt to keep in step with current Internet applications, but not all will support the newest features on the Web. Find out about browser options, and keep up with the newest versions of your browser, at **David J. Graffa's Browser Watch Page**: **http://browserwatch.internet.com/**

You can find a list of Macintosh browsers at: **http://darrel.knutson.com/mac/ www/browsers.html**

Navigating basics

Once you have connected to your Internet service provider and double-clicked on your Web browser software, you are ready to start navigating.

When you first start your Web browser, it will connect to a Web server and display an initial (or "home") page. Depending on the browser you are using and your ISP, the home page may be that of your service provider, or it could be the Netscape start-up page (or Internet Explorer's, if you're using that browser). (Later on we'll tell you how to change the page that comes up first.)

Generally, these home pages have been set up to make it easy for you to find useful information. For example, your ISP may provide links to local businesses and govern-  ment services, as well as a gateway link to one of the popular Internet directories. Both Netscape and Explorer provide you with navigation buttons and features for easy access to searching tools and other gateway sites.

Links to new pages of information are highlighted — that is, they are generally brighter and often larger than other text. Sometimes they are underlined. Pictures also can be links. If you're not sure if something is a link, try clicking on it. You can also move your mouse slowly over the mouse pad and notice when the cursor on the screen changes to a hand icon (for grabbing!). When the hand appears, you can click to move to that site.

Once you've clicked on an active link, the cursor will change to an hour glass. BE PATIENT as your browser locates the computer on the other end and sends a request to it. If you are not yet used to working online, it's easy to become impatient with the length of time it takes for a page of information to come back and be displayed on your desktop. Clicking again won't help; it just confuses the computer. It takes especially long for pages to load if there are many pictures, or if you are connecting through a telephone line with a slower modem.

In Netscape the computer address for each link will appear at the lower left of your screen. This address, called a *URL* (for *uniform resource locator*), changes as you move your cursor over different links on a page. Once you've clicked on a link, you can watch this spot to monitor the progress of your request being transmitted.

Hyperlinks are only one means of navigating the Web. Both Netscape and Internet Explorer use a toolbar at the top of the screen. The arrow keys (bearing small icons pointing backwards and forwards) move you back and forth through pages that you have already accessed. For quick access to recently visited pages, click on the down arrow in the site address window, or click and hold the back arrow icon.

In Netscape you can also use the **Window | History** option from the pull-down menu to track which sites you've already visited. In Internet Explorer, click on the **History** button displayed on the toolbar to bring up a list of recently visited sites. Click on any sites you want to return to. The button that depicts a house will take you back to the opening (home) page.

In Netscape and Internet Explorer you can also click on the **Search** button on the browser toolbar for quick access to a number of Internet search sites. (We discuss search engines in detail in Chapter 3, but to preview how different search engines work, try searching the same term using several of the various search engines presented by your browser.)

URLs

Uniform resource locators are "addresses" that specify the computer and location on the Internet for different types of documents and resources. Every page on the World Wide Web has its own unique address. (This accounts for the excessive length of some Web addresses!) The first part of the URL (before the colon) indicates the access method or the type of resource you want to retrieve. The part of the URL that follows the double slash (//) specifies a machine name or site, often along with subdirectories at the site and the name of a file.

Here are some examples:

http://www.eriche.org/About/publish.html   This is a Web site. The *http://* stands for *hypertext transfer protocol*. Many URLs for Web pages include *www* after the *http://*, and since most URLs do refer to Web sites, the *http://* is commonly omitted. However, not all URLs refer to Web sites.

file://wuarchive.wustl.edu/mirrors/msdos/graphics/gifkit.zip   A URL that starts with *file://* is used to access a specific file on the Internet. A slightly different format is used to access a file on your own hard drive.

file:///c|/netscape/bookmark.htm   This is an example of a URL that might be used to retrieve a file from your computer's C drive. Notice that, in this case, there are three slashes after the colon rather than two.

ftp://www.xerox.com/pub/   URLs starting with *ftp://* are used to access and transfer files. This URL would get you into the file listing for the "pub" directory at this site. FTP is an older Internet technology, but it's still sometimes used as a way of accessing software and uploading files.

telnet://dra.com   A telnet URL will access a login screen for a remote computer. In order to access a telnet site, you need to have telnet software, and must then set up your Web browser to call up the telnet software as a helper application (telnet is explained in Chapter 4).

news:alt.hyptertext   If your browser has been configured to point to your newsserver (or a public newsserver), an address like this gives you access to newsgroups via your Web browser.

gopher://liberty.uc.wlu.edu/   This is a URL for a gopher site. Gophers were one of the original ways of organizing information on the Internet. They have now largely been replaced by the World Wide Web, but you may occasionally bump into a reference to a gopher site.

Once you have clicked on a link to access a new Web page, the URL for that page will also appear in the window near the top of your browser (labeled "Location" or "Netsite" in Netscape and "Address" in Internet Explorer). Click on a link, and watch as the URL changes to match that of the document being retrieved.

The quickest way to access a Web site for which you have a specific address is to clear the window displaying the current URL and put in the URL for the site you want to go to. (Netscape and Internet Explorer locate the URL window at the top of the screen.) To put in a new URL, simply place your cursor in the field and click. The click highlights the existing URL. Clear the field by using the Delete key on your computer keyboard. With the cursor still in the field, you can now simply type in the URL for the Web page you want.

You can also use the pull-down menu option for **File | Open** on your browser to open a new location. Most newer browsers let you drop the *http://* part of a Web address, but you must type in the address for your site very carefully. Computers on the Internet cannot locate a site if a character is missing, or if you don't use upper- and lowercase letters correctly, or if you've typed a hyphen (-) instead of a tilde (~).

Initially, you may not know many URLs. But once you start surfing the Internet, you will quickly develop a list of interesting sites

ZDNet (www. zdnet.com/), from the publishers of *PC Magazine* and *MacUser*, is a popular source for finding out about new hardware and software options. This site offers advice and how-tos for beginners and advanced users alike.

There are many other good sites linked to print publications. A list of computer publications on the Internet is available at the **FCN Development Center**: **www.state.fl.us/fcndev/ magazines.phtml**

Web sites are constantly changing; in particular, directory names and filenames may quickly go out of date. If a URL does not seem to work, check each character to be sure that you have entered it correctly. Then, try deleting the final filename and/or directories. Once you've accessed a specific location, you can often find the exact information you're searching for just by following the links. If you still are not successful, try finding the item using the name of the site in quotes or unique key terms with a comprehensive search engine such as **Fast Search (www. alltheweb. com/)** (we describe search engines in detail in Chapter 3).

tech.ease

When referencing a Web site in an electronic mail message, don't omit the *http://* part of the URL. By preceding the Web address with *http://* you will create an automatic link. Most newer mail programs will recognize hypertext links and other HTML formatting tags. You can check to see how this works by using your mail software's HTML formatting options in an electronic mail message that you send to yourself.

and potential resources. These days, URLs are visible everywhere. Watch for them in newspapers, in magazines, and on television. Columnists sometimes publish the URL for their Web page, and there may be URLs for businesses and products that are advertised. (For example, the URL for Tide detergent is *www.tide.com/*. The site features a downloadable stain-removing guide.) Radio programs, too, often mention their Web address at the end of a show. You will see URLs displayed and exchanged at conferences, and college instructors often refer their students to useful Web sites.

Browser features

Learning about the navigation features available on your browser is a good investment of time. Many browsers allow you to customize features, such as the size of the print that displays and how long links will be remembered in the History file. To learn about the features on your particular browser, start by exploring the menu options at the top of the screen, and use the Help function for the program. Here are some basic features that are available on most browsers:

- viewing Web pages and accessing FTP sites
- viewing multimedia files with the addition of helper files or plug-ins (these are discussed in Chapter 8)
- viewing newsgroup discussions and reading electronic mail if you have set up these options (many people use separate software for these functions, such as Eudora Mail for reading mail)
- printing Web pages
- copying text from a Web page for pasting into another document
- saving Web pages as HTML files (which include all the formatting codes used by your browser) or as text files, which will then let you import the text content of a site
- saving images by clicking on the right mouse button when the mouse is positioned on a picture
- setting up bookmarks or favorites, which let you save and categorize Web site references so you can easily return to a site
- tracking sites you've been to in a History file, so that you can jump back to a site you accessed earlier without having to backtrack screen by screen
- viewing the source code for a document (this feature gives you a look at all of the cryptic-looking codes that go into HTML tagging, which we describe in Chapter 7 on writing for the Web).

Setting preferences

Many of the options for your browser are pre-set, and for the most part, you will want to stick with these. There are a few, however, that you may wish to change.

Starting page. Usually, browsers will load a specific Web page (commonly that of your Internet service provider) when they are first turned on. An option is available to change this URL setting to one that you might prefer, such as the URL for your favorite search engine or a Web directory such as Yahoo! or Snap. In Netscape, look for this option under **Edit | Preferences | Navigator**. In Internet Explorer, you can change your home page under **Tools | Internet Options | General**.

Image loading. Your browser has a setting for turning off the image loading and then turning it on again when you want to access the graphics on a page. If you don't mind viewing pages without all the pretty pictures, this feature can save you time. Find the **Preferences** or **Options** menu on your browser and click to toggle this option on or off. With the Opera browser, you can access this feature by clicking on the camera icon at the bottom of the screen.

Title bars and button bars. You can increase the size of the Web page window by turning off the screen display for these features. Usually this is a toggle selection, which allows you to turn a feature on or off with a single click. Look for the title bar display option under your browser's **View** menu.

Visual display. If you want to increase the size of the print that displays for Web pages, it is possible to do this on most browsers. It is also possible to change the default color setting for the browser background and links. Check under browser **Preferences** or **Options**.

Mail and news. These options allow you to specify which program you will use for electronic mail and reading newsgroups. The **Mail** and **News** preferences under Netscape **Options** tell your computer where to go on the Internet to get your mail, and allow you to specify a range of other mail/news options. Internet Explorer asks you to select your mail program under **Tools | Internet Options | Programs**, and a set-up wizard is available if you are using Explorer's Internet Mail.

Security. Security preferences will become increasingly important as more and more financial transactions are carried out on the

Internet. Don't be alarmed by the warning messages that may unexpectedly appear on your screen — such as a warning that you are sending unencrypted information — unless you are sending sensitive information, such as a bank card number. You can turn off these warning messages by accessing the security options on your browser. To find out more about the network and security features, use your browser's Help feature.

Browser hotlists

Most browsers have a feature that allows you to save a list of sites that you want to return to. In Internet Explorer, this list is called "Favorites"; some other browsers use the term "hotlist." Netscape calls this list "Bookmarks." Having a well-organized set of bookmarks is a great time saver — in effect, it gives you a personalized slice of the Internet.

To add a bookmark to your personal list, use the **Bookmark | Add** (or **Favorites | Add**) feature at the top of your screen. You can also click on the right mouse button. (Learning to use some of the options available with a right-click of your mouse can be a good time saver.) This will open a pull-down menu with a number of different options, including Add Bookmark or Add to Favorites. If your cursor is positioned randomly on the page, clicking on the Add Bookmark (right mouse button menu option) will save the current page, but if your cursor is positioned directly over a link, a bookmark for the link will be saved.

Once you have set up a bookmark, you can access it by clicking on the Bookmark button in Netscape or on the Favorites button in Internet Explorer, and then clicking on the Web page reference in your list of saved bookmarks.

Setting up a hotlist is really easy. What's not so easy is to avoid amassing an unwieldy list of 5,000 bookmarks. In Chapter 6, we discuss how to manage information overload, including how to organize a bookmark list.

Tips for using browsers

When your browser stalls. If a page seems to take forever or refuses to load, click on "Stop," then click the Reload or Refresh button. If a page still refuses to load, try again later. The computer server from which you are requesting the page may be temporarily out of commission. If you bump into a situation where the Back button doesn't seem to want to move you from the current page, use the Go button to select an earlier page. Watch out for situations in which a site opens a new browser window for you. You will need to switch back to the original window in order to find your navigation list.

Step on the gas. You can speed up the time required to download Web pages by electing not to download images. This will shorten your download time considerably. Once the text for a page is available, you can later download images one at a time as you want them, or download them all after the text has displayed. In Netscape, use **Edit | Preferences | Advanced** to turn off the automatic image loading. Then use **View | Show Images** to toggle this option on and off. Click on the Images icon on the toolbar to quickly load a page plus images. In Internet Explorer, you can turn off the images using the **Tools | Internet Options | Advanced** menu. A toggle (on/off) switch for pictures is listed under Multimedia.

Retrace your steps. Your browser will save references to pages you have recently visited from one session to the next in the History folder. In Netscape, you can access the history list under **Communicator | Tools | History**. When the history list is displayed, you can sort the list by title or location using the View menu. You can also search the list for a particular word or

FIGURE 2-5

Internet Explorer history list

date, using the **Edit | Search History List** menu. In Internet Explorer, click on the History button to display the list.

Foil those frames. Some Web sites offer an index list of available topics in a window (frame) that is separate from the page that is displayed when you click on a link. This can be annoying when you want to follow a link to a source outside that particular Web site. Use your right mouse button to open the link in a new browser window. In Netscape, you can also right-click on the link; copy the link location and paste it into a new browser location window.

Find a needle. You can search for a particular string of text within the page you are currently viewing using the **Edit | Find in Page** menu option. Use the "Match Case" search option if you want to match capital letters. This is a useful technique for finding what you need in lengthy text documents.

Share your bookmarks with a friend. In Netscape, bookmark files are really just glorified HTML files. This means that if you were to save your bookmarks using the **File | Save** option from within the Edit Bookmarks screen, you could open the file from the main Web browser screen just as though you were opening a Web page. Some people use their bookmark file as their browser start-up page. You can also store your bookmarks online at **MURL** (**http://murl.com/**). MURL is handy if you need to access your bookmarks from more than one location, or want to make them available to a friend.

Save information from a Web page. You can use your browser's Copy and Paste functions to save information from a Web page. In Windows, if your word processor is already open, you can use the Alt/Tab key combination to move back and forth between your browser and the word processing file to which you want to copy the information. If you want to save the complete text of a Web page, use the **File | Save** menu option. Internet Explorer will capture your favorites offline through the "Make Available Offline" checkbox; you can update these saved files using Synchronize in the **Tools** menu. To save an image from a page, place your mouse over the image you want to save and select **File | Save Image As**.

When you're too tired to think. Get your browser to think for you. Internet Explorer's Related Links feature will open up a sidebar window with links related to the page you are currently viewing. In Netscape, you can use the Smart Browsing feature. Select Smart Browsing under **Edit | Preferences**. This will place a "What's Related" button at the top right of your screen. Click here for a list of related sites.

Alexa is a popular utility for finding related sites. You can download a copy from: **www.alexa.com/**

FIGURE 2-6

Netscape Quick
Reference Cards are
available from http://help.
netscape.com/products/
client/communicator/qrc/
qrcfrnt.htm

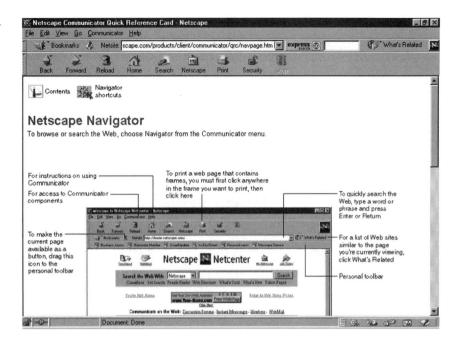

Portal sites

Web pages that offer a mix of directories, news, online shopping, and gateways to online discussions and live events are called *portals*. Many of the established Internet search engines have transformed themselves into Web portals to attract a larger audience. Select a favorite portal and set it up as your browser home page.

All of the following sites are good places to start exploring.

About.com
www.about.com/
A Web resource with a human face! As well as links to various online resources, About.com includes articles on the topics concerned. Check out the "Guide to Web Searching."

GO Network
www.go.com/
Home of the Infoseek search engine, this is now a portal site that will also point you in the direction of food, drink, shopping, and even romance (as well as some useful research sites).

LookSmart
www.looksmart.com/
An easy-to-navigate directory of higher-quality Web sites. If you can't find what you're looking for, the editors at LookSmart will help. Click on LookSmart Live.

NetGuide
www.netguide.com/home

NetGuide offers new sites, best sites, live events, and Internet tips and tricks.

Scout Report Signpost
www.signpost.org/

Funded by the U.S. National Science Foundation, this site provides information on more than 3,700 of the best Internet resources for research.

Snap
http://snap.com/

Snap is a more recent Internet directory service from NBC and CNET. It is another popular Web portal, and a serious rival for Yahoo!.

Sympatico
http://www1.sympatico.ca/

A Canadian portal site with excellent links to news, discussion groups, general interest topics, and a nice collection of computer tips and tutorials.

Yahoo!
www.yahoo.com/

For many people, Yahoo! is a favorite starting point on the Web.

Netsurfer Digest delivers news about the Web to your e-mail box once a week. To subscribe, visit **www.netsurf.com/**, where you can choose to receive any of four publications: *Netsurfer Digest, Netsurfer Education, Netsurfer Science,* or *Netsurfer Books.*

FIGURE 2-7
GO Network is a popular portal site.

The Internet Handbook for Writers, Researchers, and Journalists

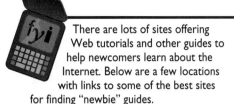

There are lots of sites offering Web tutorials and other guides to help newcomers learn about the Internet. Below are a few locations with links to some of the best sites for finding "newbie" guides.

Best of the Internet Tutorials
www.bgsu.edu/departments/tcom/tutors2.html

Help Web
www.imaginarylandscape.com/helpweb/

ICYouSee: A Guide to the World Wide Web
www.ithaca.edu/library/Training/ICYouSee.html

Interlinks: Internet Navigator and Resource Locator
http://alabanza.com/kabacoff/Inter-Links/

Internet Guides, Tutorials, and Training Information
http://lcweb.loc.gov/global/internet/training.html

Internet Learner's Page
www.mnsfld.edu/depts/lib/learn.html

Internet Learning Resources
www.rgu.ac.uk/~sim/research/netlearn/callist.htm

Learn the Net
www.learnthenet.com/english/index.html

Babel Fish (http://babelfish.altavista.digital.com/) is a text translation service available on the Web. Paste in text, or submit a URL, and the text or Web page will be translated for you. You can select English, and your text will be translated into (or from) French, German, Italian, Portuguese, or Spanish.

Dancing with your browser: Other Internet applications

Web pages are rapidly growing beyond the simple display of text and still pictures. Today, slick new applications such as audio, video, computer conferencing, panoramic viewing, and multimedia are accessible over the World Wide Web. Although from a research perspective, these are used less often than text Web pages, you will find these new technologies useful resources to know about, particularly if you are interested in distance learning or virtual work environments where you can meet and work with colleagues online. Here is a brief summary of some of the technologies that are accessible using a Web browser and helper files.

Streaming and other media

Streaming media provide sound and video broadcasts over the Internet. They let you listen or view a broadcast without waiting for the entire file to download.

One of the most popular technologies for accessing streaming audio is from **Real Networks.** With their RealAudio you can sample the latest CD or catch a CBC radio interview. CNN and ABC news offer Real news broadcasts, and there are a host of talking books in RealAudio format. For those with a taste for excitement, there are even live police broadcasts available from police scanners in New York and Los Angeles (**www.policescanner.com/**).

To listen to RealAudio, you must download and install a Real player. This helper application is available free from:
www.real.com/

Sites featuring RealAudio commonly provide a link to the player. In addition to the player, you will require, at a *minimum*:

- 90 MHz Intel Pentium processor or equivalent with 16 MB RAM (for Macintosh, 604 PowerPC with 32 MB RAM)
- 16-bit sound card
- speakers
- 14.4-baud or faster modem connection (28.8 Kpbs for video and music)
- Windows 95 or 98 (for Macintosh, OS 8.1 or later)

Broadcast radio on the Internet is not perfect, but like everything on the Net, it's improving. With a slower connection, the quality is likely to be choppy. If you plan to access audio files frequently, consider investing in a cable or DSL modem (see Chapter 8). You can also try accessing content during non-peak hours (that is, outside U.S. business hours and weekend evenings). Researchers and journalists will soon be able to access an increasing number of news and educational broadcasts from around the world.

Try these sites to sample some of the RealAudio broadcasts that are currently available:

AudioHighway
www.audiohighway.com/

BBC World Business Report
www.bbc.co.uk/worldservice/worldbusinessreport/

Broadcast.com (Check here for AudioBooks)
www.broadcast.com/

CBC Radio
www.radio.cbc.ca/

Current Awareness Resources Using Audio and Video
http://gwis2.circ.gwu.edu/~gprice/audio.htm
Links to audio/video services for monitoring current events.

MediaBay
www.mediabay.com/
Preview downloadable audiobooks and sample old-time radio shows.

National Public Radio
www.npr.org/

OnTheAir
www.ontheair.com/

Real Guide
http://realguide.real.com/

When.com
www.when.com/

Check out the Web events section for audio and video broadcasts on the Web.

MP3

This is another audio format available on the Web. Audio files are very large, but MP3 technology can compress them so that they can be more readily downloaded and stored on your computer. By far the bulk of MP3 files are music files, but some audio books and author interviews are also available. Because MP3 is a convenient way to distribute audio files, it is also a format that will increasingly be used for distance learning.

The RealPlayer can play MP3 files, but there are other MP3 players are available from **Tucows Music** (**http://music.tucows. com/**) and **Winamp** (**www.winamp.com/**), which offers a popular freeware MP3 player. The Web site **MP3.com** (**http://help.mp3. com/help/**) offers an installer program to help new users and non-geeks get started. There are even portable MP3 players that will let you take downloaded MP3 files to the beach. To search for MP3 music files on the Web, visit **Dimension Music** at:

www.dimensionmusic.com/

Video on the Web

Although video has been available over the Internet since the early nineties, is has only recently become a practical application. Because video files are *really large*, video distribution over the Internet has been hampered by a lack of bandwidth.

Bandwidth describes the size of the channels or connecting links through which information flows. In the past, bandwidth has been hampered by such things as the distribution capacity of standard telephone lines and slow modems. These days, however, with the availability of higher-speed lines and cable connections, as well as new compression techniques, video has emerged as one of the fastest-growing areas of Web development.

Bandwidth

Researchers and journalists will value the availability of up-to-the-minute video news broadcasts, online lectures, and conferences that are now distributed over the Internet. Two particularly popular technologies for distributing video are RealVideo and QuickTime. If you have an adequate computer, you'll find that setting up the software to receive video is relatively painless.

For RealVideo, the recommended configuration is:

- 166 MHz Intel Pentium processor or better with 32 MB or more of RAM
- 28.8 Kbps or better modem (some newer video files require a 56 Kbps or better modem)
- 16-bit or better sound card
- speakers
- 65,000-color or better video display card
- Windows 95/98.

In the Macintosh world, the following is recommended:

- Mac OS 8.5 or later
- 64 MB RAM
- 65 MB virtual memory
- G3 233 (or faster) PowerPC.

You can download free video players from these sites:

QuickTime
www.apple.com/quicktime/

RealPlayer
www.real.com/player/ (the RealPlayer 7 Basic is free)

Although a video presentation may initially appear in a small viewing screen, both RealVideo and QuickTime allow for a larger screen display. On the RealPlayer, click on the small magnifying glass to access the enlargement option. In QuickTime, access the Double Size and Fill Screen options under the **Movie** menu. Be aware, however, that many older video clips cannot be enlarged, and older videocards may need to be updated to accommodate this feature.

Also take note of the range of preferences available that can affect play. For example, under the RealPlayer's **Options | Preferences,** you can reduce picture quality slightly to improve playback on a less powerful computer.

You may want to sample some of the "channels" that come already configured with your player. The RealMedia Player offers news stations and science and technology channels. You can customize these and add your own favorites.

Here are some examples of video resources that you might find interesting to sample.

C-SPAN
www.cspan.org/
Public affairs programming.

Columbia News Multimedia Archive
www.columbia.edu/cu/news/media/index.html
A selection of Web videos from Columbia University.

Court TV
www.courttv.com/
Live broadcasts and video archives for high-profile court cases.

Desktop Video for Education
www.apple.com/quicktime/showcase/education/index.html
A source for video-based online learning.

FedNet
www.fednet.net/
Hearings, debates, and press conferences. A subscription is required for access to archived material.

Foreign TV
www.foreigntv.com/
Global video programming: news, travel, lifestyles, and culture.

Journal E Media Lab
www.journale.com/medialab/index.html
For the latest in online storytelling technology. Includes QuickTime video.

FIGURE 2-8
QuickTime TV: live QuickTime events

Want to create your own audio or video productions? Check out the **RealSystem G2 Production Guide** at:

http://service.real.com/help/library/guides/production/realpgd.htm

or QuickTime's authoring link at:

www.apple.com/quicktime/authoring/

Travel View
www.travelview.com/Streaming_videos_travel.htm
Video clips for more than forty destinations.

VideoSeeker News and Business
www.videoseeker.com/vlist/news.html
A good collection of news video sources.

Yahoo!broadcast
www.broadcast.com/video/
The video channel at Broadcast.com includes a good selection of educational broadcasts.

Web conferencing

Virtual communities are cropping up everywhere on the Net as more and more people learn to use online communications tools. While the Web itself is reported to be still growing at a rate of 50% a year, online communities have been shooting up at a rate of 20% per month.

People can communicate on the Internet in several different ways, the most common being electronic mail. There are also discussion forums — called newsgroups and listservs — that use mail servers to exchange messages. (We discuss these groups in Chapter 5.) Another way to participate in electronic discussion groups is through your Web browser, by joining a Web-based computer discussion. You can even start your own, using some of the free conferencing environments available on the Internet.

In a Web conferencing environment, messages are grouped by topics and subtopics. You can review comments made by other contributors and submit your own comments — either to the group as a whole, or to an individual. The distinguishing features of Web conferencing are that commentary is usually structured (with related messages grouped together), and messages are posted directly onto the Web. Frequently it is possible to view messages that have been posted months earlier, making it easy for newcomers to catch up with what's being discussed.

Web conferencing tends to be more formal than newsgroup forums. Conferences may be moderated; they may occur within a set time frame, and may be intended to facilitate discussion among a specific group, such as students enrolled in a distance learning course.

There are thousands of Web conferences. Delphi attempts to track Web-based discussion groups and puts the current count at 80,000, though it is likely that not all of these are active discussion communities.

To sample a Web-based conferencing environment, try one of the following sites:

Delphi Forums
www.delphi.com/
Delphi can put you in touch with forums on topics ranging from bioethics to frugal living.

eGroups.com
www.egroups.com/
Here you can sample existing online communities or set up your own.

Excite Communities
www.excite.com/communities/
Join a community or set up your own private or public discussion.

Forum One
www.ForumOne.com/
Search for discussions using a keyword, or sample one of the recommended forums.

Hungryminds
http://hungryminds.egroups.com/
Hungryminds offers mini-courses and invites you to participate in a "knowledge-sharing" group.

Salon Magazine: Table Talk
http://tabletalk.salon.com/
Lively discussion and regular guest speakers.

Sympatico Discussion Forums
www.ns.sympatico.ca/forums/
A good resource for accessing Canadian discussion groups.

Utne Cafe
www.utne.com/
A number of print magazines, such as the *Utne Reader*, also support discussion forums of interest to their readers.

The Well
www.well.com/
A long-standing online conferencing forum. Participation currently costs $10 U.S. per month.

---

fyi Free Web-based conferencing and chat environments are available from a number of sites. Examples include **eGroups.com** and **Excite Communities** (listed in the text) and **Yahoo! Clubs (http://clubs.yahoo. com/).** You can find out about other conference-hosting services at: **www.forumone.com/hosting.htm Conferencing Software for the Web** is a comprehensive guide to Web conferencing software programs. It is available at : **http://thinkofit.com/webconf/** This is a very useful site that also includes links to conference hosting services.

PDF files

If you are a journalist or a researcher, you will undoubtedly encounter PDF files. PDF stands for *portable document format*. This file format is designed to preserve the original look of a print document (headlines, columns, graphics, etc.). Many agencies find it convenient to make information available as PDF files, rather than convert the files to the Web page file format known as HTML.

PDF can prevent illegal copying of material, and it ensures that a document will look the same regardless of which browser — or which computer platform — you are using. Many magazine articles, newsletters, reports, and forms (such as tax forms from the IRS) are accessible over the Web in PDF format. **Pennsylvania State University (www2.hn.psu.edu/faculty/jmanis/jimspdf.htm)** makes available classical works of literature in PDF format.

PDF files require the use of a helper application known as a *PDF viewer*. The most commonly used PDF format on the Internet is **Adobe Acrobat**. To read Acrobat files, you require the Acrobat Reader, which is free to download. Most sites that provide information in PDF format also provide a link to the viewer. Usually, you need only click on the viewer link to download it to your own computer. Once you have installed the viewer, your browser will know how to find it whenever you need to access a PDF file.

You can find out more about PDF files at these sites:

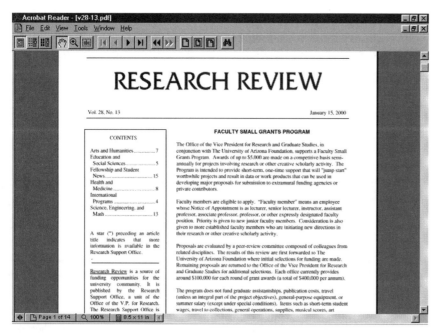

FIGURE 2-9

The University of Arizona publishes *Research Review* in portable document format.

Take time to explore the viewer's features, such as increasing the size of a display for easier reading. Editing features will vary. For example, although most PDF viewers will allow you to view and print a document, you may not be able to cut and paste from it. You can, however, often copy individual pages electronically by using the **Edit | Select All** menu option.

Online chat

Chat is a term used for online discussions that take place in real time. Some chat groups require that a piece of software be downloaded onto your local system, while others are virtual discussion spaces that appear when you access a chat site online. Although some chat events feature interesting topics, such as the real-time chats sponsored by About.com (e.g., on animal rights, career development, etc.), text-based online discussions are most often superficial and difficult to follow. Many people join chat groups just for fun.

Chat software allows you to open up a channel on the Internet and converse in real time with someone else on the Internet. Some sites, such as Time-Warner's Pathfinder service, provide a group chat environment where you can interact with a guest speaker. **Yahoo!** (**www. yahoo.com/**) and **About.com** (**www.about. com/**) both list scheduled chat events.

Desktop messaging tools are probably more valuable for researchers than online chat groups. Tools such as **ICQ** (**www.icq. com/**), **PoWWow** (**www.tribal.com/**), and **Excite PAL** (**www.excite. com/communities/pal/home/**) are called "instant messaging" software. Newer versions of Netscape come bundled with AOL's Instant Messenger. Macintosh users can try **Gerry's ICQ** (**www.chicoweb. com/~gerryicq/index.shtml**).

Instant messaging software allows you to connect directly with colleagues who are online in a text-based chat environment. Desktop chat software may also include a number of interesting features, including easy ways to post or exchange files and the ability to cruise the Web as a group. With a computer microphone or headset and speakers, you can also send voice messages. A new AOL product called **AIM Talk** adds voice messaging capabilities to AOL's popular messaging software.

You can find out about a range of other chat software and Webphone products at **Tucows** (**www./tucows.com/**) and at the **Dave Central** software archive (**www.davecentral.com/sitemap.html**).

Desktop videoconferencing

There are now a number of inexpensive options for desktop videoconferencing. Videoconferencing systems offer video communications as well as such features as remote desktop sharing (where two

people can view and work on an application at the same time); a whiteboard for sharing graphics, slides, and other displays; file and screen snapshot exchange; and "Web-walks," in which a group can surf the Web together.

Desktop videoconferencing is becoming particularly prevalent for online conferences, presentations, and distance education. It is also gaining interest from people who work away from the office, but still want to be able to connect with co-workers online.

An example of a desktop video conferencing product is Microsoft's **NetMeeting** (which can be downloaded from **www.microsoft.com/windows/NetMeeting/**). Although some conferencing functions can operate without the video display, to fully participate in desktop videoconferencing, you will need a piece of equipment called a Webcam (a small camera that attaches to your computer). An entry-level Webcam can be purchased for about $100 U.S. You will also need conferencing software, such as NetMeeting or **CU-SeeMe** (available from **www.wpine.com/**), and you must connect to a conferencing server.

You can find more information about desktop audio and video-conferencing at About.com:

http://netconference.about.com/internet/netconference/

A last word

The Web is always changing. Newer technologies include WebTV, which lets you surf the Net using your television rather than a computer, and portable devices, such as MP3 players and cell phones with Internet access. Faster modems and new technologies for delivering services and exchanging information are paving the way for e-commerce and online collaborative work environments. The drawback is that the technology sometimes runs ahead of our ability to keep up with all the new possibilities it offers.

This introductory chapter has given you a glimpse of some the applications and information sources available on the Web. We have dealt with the fundamentals of Web navigation: browsers,

URLs, and multimedia applications. You can build on this information as you become acquainted with other features of the Internet. Don't be overwhelmed by your technowhiz colleague's knowledge of the very latest Internet gizmo. The most important thing is to have a good understanding of how the Internet can be useful to *you*.

In the chapters to come, we'll discuss more ways to find what you're looking for on the Internet, and identify specific Web sites that are especially valuable for researchers and writers.

Further reading

Carroll, Jim, and Broadhead, Rick. *Canadian Internet Handbook.* Toronto: Prentice Hall, 1998.

Internet Guides: The Teaching Library Instruction and Guides to the Internet
www.lib.berkeley.edu/TeachingLib/Guides/Internet/

The Internet Index Home Page
http://new-website.openmarket.com/intindex/index.cfm

Odd de Presno Online World Resources Handbook
http://login.eunet.no/~presno/index.html

"Undocumented Internet Secrets." *PC Computing,* October 1999, p. 154ff.

Web Browsers Open FAQ
www.boutell.com/openfaq/browsers/

White, Nancy, Boettcher, Sue, and Duggan, Heather. *Online Community Toolkit*
www.fullcirc.com/community/communitymanual.htm

Witulski, Meredith. "Stop, Look & Listen: Innovative Uses for Audio & Video on the Web." *Smart Computing in Plain English*, January 1999.
www.smartcomputing.com

<small></small>

CHAPTER

3

Search Strategies and Techniques

"The Internet is not like the computer on Star Trek. You can't just say: 'Computer, who are the ten biggest crooks that donated money to the sleazebag politician in my city?' and wait a few seconds for the answer. The Internet will not make stupid reporters smart. But it will make smart reporters smarter. The Internet is a vast, largely unorganized, ever-changing library (in fact, many of the world's best libraries are actually on the Internet). And — like any library — you have to do the hard work to find the nugget of information you want. The books don't walk off the shelves into your hands.**"**

— JULIAN SHER, *MEDIA MAGAZINE,* WINTER 1995.

Trying to find information on the Internet has been likened to trying to get a sip of water from a fire hydrant. With just a few keystrokes, it's easy to flood your computer screen with endless lists of possible references. Finding and isolating the useful material can seem daunting. There are, however, some simple search strategies and techniques, as well as sophisticated tools that you can use to find what you want quickly. Once you develop some skill using these, the results will be rewarding.

The Internet's phenomenal growth has made it critical for researchers to fine-tune their online search skills. With hundreds of millions of Web pages on the Net, you need to know where to start looking — and which search tool to use in different circumstances. Otherwise, your Internet searches may be about as efficient as looking for a lost contact lens in the sand on the beach. You may enjoy the heat of the sun and the sound of the waves, but you're not likely to find what you're looking for.

This chapter will provide an overview of the tools and strategies you can use to make your searches both pleasant and successful.

CHAPTER HIGHLIGHTS

- ◼ **Searching the Web for information**
- ◼ **Subject directories — a bird's-eye view**
- ◼ **Search engines — the most comprehensive results**
- ◼ **Metasearch tools**
- ◼ **Starting pages for journalists — a place to browse**
- ◼ **Comparing search tools**

Searching the Web for information

"[The Internet] has turned into one of the most important journalistic tools since the invention of the telephone. It is hard to overstate how useful the Net has become. It seems as if some virus has gotten loose that impels people to put every scrap of information known to man online."

— *Stephen C. Miller, The Freedom Forum Online*
www.freedomforum.org/technology/1997/10/stevespeech3.asp

The Internet is a storehouse of information, pictures, sound, and even video, so vast it is difficult to comprehend.

You can log onto NASA's computers and look at the latest space pictures before they are published. You can read tomorrow's *Jerusalem Post* online hours before you can get a hard copy of it in North America. You can search a database at Johns Hopkins University for some of the latest research on prostate cancer. You can listen to radio shows live from around the world. You can even track the latest on an approaching hurricane before you hear about it on the evening news.

If you are a writer or a researcher, much of the information you need is probably out there — somewhere — online, and it is probably indexed or catalogued somehow. But the Internet wasn't set up by librarians who organize things in a logical way and provide a central index to make them easy to find. Nor was it organized by journalists who need information quickly to meet tight deadlines. Still, it has become an essential tool for writers, researchers, and journalists.

In the early days of the Internet, researching online meant trying to find all the relevant documents on a particular subject. Today, the sheer size of the Internet makes that impossible. Now, you'll want to pinpoint a few key documents without having to wade through a lot of junk.

The first thing you need is a plan for your search.

An excellent list of ten friendly tips to improve your Internet searching can be found at:
www.researchbuzz.com/ excerpts/10friendly.htm

A great resource for factual information about countries around the world is the **CIA World Fact Book**. No, it doesn't provide any classified information about spies, but it does offer political, social, and economic information about places you may not even have heard of. It is updated annually and is located at:
www.cia.gov/cia/publications/ factbook/index.html

Developing a search strategy

When you log on to the Internet to find something, the last thing you should do is, in fact, the *first* thing most people do: head straight to your favorite search engine and type in a simple key-word. That's a sure way to get thousands, if not millions, of "hits" — or Web sites containing that keyword. Sifting through the first ten pages of a list of ten thousand hits is not the most effective way to find something.

It's also not effective because it's estimated that even the best search engines find less than 20% of what is out there online. Contrary to popular belief, search engines don't actually search the Internet; they search only their limited databases. (More on that later.) So, much of the Internet is actually hidden from search engines, or won't be found with simple keyword searches. Often, there are better places to start your search than a search engine — and better ways to use a search engine than to search for simple keywords.

What's more, all search tools are not equal; each works differently. Understanding the differences can help you choose which one is right for you, depending on what you are looking for at the time.

So, you need a search strategy. For each search, consider the following questions:

- What's the best place to find this information?
- What's the best search tool for finding this kind of information?
- What's the best search term to use?

The best place to start...

...depends on what you are researching.

Let's say you are preparing for a trip to Indonesia where you are planning to write a travel piece. If you want to research news stories about recent political unrest in the country, you shouldn't start by heading straight to a search engine. Instead, you should consider which news organization you might trust, find its Web site, and search there for recent stories on Indonesia.

For a thumbnail sketch of Indonesia, why sift through all the irrelevant hits that a search engine will turn up? Instead, the CIA World Fact Book can give you basic information about the politics, climate, geography, languages, and religions of Indonesia. (More on the CIA World Fact Book and other such useful sites in the next chapter.)

If it's travel information you want, you might try Fodor's Resource Centre online, just as you would look for Fodor's travel guides in a bookstore or library.

In other words, using a search tool to find the *Washington Post*, the CIA World Fact Book, or Fodor's online would probably be more efficient and effective than using it to search on the keyword "Indonesia."

Before you begin your search, it's useful to figure out exactly what information you need and then where you are most likely to find it. For example, if you are doing some research for an article on school violence, you should consider the different pieces of information that you will need. You would probably want statistics from law enforcement authorities to show whether the problem is growing and, if so, how significantly. You would probably also need examples of incidents across the country to illustrate the problem. You might want to find out about school board policies toward school violence and how they have changed in recent years. You would also want to get in touch with experts who have studied the problem and have advice for educators and parents.

You could probably find leads to all that information online — but not all at the same Web site. Instead, figure out where each piece of information you need would most likely be found, and search for those Web sites.

Search tools

"The irony of the Internet is that its greatest virtue — its richness — is also its greatest flaw. With nearly a billion Web pages already, this still-young medium threatens to drown us all in information, as the sorcerer's apprentice was nearly drowned in water when he wished too hard for help. That's why search engines have become the biggest draws on the Web. We tell them what we want; they look for it."

— *Penelope Patsuris with Emily Manzo*, Forbes Magazine, *September 13, 1999.*
www.forbes.com/forbes/99/0913/6406035a.htm

The same search using different search engines or search tools can turn up very different results. Often, people decide to stick to one search tool based on past experience and give up trying to use others. That's a mistake.

It's important to understand the differences among search tools so that you'll know which one to use for a given search. The biggest difference, which is often not well understood, is between *subject directories* like Yahoo! and *search engines* like AltaVista. Contrary to popular belief, neither one searches the entire Internet. What they search, instead, still makes them very useful — but not for the same things.

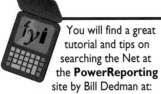
Subject directories — a bird's-eye view

Like the card catalogs that once existed in libraries, subject directories (also called *subject trees*) are databases full of useful information that you can search easily to help you locate items in the collection. Subject directories online organize Web sites into a hierarchy of categories. Each category contains links to subcategories, linking Web pages that contain information on broad topics.

Subject directories don't try to be comprehensive. Instead, they set out to include only the best or most important information on a topic. Each Web site is reviewed by librarians or editors and judged for its suitability to include in the collection. So, if you're starting your search using a subject directory, you don't have to worry about finding Web pages created by fourth graders, or sites containing pictures of Uncle Harry's pet schnauzer. But since it is not humanly possible to review and assess the millions and millions of Web pages out there, the collections are also small — at least in Internet terms. Subject directories may include tens of thousands of Web pages, but that's only a fraction of the Web sites online.

Think of subject directories as the tool that helps you find the haystack. Other tools will help you find the needle.

Yahoo!
www.yahoo.com/

"For users overwhelmed by the mind-boggling number of 'hits' produced by simple searches in the 100-million-page indexes of the biggest search engines, Yahoo!'s helping human hand is blessed relief. It's not surprising that this innovative guide to the Web became the top site on the Web itself. Now Yahoo!'s imitators are legion, with even the busiest search engines rushing to add subject directories, topical 'channels,' and rated site reviews. They're all covering the same bases."

— *Nora Paul and Margo Williams,* Great Scouts! CyberGuides for Subject Searching on the Web. *CyberAge Books, 1999.*

Yahoo! is, by far, the most popular subject directory, and it deserves a prominent place on your bookmark list. Its collection of Web sites is small by Internet standards, but it's still an extensive index of the best of the Web.

You can search Yahoo! in two ways:

- You can drill down through its categories by clicking on one of the broad subject categories on the home page, then clicking on the appropriate subcategory, then perhaps another sub-subcategory, until you find something related to what you're looking for.
- Or, you can use the search field on the home page to search the entire Yahoo! collection of Web sites by keyword.

When you first go to Yahoo!, you'll find a general index of broad subjects such as Arts, Computers, Health, News, and

FIGURE 3-1

Yahoo's home page

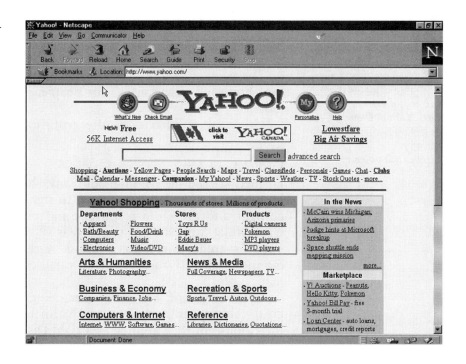

Reference. Each heading is subdivided into dozens of subheadings that lead to further subheadings, which you can follow until you get to the specific information you want. In all, hundreds of thousands of Internet sites are listed here with short descriptions of each. If you are looking for something useful to start your research you will probably find it here, or something close to it.

Yahoo! is an ideal place to find general information quickly, as well as starter sites that can lead you to more specialized information. It's also a great tool to find official sites for organizations, groups, and government departments or agencies.

Searching is straightforward and based on keywords. Just enter your search term in the field and click Search. From the home page you can search the entire Yahoo! collection.

You can click on the link to Advanced Search and refine your search in various ways, such as by date. You can also choose a category and then simply search that category rather than the entire collection.

Yahoo! presents you with a list of relevant links and shows you under which category and subcategory the links were found. The results will give you titles as well as descriptions of the pages that match your query. You will also get a link to the category from which those pages derive, enabling you to explore further information you may not have considered.

If Yahoo! can't find what you want, it offers links to other search engines at the bottom of its search results pages. These may help you find more specific information.

These days, Yahoo! also provides lots of links to sites where you can shop, find news, search for people, get your stock quotes, and more.

Other subject directories offer features not available at Yahoo!.

About.com
http://about.com/
Formerly called the Mining Company, this is a network of sites led by expert guides. It hires people to mine the Internet for original content and premium resources and put together collections of worthwhile Web sites in their areas of expertise. You can use the site to search the resources found by these experts, or send your questions directly to About.com's guides, who will respond by e-mail.

For example, if you were researching panic disorder, you could go to About.com and click on Health from the main page. From there, look for the subcategory called Diseases and click on the link to Panic/Anxiety Disorders. There, you will find a great collection of different links — to information about the disorder; to news stories with related information; to chat rooms where sufferers share their stories; to books on the topic; to a list of the most frequently asked questions about the topic, and more. You will also find a picture of your expert guide, a link to her biography, and an address that you use to send her questions. It's like having a trusted friend to turn to when you are looking for some guidance on a subject she knows well.

LookSmart
www.looksmart.com/
LookSmart is another collection of quality Web sites, all accessible through a well-organized, easy-to-navigate directory of familiar categories and subcategories. LookSmart employs more than 200 editors to comb the Web, reviewing and categorizing only what they consider useful sites. It also offers links to City Guides for local information on weather, area activities, movies, restaurant reviews, and links to local businesses.

If you can't find something you're looking for, you can click on the link to LookSmart's unique feature, LookSmart Live. There, you will be asked to fill in some fields explaining what you are looking for. LookSmart promises that some of its 200 editors will find it for you and send you a response by e-mail within twenty-four hours. If you're in a real hurry, click on the link to LookSmart Live Express and, for a small fee, you can get your answer in an hour.

Check out the **National Library of Canada**'s subject tree, Canadian Information by Subject, located at:
www.nlc-bnc.ca/caninfo/ ecaninfo.htm

Magellan
http://magellan.excite.com/
Magellan is another subject index that can be searched by keyword. What makes it different is that it rates sites in its database and provides a list of recommended sites, along with a list of other sites, for anything you find in its subject index. You can also search by keyword. Magellan looks not just for the keyword, but also for sites that contain words related to the keyword.

More subject directories

The next section of this chapter will talk about an entirely different kind of search tool — search engines. But because many search engines have seen how popular subject directories are with people who are looking for quality sites, they now include subject directories at their Web sites, too. You will find subject directories at almost all the popular search engines such as AltaVista, Excite, Infoseek, Snap, and the GO Network. But since their subject directories are only one of many services offered at those sites, they are often not as good as those you find at sites that focus only on providing a quality subject directory.

In addition to general interest directories such as Yahoo!, About.com, and LookSmart, there are subject-specific directories covering everything from agriculture to zoology. There are several sites that can help you find them.

One of the best is the **Argus Clearinghouse**, which is a subject catalog of subject catalogs. It is a highly selective collection of topical guides chosen and rated by their staff of librarians. The list is updated frequently; any guides that are not revised regularly are dropped from the list. You will find the Clearinghouse at:

www.clearinghouse.net/

Another place to search out subject directories is the **WWW Virtual Library**. This is the oldest catalog of the Web created by the Web's founder, Tim Berners-Lee. You can view the listings alphabetically, click through the hierarchies, or search by keyword. You will find the WWW Virtual Library at:

www.vlib.org/

If you are looking for a scholarly collection of directories on the Web, you will find it at **Infomine**:

http://infomine.ucr.edu/

You'll find more links to good subject directories in Chapter 4 of this book, as well as in Appendix A.

While subject trees are a great place to start, they are not comprehensive. They rely on human diligence to maintain them, and it is not humanly possible to keep up with the phenomenal growth of the Web. To conduct a more thorough search, you will have to use one or more of the Internet's search engines.

UnCover Web
http://uncweb.carl.org/

Of particular interest to professional and academic researchers, UnCover is a massive index to a wide range of multidisciplinary journals and magazines maintained by the Colorado Alliance of Research Libraries.

The database is very up to date and includes more than 18,000 journals and magazines and brief descriptive or bibliographic references to more than eight million articles that have appeared since Fall 1988. UnCover includes periodicals from all subject areas, but concentrates heavily on the sciences and social sciences. It adds new citations daily.

You can search the UnCover database for free. If you find something you want, you can have it faxed to you within forty-eight hours for a small fee. Some articles can also be ordered for delivery directly to a desktop computer and can be viewed by a special viewer available from UnCover.

From the main Web page, you'll find the link to search the database first. You can search on the database without registering. But before you can order any articles, you'll have to register by filling in some basic information and choosing a password. Your profile will be saved for future searches.

You can search by keyword, author's name, or journal title. UnCover will provide a list of article titles and their publication dates. You can click on the title for the full bibliographic information — all you need to find the article in a library and/or order the article.

Other services are also available at this site, but most require a subscription. UnCover Express, for example, is a service designed for people in a hurry. It promises delivery of a select group of articles within an hour. UnCover Reveal is an automated service that delivers the table of contents of your favorite journals directly to your e-mail box. With Reveal, you can also create search strategies for your favorite topics. Keyword or author searches result in a list of individual article citations. Articles may be ordered from UnCover by reply e-mail, or by printing the list and faxing the order to UnCover.

Search engines — the most comprehensive results

"We live in a wired age of palm-this and palm-that, beepers and Net-connected cell phones, e-mail and voice mail. A fast, user-friendly search engine that doesn't assault us with thousands of irrelevant citations may be the only thing that saves us from a lifetime of infopsychosis."

— *Sam Meddis, "On the Web," USA Today, October, 1999.*
www.usatoday.com/life/cyber/ccarch/ccc002.htm

Search engines are the most sophisticated, most comprehensive tool you can use to search the Net for information. But they are not as intuitive as subject directories, and they do not all work the same way.

Like subject directories, search engines don't search the entire Internet. But unlike subject directories, they don't use human beings to review and compile lists of useful Web sites. Instead, they use programs called robots or spiders to scour the Net. Quietly and persistently, these programs go from hyperlink to hyperlink, and when they find new documents, they add the material to their indexes or databases.

When you use a search engine, you are searching only *that search engine's database* for the keyword or keywords you have chosen. The engine finds and displays a list of links to Web sites where those words were found. What's more, even the most powerful search engine, with the most sophisticated program, doesn't have every Web site out there in its database.

Still, all search engines have huge databases and will, most likely, return impossibly long lists of matches or "hits." It is easy to be overwhelmed at the prospect of sifting through them all. For researchers and journalists, hundreds of thousands of hits are almost as useless as no hits at all. So, you will need to develop a few strategies and learn a few tricks to get more manageable, relevant results.

Each search engine uses a program that works a little differently and gathers a different collection of raw data. So when you send a search engine out looking for a keyword, the results will vary depending on which search engine you use. To find just what you want, it's best to learn how to use several of them. Different engines require you to refine your searches differently. For example, the rules about searching for phrases can vary.

Understanding the differences among search engines is the key to choosing the right ones and using them most effectively.

Google
www.google.com/

> "Once you type in a description of what you're looking for and click, Google seems to exhibit inscrutable magic. More often than not, the first link listed gets you exactly where you want to go. ... In the opinion of this oft-frustrated Web surfer, Google is the first search engine that consistently works."
>
> — *David Kirkpatrick, "What's a Google? A Great Search Engine, That's What,"*
> Fortune, *November 8, 1999.*

Google is the best new search engine to come along in years. Unlike other search engines, which are now offering subject directories, free e-mail, chat rooms, online shopping, etc., Google is (so far, at least) a no-frills search engine that aims to do one thing well — find relevant sites fast. It seems to offer a unique blend of the best features of both subject directories and search engines. It consistently finds relevant sites fast, the way Yahoo! does, but it searches a database as

FIGURE 3-2

Google's home page

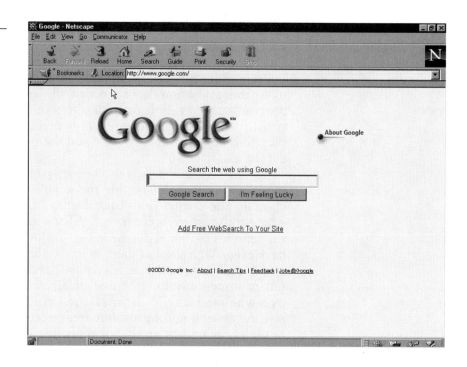

comprehensive as some of the bigger search engines, such as AltaVista and Infoseek.

Google quickly gained a reputation for effectiveness because it was the first search engine to use a new formula for ranking its results. Older search engines generally ranked sites according to how many times a search term appeared on a page, or how prominently it appeared. Google's sophisticated program ranks Web sites based on how popular they are with other popular or important Web sites. For example, the more sites that include links to a particular page, like the American Cancer Society, the more likely it is that page will pop to the top of Google's search results. This means that Google turns up prominent Web sites whose main focus is the issue you are researching, rather than ones that happen to mention the issue in passing.

Google's list of results is also clean and easy to read. Each URL is followed by a brief description of the site — not just the first few words on the page. Each item is followed by a link to Google Scout, which will find sites related to that particular URL.

When you do a search at Google, you can choose to skip the results list completely and go straight to the first hit on the list by pressing the button labeled "I'm feeling lucky" rather than the Google Search button. For example, if you type in the name of the Irish political party, Sinn Fein, and click on the "I'm feeling lucky" button, you will go straight to Sinn Fein's home page.

Google makes searching using keywords fairly simple. All you need to do is type in a few descriptive keywords and click on the Search button. It looks only for pages with all those search terms on them. If you want to search on specific phrases, you can put quotation marks around the exact phrase. With Google, it doesn't matter whether you use uppercase or lowercase letters. All letters are understood as lowercase, no matter how you type them.

You can also use Google to search for any pages that link to a particular site. For example, by typing *link:www.google.com/* in the search field, you will get a list of all the pages that link to Google's home page.

Google is an excellent tool for finding official information and popular sites. But other, older search engines are still better for some searches. And, they offer more sophisticated ways to refine searches than Google does.

More search engines

Albert

www.albert-inc.com/

This is a new search engine, developed by a French company. It promises to track your search patterns and limit results to what it thinks you want, based on your past search history. To use the search engine, click on the button labeled Use Albert Now.

AltaVista

www.altavista.com/

AltaVista is still one of the most popular, sophisticated, and comprehensive search engines on the Net. It has one of the largest indexes, and returns consistently useful information at lightning speed. AltaVista lets you refine searches in more sophisticated ways than most other search tools. It also allows you to search more than just the Web — for example, it will find news stories, discussion group postings, products, images, and video and audio clips. You can search for material in a wide range of languages, as well.

The new and improved version of AltaVista, launched late in 1999, now organizes its results list so that only one Web page per site makes it into the top list of results, thus cutting the clutter of a lot of Web pages from the same site. If there are more pages at the same site, it displays a link below the URL description which you can click to see the other pages. Some hits also include a link to a company fact sheet that takes you to detailed information about the company that owns the Web site.

AltaVista allows you to conduct simple searches, advanced searches, or searches for images, audio, and video by selecting the correct tab at the top of the page. It also searches more and better news sources for current news than ever before.

fyi Google has a separate Web page called **Google Uncle Sam**, which allows you to search U.S. government sites only. It's at: www.google.com/unclesam

FIGURE 3-3

AltaVista's new look

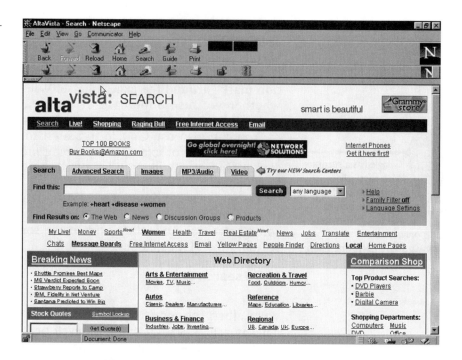

To make a simple query, just enter a keyword or phrase in the search field and click the Search button. You will be presented with a list of hits that include all the keywords you entered, no matter the order in which you entered them. The list will provide hyperlinks that you can click to go directly to the site described. Like other search engines, AltaVista ranks its results, though not as well as Google. You will generally find the best hits near the top of the page and less relevant ones farther down.

Be warned, however: simple searches using single words or series of words can result in hundreds of thousands of hits. To get more manageable results with AltaVista, there are a several things you should do:

- You can direct AltaVista to search for phrases rather than individual words by putting the words in double quotes. For example, if you searched using the words *lung cancer* you would get thousands of references to lungs and thousands to cancer, but by using quotation marks around "lung cancer" you will get hits only on pages where both words are used together.
- If you want to be sure each word you are searching is included in any pages found, you can put a plus sign in front of the word, without a space. For example, you could search on *+paul +newman +sting*. Similarly, you can exclude words by using a minus sign in front of the word. For example, you could search on *+clinton -lewinsky*.

- Unlike Google, AltaVista is case sensitive, so if you use capital letters in your search term, AltaVista will find only sites where capital letters were used in the same way. If you use lowercase letters, however, it will find lowercase, uppercase, and mixed-case versions of the words. So, the safest thing is always to use lowercase letters.
- It's also possible to use a *wildcard* when searching AltaVista to ensure that a number of possible variations on a word are included in search results. The wildcard symbol is the asterisk (*), and means "anything can go here." For example, if you are looking for information about Mexico, you could type *Mexic** in the search window to ensure you get hits that include the words Mexico, Mexican, and Mexicans.
- There are several other ways you can refine your search. For example, you can search for Web sites by specific domains: if you want only U.K. sites, you can add *domain:uk* to your search term. For a full list of other ways to refine your searches, click on the link to Help from AltaVista's main page.
- You can narrow your search by choosing an advanced, rather than a simple, search. Just select the Advanced Search tab from AltaVista's main screen. Advanced searches allow you to use what are called Boolean operators. That just means you can use the words AND, OR, NOT, and NEAR to refine your searches. For example, you could search for *(smoking OR tobacco) AND "lung cancer."* The advanced search page also allows you to search by date, so you can restrict your search to a certain period of time. Detailed but clear instructions about how to use the advanced search page can be found by clicking the link to Advanced Search Help.

fyi

AltaVista also offers separate pages to search for a wide range of international sites. If you want Canadian information, you will find **AltaVista Canada** at: www.altavistacanada.com/

Direct Hit
www.directhit.com/

Direct Hit calls itself a "popularity engine" and promises highly relevant results fast. It ranks sites according to how popular they were with previous searchers who conducted searches on the same terms. It claims to monitor, anonymously, which sites searchers access and how much time they spend there. The more often a site is accessed and the longer it is used, the higher it is ranked the next time someone searches on that term.

If you are searching on an obscure topic, however, Direct Hit may not find anything. If no one has located topics on the subject before, the site will not have anything to rank.

Ejemoni
www.ejemoni.com/

This is a new search tool that was expected to be available in 2000. It promises to allow users to enter paragraphs or entire documents as search terms to give even more context to a search. Company officials say entire documents can be scanned by the search engine, to evaluate the words in context and assign a numeric value. The engine will then search through its index for a Web page or document that has a similar numerical value or "meaning."

Excite
www.excite.com/

Excite is different from other search engines in that it searches not just by keyword, but by concept. In other words, it tries to find *what* you want, not just what you *say* you want. In librarians' terms, it uses "fuzzy logic." It's a great tool when you are not sure of the exact term to search on.

Concept searches find documents related to the idea of your keyword or keywords, not just documents explicitly containing the search terms you enter. This method works best when you provide more than one search term. For example, searching on the words *retired people* will also find pages where seniors and the elderly are mentioned. (You can use the plus and minus sign directly in front of a keyword to ensure it is either included or excluded from the search.) Excite's results list also offers a link below each hit called "Search for more documents like this." If you click on it, Excite will use that document as the basis for another search for more sites similar to the one you selected.

Like AltaVista, you can use Excite to find more than just Web sites — you can search current news and online discussion groups as well. At the bottom of Excite's home page, you will find a link to search for audio and video online.

Excite doesn't make it easy to find, but there is a link on its home page to Advanced Search. By clicking on it, you can get to a page where you can use Boolean operators. Excite makes them easier to use than AltaVista by offering pull-down menus to help you choose your search terms.

Excite has now moved from being a search engine to a portal site that offers a subject directory, e-mail, chat groups, news, weather, and stock reports. You can personalize Excite's home page so that it displays the news you are most interested in, the weather in your area, and the stocks you care about.

Fast Search
www.alltheweb.com/

Also known as All the Web, this search engine claims to have the biggest database of all the search engines online and promises soon to have everything on the Web in its database. Despite its overwhelming size, it also promises relevant results quickly. It allows searching in a wide range of languages and includes audio and video on the Web.

Like most search engines, Fast Search allows either simple or advanced searches. With a simple search, you can search on an exact phrase by putting it in quotation marks. You can require that a word be in the document by putting a plus sign directly in front of it, or exclude words by using a minus sign. For advanced searches, Fast Search offers easy, pull-down menus to help you choose your search terms.

HotBot
http://hotbot.lycos.com/

HotBot is popular because it's up to date, incredibly fast, and makes refining your searches very easy. Here, after typing in your search term, you can modify your choices with the help of three pull-down menus on the left of the page. The first allows you to choose whether you want HotBot to look for pages with all the words, any of the words, or the exact phrase. The second allows you to choose whether you want pages updated in the last few days, weeks, months, or years. The third allows you to choose what language you want to search.

Like AltaVista, HotBot allows you to use an asterisk (*) as a wildcard, and it is case sensitive if you use capital letters in your search terms. If, however, you use lowercase letters, it will search for both lowercase and uppercase versions of the term.

HotBot offers an advanced search page that allows you to refine your searches in very detailed ways, such as by language, date, and even domain, and its pull-down menus help you make your choices. It also allows you to search for video, audio, and other multimedia features. However, HotBot's database is not quite as big as some of the other search engines.

Infoseek
http://infoseek.go.com/

Infoseek, like Excite, has become a portal site with lots of other features besides its search engine. It is now part of Disney's GO Network. The search engine has long been popular because it is fast and comprehensive, and provides generally relevant results. It allows you to search the Web, current news, and Internet discussion groups. It highlights your search term on the pages it finds. One of the new things it offers is the option to search for information on companies.

Like the others, Infoseek allows you to search on phrases by putting them in quotation marks. You can also include words by putting a plus sign directly in front of the words you want, so that *+computer games* will get you pages that have the word computer in them and may have the word games also, but *+computer +games* will find only pages with both words. It, too, is case sensitive if you use any uppercase letters in your search terms.

Infoseek's advanced search page offers pull-down menus to help you modify and refine your search terms.

InvisibleWeb
www.invisibleweb.com/

InvisibleWeb consists of searchable information resources whose contents cannot be indexed by traditional search engines. These include databases, archived material, and interactive tools such as calculators and dictionaries.

Karnak
www.karnak.com/

This search engine is aimed at serious researchers. It stores your searches on its server and keeps searching for several days. Karnak will e-mail you with new links and Web sites related to your search. The basic services are free; other premium services are offered for a fee.

Lycos
www.lycos.com/

This is another search engine turned portal that offers links to a huge range of services. Its search engine allows you to conduct simple and advanced searches using many of the same rules as other search engines. But its database is not as large as some others.

Northern Light
www.northernlight.com/

One of the most highly rated search engines online, Northern Light is fast and comprehensive, and searches news and business sources as well as the Web. Its current news search feature is one of the best online. It allows simple searches with most of the same features as AltaVista. It also offers "power searches," which allow you to refine your search terms.

Northern Light has some unique features, such as sorting its results into well-labeled custom folders along the left-hand side of the page. You can open those folders to find the specific results you want, rather than wading through a long list of a wide range of results. In addition, Northern Light searches more than just the Web. It also searches what it calls its "Special Collection" of popular and academic magazines whose content is not found on the Web. You can search the Special Collection for free and get a reference for the article, which you can use to find it in the library. Or, you can order the full text of the article for a small fee.

Northern Light also offers links to search business-only and investment information sources.

Oingo
www.oingo.com/

This new site calls itself the first "meaning-based search tool." It searches for the meaning of your keywords rather than the literal

FIGURE 3-4

Oingo, a "meaning-
based" search tool

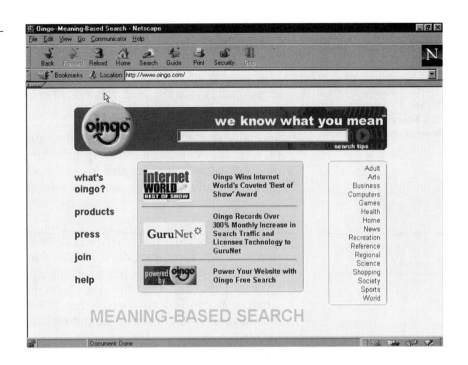

text. Oingo says this is a more human, more intuitive way to search.
When you type in a search term, Oingo will return a box with a
pull-down menu of choices about what you might be looking for.
For example, if you type in the word "dolphins," Oingo will come
back and offer you choices such as the football team or the toothed
whale. When you refine your choice, it will search again and come
up with relevant hits.

Snap
http://home.snap.com/

From CNet and NBC, Snap is both a search engine and a directory.
It has a large database, and searches can be refined in a number of
ways. It's very good for finding popular sites.

tech.ease

Desktop search software can speed up
searching for information. These products offer features beyond what is available through basic Net search engines.
For example, **Express Search (http://
express.infoseek.com/)** will let you
save searches and re-run them, and
incorporate predefined customizable
categories into your search.

Alexa (www.alexa.com/) travels
the Web with you and suggests other
sites that relate to the one you are currently visiting. It will also monitor traffic
on a site, relative to other sites.
Copernic (www.copernic.com/)
lets you preselect search categories and
highlights search terms in the results.
Flyswat (www.Flyswat.com/)

analyzes the content of any Web page
you visit and provides hundreds of links
to related sources of additional information.
Visit **Tucows (www.tucows.com/)**
to find out about a range of other
browser "searchbots."

Webcrawler
www.webcrawler.com/
Yet another Web search engine turned portal site. Its search engine offers many of the same features as others. It was more impressive in the past, when the field was not so crowded.

Specialty search engines
Specialty search engines are tools that allow you to search databases of Web sites containing very specific kinds of information. We will mention a few here. Chapter 4 and Appendix A include descriptions of many more.

FindLaw
www.findlaw.com/
A Yahoo!-like directory that provides a vast array of legal information — from Supreme Court decisions to law review articles. Don't be fooled by the home page, which appears to be dominated by links to U.S. sites. One link on the main page takes you to a page where you can link to a vast array of legal information from more than seventy-five countries, including Canada.

Fodor's Resource Centre
www.fodors.com/resource/
Not surprisingly, this one's a great resource for travel information from an organization that has gained a reputation for producing excellent travel guides.

Hoover's Online
www.hoovers.com/
This site provides a lot of free information on, and links to, the Web sites of all publicly traded and many private U.S. companies, as well as other large companies. All you need to know is the company name, or even just part of it.

Law Enforcement Links Directory and Police Search Engine
www.leolinks.com/
An amazing, huge collection of links to a wide range of law enforcement sites around the world.

Livelink Pinstripe
http://pinstripe.opentext.com/
Another source for business information where you can search by industry.

MapBlast
www.mapblast.com/
A great resource for all kinds of maps from around the world.

NewsTrawler
www.newstrawler.com/

Most online news organizations have archives that can be searched by keyword. This tool allows you to search multiple news archives at once. It can access hundreds of newspapers and broadcast news archives around the world. You can register and choose the ones you are most likely to want to search. Then, each time you go to the site, you are presented with your list of favorites. You can search any number of them simultaneously, and receive a list of results from each of the archives you choose.

Political Information.com
www.politicalinformation.com/
Strictly American, this site indexes thousands of Web sites for those interested in political campaigns, political policy making, and political news.

Statistics Every Writer Should Know: Finding Data on the Internet
http://nilesonline.com/data/
A guide to Web sites that have statistical information compiled by the executive producer of the Web site of the Denver *Rocky Mountain News*.

StreetEye
www.streeteye.com/cgi-bin/allseeing.cgi
A metasearch engine for investment information.

The Terrorism Research Centre
www.terrorism.com/
A collection of links to quality resources on terrorism. The site also features essays on current issues involving terrorism.

Metasearch tools

In addition to the individual search engines, there are sites that allow you to submit your query to several search engines at the same time. They are not as useful as they might seem, though, because they generally use the most basic-level searches at each of the major engines. They don't allow you to refine your searches in very sophisticated ways, and so don't handle complex searches well.

AskJeeves
www.askjeeves.com/
This popular search tool is ideal for rookie searchers because it allows you to ask questions in plain English rather than coming up with precise search terms. It responds to your questions with one or more closely related questions to which it knows the answer, along with the answers from a variety of search engines. It's great for simple questions, but not for complicated searches.

FIGURE 3-5

AskJeeves

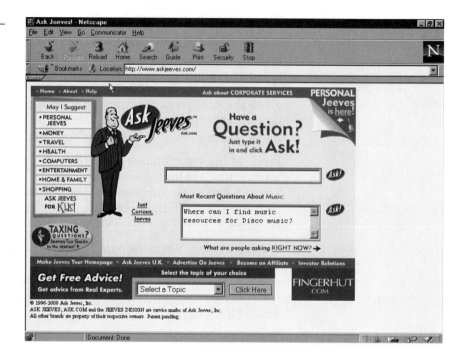

C4

www.c4.com/

Formerly Cyber 411, this one offers you the option of asking a question in plain English or using keyword search terms. Though you can't do much to refine your search terms, you can customize your search by choosing which of the top search tools you want to use. The results are returned with a note about which search engine found them. You can also search beyond the Web to include current news, financial news, and discussion groups.

Dogpile

www.dogpile.com/

This site is remarkable for more than just its tacky name. Its speed and flexibility set it apart as a powerful metasearch site. Dogpile allows you to choose which of up to eighteen search tools you want to conduct your search and the order in which you want the results presented (for example, findings from Yahoo! first, then AltaVista, then Excite, etc.). It was developed by a guy named Aaron Flin who says he got tired of using Yahoo! and finding almost no results, then turning to AltaVista and getting 30,000 hits. Unlike other metasearch sites, Dogpile also allows you to refine your search terms using Boolean operators. But it doesn't sort the list to get rid of duplicates.

Gogettem

www.gogettem.com/

This site sends your search to up to eighteen other search tools at the same time. You can choose which ones you want used. The difference is that it opens each search engine you choose in a different browser window. So, if you choose six search engines, suddenly you will have six different versions of Netscape or Explorer open — one for each search engine.

Inference Find

www.infind.com/

Inference Find uses six of the best search engines on the Web at the same time. It is unique in the way it merges the results, removes redundancies, and clusters the results into neat, understandable groupings. It is an intelligent multisearch tool.

Mamma

www.mamma.com/

It calls itself the "mother of all search engines," conducting parallel searches of several popular search engines. It properly formats the search term for each engine. It also organizes the results into a uniform format and presents them by relevance and sources. So, you get a relevant, comprehensive, easy-to-follow list of results.

MetaCrawler

www.metacrawler.com/

MetaCrawler, now operated by Go2Net Inc., is a highly rated multisearch site that sends your query to several search engines at once, organizes the results into a uniform list, drops duplicate results, and then ranks the remainder by relevance.

Profusion

www.profusion.com/

This tool gives you the largest number of options for tailoring your search and displaying the results.

SavvySearch

www.savvysearch.com/

This search tool allows you to search from among 200 different Web databases at the same time. You can customize it to search the ones you want, and it integrates the results well.

Starting pages for journalists — a place to browse

Starting pages for journalists are Web pages designed to provide you with a useful set of links to the kinds of sites journalists generally need. They're one-stop shops for all your basic needs. Just scan the list of topics and select a link that interests you — no searching skills or strategies are required. Many writers and journalists make

Ixquick is a new metasearch tool that is smarter than most. It is fast and comprehensive, searching 14 search engines, ranking the results and identifying which engine found each result. It is one of the few metasearch tools that allows you to do advanced searches and it knows which engines support which kinds of searches. When it finds pages with multiple engines, it only lists them once. You'll find Ixquick at:

www.ixquick.com/

Need census data or financial information? Check out a great collection of links to statistical resources at: **www.columbia.edu/cu/ libraries/indiv/jour/subject/ stats.html**

For the **U.S. Census**, which gets an update in 2000, check out: **www.census.gov/**

For Canadian statistics, go to **Statistics Canada** at: **www.statcan.ca/start. html**

these sites their home pages so that when they open their browser, these pages open automatically.

If you have access to the Internet at work, your place of employment may have a starting page with links to information you need on the job, such as the e-mail addresses of your colleagues. If you access the Internet through a commercial service or ISP, you may get their page, or Netscape's home page, when you log on. If you use one of the portal sites such as Excite, Infoseek, or Lycos, you will get a set of links that you may even personalize. All these pages will provide useful links to explore. But for writers, researchers, or journalists, there are a few specific sites designed especially for them.

The Beat Page
www.reporter.org/beat/
A jumping-off point for journalism resources, organized by subject or beats, maintained by investigative reporters and editors in the United States.

European Journalists Page
www.demon.co.uk/eurojournalism/media.html
Sites and resources of interest to journalists working in or covering Europe.

FACSNet
www.facsnet.org/
A collection of selected online resources for reporters produced by the Foundation for American Communications (FACS), an independent, nonprofit, educational institution based in Los Angeles. It includes a good database of expert sources.

Interested in finding out more about the top stories in the news in the United States this week? Check out the **Poynter Institute for Media Studies Links to the News** at: **http://poynter.org/dj/ shedden/index.htm**

Internet Journalism Resources
www.moorhead.msus.edu/~gunarat/ijr/
A well-designed page with a great collection of search tools and other resources for journalists. It's maintained by Shelton Gunaratne, a journalism professor at Moorhead State University in Minnesota.

Journalism Access
http://mindy.mcadams.com/jaccess/index.html
A small collection of useful links, including some offbeat ones you won't find easily elsewhere. It's maintained by Mindy McAdams, a journalism professor at the University of Florida and one of the authors of this book.

JournalismNet
www.journalismnet.com/
This is an extensive collection of great links for journalists. It has an international flavor, including links not just to U.S. sites, but Canadian, U.K., and other European sites, as well. It also features the top search engines right on the main page. The site is main-

FIGURE 3-6

JournalismNet

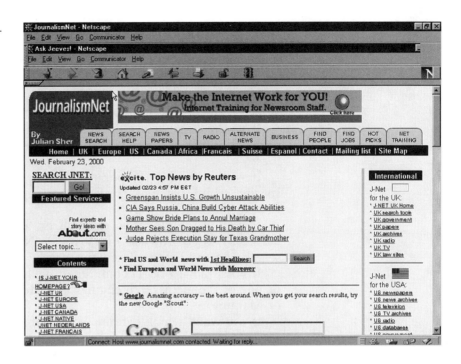

tained by Julian Sher, a Canadian television producer now living in the United States, who trains reporters around the world about Internet research techniques. His site also features a "Pick of the Week" — a site that Sher highlights every Sunday of special interest to writers, researchers, and journalists online. It's a great way to find out about new sites. You can check his list of past "picks" going back to 1997.

PowerReporting
http://PowerReporting.com/

A no-frills collection of some of the best links for journalists to Web sites, search tools, and government and company information. It has a great list of the top 100 Web sites for journalists. It also organizes links by beats for beat reporters. The site is maintained by Bill Dedman, a reporter for the *New York Times*, who trains reporters in computer-assisted reporting and online reporting techniques. His site also includes an excellent primer on searching on the Internet. The site has a strictly U.S. bent.

Teaching Journalism Online
www.carleton.ca/~mmcguire

A small collection of links to Internet search tools and other sites for people who teach Internet research techniques and online journalism. It's maintained by Mary McGuire, a journalism professor at Carleton University and one of the authors of this book.

Comparing search tools

> "Knowledge is of two kinds. We know a subject ourselves, or we know where we can find information upon it."
>
> — *Dr. Samuel Johnson*

Which is the best search tool? It depends.

If you're just browsing, or are looking for general information on a broad topic, start at Yahoo! or one of the other subject catalogs.

If you're looking for popular and/or important Web sites for a specific group, company, organization, agency, or issue, try Google first, or HotBot.

If you're doing serious research on an issue that is difficult to define by keyword, use AltaVista or Northern Light's advanced search pages to try to refine your search.

If you want to be as comprehensive as possible, try Fast Search or one of the metasearch engines like MetaCrawler, Inference Find, or Mamma.

If you want help in defining your search, try Oingo.

And, if you have a simple question, try AskJeeves.

In the end, it's best to bookmark several search tools and use different ones at different times. When you use them, too, don't settle for making simple queries. Read the Help menu; try some advanced search techniques; follow some of the tips and tricks on pages 70–71. The time you spend mastering a few search techniques will be time saved sifting through useless results.

A last word

Don't restrict yourself to broad search engines that search only the Web (or at least as much of the Web as will fit in a single database). These days, a growing number of specialty search engines are there to help you search for just about any kind of information.

fyi For a comprehensive list of over 500 Internet search tools, check out the **All-In-One Search Page** at:

www.allonesearch.com/ For a well-organized set of links to the vast array of search tools available online, visit the **Indiana University Bloomington**

Libraries page on Internet Quick References: **www.indiana.edu/ ~librcsd/internet/ _Searching_the_Web/**

FIGURE 3-7
Search tools at a glance

SUBJECT TREES	URLS	COMMENTS
About.com	about.com/	General index compiled by expert guides who will answer your e-mail
LookSmart	www.looksmart.com/	Online editors help you search
Yahoo!	www.yahoo.com/	Great general index
SEARCH ENGINES	**URLS**	**COMMENTS**
Albert	www.albert-inc.com/	Tracks your search patterns
AltaVista	www.altavista.com/	A leader among search engines
Direct Hit	system.directhit.com/	Ranks results according to popularity with past searchers
Ejemoni	www.ejemoni.com/	Searches context, not just keywords
Excite	www.excite.com/	Good for concept searches
Fast Search	www.alltheweb.com/	Searches more of the Web than most
Google	www.google.com/	Consistently provides the most relevant hits
HotBot	hotbot.lycos.com/	Fast, easy, and very popular
Infoseek	infoseek.go.com/	Consistently good
InvisibleWeb	www.invisibleweb.com/	Searches databases not included by other search engines
Karnak	www.karnak.com/	Saves your search, updates while you are offline, and e-mails updates
Lycos	www.lycos.com/	Reliable and comprehensive
Oingo	www.oingo.com/	Helps refine your keyword search based on meaning
Northern Light	www.northernlight.com/	Offers unique features and search options
Snap	home.snap.com/	Fast and comprehensive
Webcrawler	www.webcrawler.com/	Small but easy to use
METASEARCH ENGINES	**URLS**	**COMMENTS**
AskJeeves	www.askjeeves.com/	Takes questions in plain English
C4	www.c4.com/	Allows you to customize preferences
Dogpile	www.dogpile.com/	Searches 18 search engines at once
Gogettem	www.gogettem.com/	Opens new browser window for each search engine used
Inference Find	www.infind.com/	Uses six engines; organizes results well ▶

**FIGURE 3-7
(cont'd)**
Search tools at a glance

METASEARCH ENGINES	URLs	COMMENTS
Ixquick	www.ixquick.com/	Fast, comprehensive, and smarter than most
Mamma	www.mamma.com/	Uses several search engines; organizes results well
MetaCrawler	www.metacrawler.com/	Dependable, easy to follow
Profusion	www.profusion.com/	Lots of search options
SavvySearch	www.savvysearch.com/	Offers huge number of search tools

10 TIPS FOR BETTER SEARCHING

1. **Know the differences among search tools.** Learn to use different search tools for different searches. Some of the new tools offer unique features that make them particularly well suited to particular kinds of searches. Don't rely on one or two tools for all your searches.

2. **Decide what you need first and where you might find it.** Before you head straight to a search engine, consider where you might find the information you need. Consider using a search tool to find the agency, company, department, etc. that might have the information before doing a simple keyword search on a topic. This strategy will save you time in the long run and could be more effective, because so much of the Web is hidden from search engines.

3. **Don't be afraid to guess.** These days, you can often guess at the address of sites where you might logically expect to find information. If you're looking for a company's Web site, try typing in *www.companyname.com/*; for an organization, try *www.organizationname.org/*. But beware of near-misses: for example, if you go to *whitehouse.gov/* you will get the official site for the White House. But change the *.gov* to *.net* or *.com*, and you'll find something very different!

4. **When doing keyword searches, choose search terms carefully.** Use as many search terms or phrases that identify precisely your subject of interest. Choose unusual words. Be specific. Don't use words *about* the subject; consider which words are most likely to be found on the ideal page. For example, if you are researching contraceptive methods, those two words might not occur on the best pages. However, *birth control pill, condom*, and *IUD* might be. The more precise you are, the better your results will be. You want to avoid wading through a flood of irrelevant or inconsequential sites to get to the jewels.

5. **Know the rules for qualifying your search terms at the search engine you are using.** Should you put quotation marks around phrases? Should you use a plus sign directly in front of any word (without a space) you want included, and a minus sign in front of any word you want excluded? Most search engines require this, so that searching for *+meat +safety* will get you sites that include both words, but searching on *+meat safety* will get you sites that include meat and maybe safety. Is the search engine case sensitive, meaning you should use lowercase letters only? Can you use an asterisk for a wildcard? Read the Help page

at any search engine you are using. The rules are generally short and clear, and time spent reading them will be time saved sorting through useless hits.

6. **Use advanced or power search features when available.** The advanced search features of most search engines usually let you create more complex and targeted searches. Read the Help menu for tips on how to do advanced searches.

7. **Get to know some of the specialty indexes and search sites.** As the Internet continues to grow, finding relevant information using general search tools becomes harder. Find sites that compile databases of subject-specific information and use them, as well.

8. **Enter multiple spellings where appropriate.** For example, try *Khaddafi Quadafy Gadaffi*. If you are interested in rock climbing, try *rockclimbing* and *rock-climbing*. Most search engines look only for exact matches to your search term, and Web site creators don't necessarily use a spell checker on their sites.

9. **If at first you don't succeed, try again.** Be persistent and creative. Expect to search several times, adding and removing restrictions to find what you need. Try using synonyms, too. Try using other search tools. Don't get stuck using only one.

10. **Know when to stop or to look elsewhere.** Sometimes the information you need may be out there online, but finding it the old-fashioned way — from a book or library, or even by picking up the phone — will be faster. Other times the information is *not* out there. All the information known to humankind is not on the Web, even if it seems that way.

Further reading

Callahan, Christopher. *A Journalist's Guide to the Internet.* New York: Allyn & Bacon, 1999.

Cohen, Laura. *Conducting Research on the Internet.* www.albany.edu/library/internet/research.html

Flanagan, Debbie. *Web Search Strategies.* http://home.sprintmail.com/~debflanagan/main.html

Paul, Nora. *Computer Assisted Research: A Guide to Taping Online Information.* Third edition; revised 1997. www.poynter.org/car/cg_chome

CHAPTER 4

Beyond Search Engines: The Undiscovered Web

"If your search tools can't see ... database-driven, dynamically constructed Web pages (and most current search tools can't), you are unintentionally excluding from your Web searches:
- 12 million documents from the Library of Congress
- most data from the U.S. Census Bureau
- ERIC databases
- most daily newspapers
- vast collections of fine art owned by important museums
- more than 1,700 other information-rich databases.**"**

— KEN WISEMAN, "THE INVISIBLE WEB," *LEARNING TECHNOLOGY REVIEW,* FALL 1999/WINTER 2000. www.apple.com/education/LTReview/fall99/

When many folks first start using the Internet, they are astonished at the amount of information that is available. And chances are, what they've found is only the tip of the iceberg.

The World Wide Web may seem to hold an unprecedented wealth of sources. But the business of information storage and retrieval is not a new phenomenon — after all, the ancient Mesopotamians maintained libraries of clay tablets from about 3500 BCE!

Today, newspapers and magazines are a chief source of both news and information: visit any large library and you will see shelves of microfiche for back issues of the *New York Times*, the *International Herald Tribune*, and other major newspapers. As well, online searching of research databases, statistical information sources, libraries, and government archives has been a reality for over a quarter of a century.

Since the advent of the Web, most of the traditional agencies involved in collecting and organizing data have established a presence on the Internet. As a researcher, you will certainly want to know how to access these sources — and often, search engines are not a sure way to find these.

The last chapter gave the "big picture" of how to find your way around the Net. In this chapter, we take a closer look at some valuable research sources — available from libraries, databases, media, and government resources. Too often, these resources are the undiscovered Web.

■ **Subject guides**
■ **Libraries on the Net**
■ **Databases**
■ **Media on the Web**
■ **Government information on the Net**

Subject guides

There are a number of locations on the Net where you can find well-researched subject guides to resources for particular topics — for example, Yahoo! indices (see Chapter 3) can be used this way. You will find others listed in Appendix A.

One of the best subject trees is found at the Argus Clearinghouse (which we suggested in Chapter 3 as a good general starting point).

Argus Clearinghouse
www.clearinghouse.net/
Formerly known as the Clearinghouse for Subject-Oriented Internet Resource Guides, Argus is a repository of over 400 guides to the Internet — many of which have been developed by experts in their field. These sources differ from starting pages (described in Chapter 3) in that they are in-depth guides to selected resources on specific subjects, such as English literature or animal rights.

Argus guides are donated, and each is the work of an individual author or group. As a result, they vary considerably in terms of format and the sorts of references that are included. A guide to environmental law developed by the Indiana University School of Law at Bloomington will differ considerably from a guide developed by an environmental activist.

The advantage of the Argus Clearinghouse guides is that the best ones provide you with a narrative overview of a topic, rather than just a set of links. Another plus is that Argus quickly points you in the direction of some of the best sources on your topic. Quality is a big factor at the Argus Clearinghouse. Only the best submissions are selected for posting at the site, and each guide is rated for its content and design.

Argus guides typically list Web sites, but may also include FTP sites, Usenet newsgroups, and electronic mailing lists for a specific topic or set of related topics. You'll find similar guides elsewhere on the Net, but the Argus Clearinghouse is one place to find these resources quickly.

Another good jumping-off point is Infomine, a virtual reference tool intended specifically for university-level researchers.

FIGURE 4-1

The Argus Clearinghouse

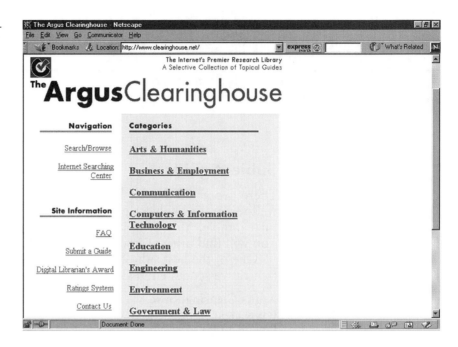

Infomine
http://infomine.ucr.edu/
Developed by the University of California at Riverside, this site offers guides to the Internet for most disciplines, as well as access to useful databases, textbooks, conference proceedings, and journals. Infomine lists virtual collections according to broad disciplines, for example: Agricultural, Biological, and Medical Resources; Government Information; Physical Sciences; Social Sciences; and Humanities. There are also components devoted to Maps and Geographic Information Systems, Visual and Performing Arts, and Internet Enabling Tools, such as a list of recommended search tools.

Here are a few more notable subject guides:

BUBL Information Service
http://bubl.ac.uk/
BUBL bills itself as a "national information service for the higher education community." BUBL Link provides excellent coverage of academic disciplines, including arts, literature, health studies, life sciences, social sciences, and technology topics. The BUBL Journals section contains tables of contents, abstracts, and full text for over 200 current journals and newsletters.

Consumer World
www.consumerworld.org/
This is a very comprehensive resource for consumer information. In

addition to the Net's latest bargains, you will find an extensive list of links to consumer organizations, consumer and general news sources, travel information, and a very good list of Internet sources including search engines, free stuff, and "Internet Wonders."

FindLaw
www.findlaw.com/
This site looks a lot like Yahoo!, but its focus is on legal topics: cases and codes, government resources, international law and trade, and more.

Healthfinder
www.healthfinder.gov/
This is a government site for health information. You can search Healthfinder or browse by topic for information on popular health issues: AIDS, tobacco, seniors, minority health, and more. There is also a selection of health-related online journals.

Voice of the Shuttle
http://vos.ucsb.edu/
A comprehensive site for humanities research, covering anthropology, history, literature, media studies, and many other social, cultural, and educational areas. Here you will also find a selection of tutorials on Internet search techniques (check the General Humanities Resources page).

You can find a directory with contact information for U.S. businesses at **The Ultimate Yellow Pages**: www.infospace. com/info.abii/index_ylw.htm This resource is organized by region and category.

A similar resource is the **BigBook**: www.bigbook. com/

For more comprehensive business information resources (some at a cost), visit **Corporate Information** at: www.corporateinformation. com/

Libraries on the Net

Like many businesses and agencies, libraries are adapting to the electronic environment. Some libraries have made their catalogs searchable over the Internet, and others are developing digital archives, so that existing print resources (such as photographic collections or academic journals) can be accessed electronically. Further, some of the most useful Web resources have been developed by librarians — most often in an effort to organize Internet materials for a particular client group, such as a university community or a business library.

If you long for the Net to be organized more along the lines of the traditional library, where you know exactly where they keep the dictionaries or the psychology books, spend some time exploring the following library resources on the Internet.

The Internet Public Library
www.ipl.org/
A fun place to experience an online library! The Internet Public Library is set up like a real building, with a Reading Room, a Reference Center, and even an Exhibit Hall that displays virtual art. You'll also find services for youth and Pathfinders, which are guides

FIGURE 4-2

Internet Public Library
Reference Center

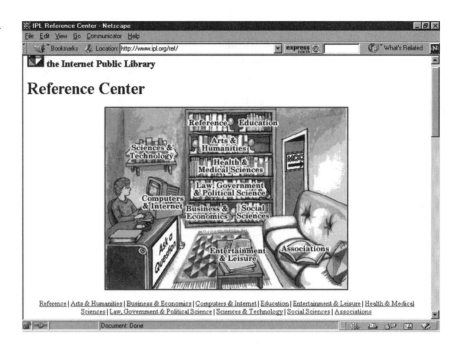

written by IPL staff that are designed to help you get started doing research on a particular topic.

Of particular value to researchers is the Reference Center, which points to a selection of Internet reference sources. You can access the general reference area for dictionaries and similar tools, or you can go to a specific subject area, such as Arts and Humanities or Business and Economics, where you will find works targeted to specific subjects. The IPL provides a detailed overview of each of the sources they have selected to include in the library. The references are not extensive, but they are carefully selected and can point you toward some useful starting-point pages.

If you visit the Reference Center, you will find many full-text books, such as almanacs, dictionaries, and encyclopedias. There are also telephone books, a currency converter, atlases, and *Bartlett's Familiar Quotations*. In the Reading Room there are books, newspapers, and magazines. You can use this area as a gateway to the many online books and periodicals available on the Internet: there are pointers to more than 2,600 books, 800 magazines, and 1,100 newspapers. And, if one of the things you miss most (as traditional library services move onto the Net) is a helpful librarian, the IPL provides an Ask a Reference Question service. You can submit a question by filling in an online form, or via electronic mail. These are forwarded to a librarian or library student, who will either return an answer or point you in the direction of (mostly Internet) sources that you can use to research the topic.

fyi Be sure to visit your local public or university library on the Internet. Many libraries provide information about local resources and events. At a university, research agency, or newspaper, the librarians may have developed a Web page that points to some of the best resources for persons in that organization, and some libraries actually offer an online reference service to their local users. You can find libraries at **Yahoo! (www.yahoo.com/)** and at **LibWeb (http://sunsite.berkeley.edu/LibWeb/)**

Library of Congress
www.loc.gov/
Another important Internet library source. The many valuable research sources here include a series of detailed background studies for seventy-one countries around the world (called Country Studies); the American Memory Collection, a digital library of historical documents and photographs; a database of bibliographies for research in science and technology and social sciences; and an Entrepreneur's Reference Guide to Small Business Information. A good way to get an overview of some of the resources available here is to browse the Alphabetical Index. You can search the library catalog for books held by the Library of Congress through an easy-to-use Web interface.

At the Library of Congress you will also find something called the *Z39.50 gateway*. This tool lets you search a variety of library catalogs and databases directly from the Web. (Of particular interest is GILS, the database for Government Information Locator Service.) With the Z39.50 gateway, you fill in a simple onscreen form — so you don't have to figure out the exact commands usually required by a catalog or database.

The Library of Congress offers a further set of subject links to the Internet, called **Explore the Internet** (**http://lcweb.loc.gov/ global/explore.html**). This service includes pointers to search engines, a number of Internet learning resources, and a particularly good set of links to U.S. government information.

Other Internet library sources
You can locate an extensive set of links to libraries on the World Wide Web at **WebCATS: Library Catalogs on the World Wide Web:**
  www.lights.com/webcats/
and at Hytelnet:
  www.lights.com/hytelnet/
Hytelnet includes instructions on how to search various library catalogs using telnet. Hytelnet also offers links to a number of specialized databases and bulletin boards. For information sources that have not yet made the transition onto the Web, Hytelnet is a useful point of access.

Also, check out the resources that follow (continued on page 79).

Librarians' Index to the Internet
http://lii.org/
This extremely useful resource includes, in addition to carefully selected subject resources, an Internet Search section with the LII's choice of search engines, virtual reference links to business and other information, and a What's New? feature. You can subscribe to the LII New This Week mailing list to receive weekly updates on some of the best new sites on the Web.

Telnet

Telnet is the application that lets you connect to another computer on the Internet, log on, and actually use the remote computer directly — rather than simply view the information, as is usually the case with a Web page. Although telnet is not used as often as it once was, there remain some resources (such as some commercial databases) that are not available any other way.

One common use for telnet is to log on to a computer where you have a second Internet account. For example, you may have a university account, and you may have a second account with a service provider or a local freenet. If you are at a conference and away from your home computer, you may be able to telnet to your home account and not have to dial long distance.

To use telnet, you will need some type of telnet software; your service provider should be able to supply this. In a Macintosh environment you can use NCSA Telnet or Nifty Telnet; in Windows you may use WinTel32, Telnet98, NetTerm, or another. If your service provider has not given you telnet software, you can obtain telnet clients for both

Macintosh and Windows from **Tucows** at:

www.tucows.com/

A telnet client enables your smart computer to pretend it's a dumb terminal. Large mainframe computers usually require you to "dumb down" your personal computer before they will recognize you. If you configured your own communications software, you may recall setting the terminal emulation. Some common terminal emulation types are VT100, VT102, ANSI, and TTY. On the Internet, VT100 is the most frequently used terminal emulation, so you will probably want to set this as a default on your telnet software. With any telnet program, you need to use the software's menu choices to configure the software and access a site. Frequently, the default settings do not need to be adjusted. Remember that you will need to be logged on to your Internet account for the telnet software to be able to access other Internet computers.

It is possible to telnet using a Web browser, but only if you have set up your browser to use telnet software as a helper application. (See Chapter 8 to find out more

about helper applications.) In this case, when you type in the URL for a telnet site (or click on a telnet link), your telnet software will automatically be activated. A telnet connection almost always requires you to log on to the remote computer you are accessing. Many systems allow you to log on as a guest.

You need two pieces of information for a telnet session:

- the address for the site that you want to connect to — for example, *lex.meaddata.com/* to telnet to a Lexis-Nexis account. In this case, from within your Web browser, you would type in the URL field: *telnet://lex.meaddata.com/*

- the logon information for the site. This could be your name and password for a personal account, or it could be a public logon, such as *guest*, on a telnet site that has been set up for public access.

Once you arrive at a telnet location, follow whatever onscreen instructions appear for using the system. You will not find telnet sites as easy to navigate as the World Wide Web, and some of the sites can be confusing, but help screens are almost always available.

Be prepared to take time to familiarize yourself with a telnet site in order to use it efficiently. Watch carefully for logging off instructions when you are telnetting to a site. On many systems, typing the **Control C** key combination or **Control]** (Control plus right bracket) may break the connection. You can also just exit from your telnet software, though it is preferable to log off from a site before doing so.

Some sites now use the Java Telnet Applet. This is a telnet program that will automatically appear on your screen when you click on the telnet link. If you encounter such a site, you will not need a separate telnet program. Just wait for the telnet application to load. Follow the on-screen instructions to access the site. The applet will disappear when you exit the page.

Best Information on the Net
http://vweb.sau.edu/bestinfo/
These resources have been chosen by librarians at O'Keefe Library, St. Ambrose University. The organization of this site will appeal to many academic researchers. Headings include Important Sites by Major, Reference Desk, and Hot Paper Topics.

LibrarySpot
www.libraryspot.com/
Links to libraries online plus a reference desk and a reading room with books, journals, magazines, newspapers, newswires, and speeches. While you're there, check out the other StartSpot sites: BookSpot, EmploymentSpot, GourmetSpot, GovSpot, LibrarySpot, ShoppingSpot, and TripSpot.

The Michigan Electronic Library (MEL)
http://mel.lib.mi.us/main-index.html
MEL offers a reference section and an exceptionally well-organized set of subject links. The links included here are selected by content specialists for quality, reliability, and relevance. The site covers many areas of general interest.

National Library of Canada
www.nlc-bnc.ca/
This resource is similar to the Library of Congress's online service. In addition to the library's own collection, the NLC provides access to a collection of Canadian online books and journals. The NLC lists Canadian information by subjects according to the Dewey Decimal System, then provides links to Web sites with more information. For these links, access:
www.nlc-bnc.ca/caninfo/ecaninfo.htm

FIGURE 4-3

Britannica.com, a searchable directory of Web sites

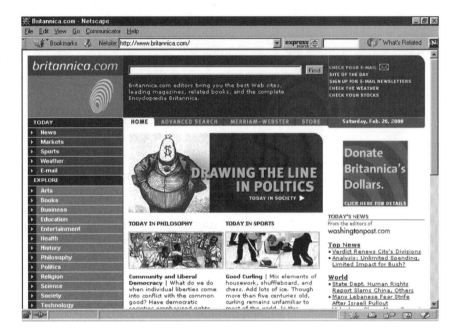

Databases

There are thousands of databases offering Internet access to information on hundreds of specialized topics. Examples include the **ERIC** database for educational research (**http://ericir.syr.edu/**) and **QPAT-US** (**www.qpat.com/**), which stores the full text of all U.S. patents issued since 1974. Many databases were established long before the Web came into being, and increasingly, organizations are attempting to make their databases available on the Internet.

Resources such as magazine archives or abstracts for research reports may also be stored in databases. Unfortunately, regular Web search engines are not able to search databases directly. As a result, information stored in databases is now often referred to as the "invisible Web." To gain access to the invisible Web you need either to visit a site that has been set up for searching databases, or to know about a database and go directly to its home site to search. Following are several good sources for locating searchable databases on the World Wide Web.

AlphaSearch
www.calvin.edu/library/searreso/internet/as/
AlphaSearch is a collection of high-quality gateway sites and databases for many different subject areas. You can search for resources by subject, or browse databases by discipline.

The BigHub
www.thebighub.com/
The BigHub provides access to over 1,500 specialty search engines for searching databases on the Web, and allows you to search these directly. The databases include business directories, science databases, and job listings. This is also a useful resource for government and health information, and for finding people on the Net.

Searchable media information sources include Newsletter Access, a directory of over 5,000 newsletters; NewsDirectory.com (formerly Ecola Newsstand), which has links to over 8,400 newspapers and magazines on the Web; and specific magazines, such as *Scientific American, Time,* and *World Watch.* You can search these resources directly from The BigHub's home page. Further, the site provides a brief description of each database and hyperlinks to listed sites. You might want to bookmark this site.

The Cornell Gateway Catalog
www.mannlib.cornell.edu/
Some of the databases listed in this resource are proprietary, meaning that you must be affiliated with Cornell University to gain access to them. But there are hundreds of databases here, some of which can be searched for free: for example, many U.S. government databases; the Journalism Periodicals Database, which references professional and academic publications for journalism and mass communication; the Economic Research Service publications database; and *Psyche: An Interdisciplinary Journal of Research on Consciousness.*

The biggest disadvantage to the Cornell Gateway is the large number of "Cornell Only" databases. Still, it's worth checking out to determine what resources might be available in your area of interest.

Direct Search
http://gwis2.circ.gwu.edu/~gprice/direct.htm
Database junkies should check out Gary Price's Direct Search, a *very long* list of many database resources on the Web. How else could you ever find about the "Nonproliferation and Arms Control Directory" or the "Consumer Price Index Historical Calculator"? Price also maintains a number of other unique lists, such as **The Speech and Transcript Center** at:
    http://gwis2.circ.gwu.edu/~gprice/speech.htm

FIGURE 4-4

A list of searchable databases is available at Lycos.

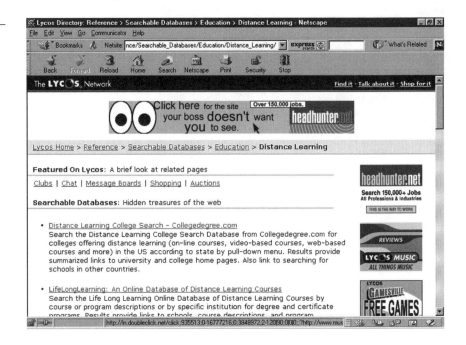

Healthgate
www.healthgate.com/index.shtml

This resource lists extensive health information databases and services. While access to most of these requires a subscription, Healthgate offers free access to the National Library of Medicine's biomedical database, Medline.

Medline is a primary medical research database that offers over eight million references to journal articles in medicine and related disciplines. Many of these references include abstracts. The Medline database can also be accessed from **BioMedNet** at:

www.biomednet.com/db/medline

Lycos Databases
www.lycos.com/

Lycos provides quick access to as many as 7,000 searchable databases. Look in the directory under Reference, and then under Searchable Databases, to find individual topics.

The National Institutes of Health
www.nih.gov/health/

This is an authoritative source for health information. Here you can find some full-text consumer health publications and search the Combined Health Information Database.

Search
http://search.cnet.com/

Search provides a listing of over 100 specialty search engines and a pull-down menu that will let you search within a particular topic area, such as business, entertainment, or news. By using a specialty search engine designed to search for database information within a particular site (such as FedStats for U.S. Federal government statistics or Hoover's Online for corporate summaries), you can significantly reduce time spent searching for factual information on the Web.

WebData
www.webdata.com/

WebData covers arts and humanities as well as shopping, travel, and stocks, and offers a number of unique search features. For example, you can enter data once and search a number of different resources.

Nice — for a price

As the material on the Net improves in quality, so do the costs. Commercial information services offer access to thousands of databases and provide much more in-depth coverage than is available from free sources on the Net. Here are some database and full-text services that you will have to pay for, but which may be worth purchasing, depending upon your research needs.

Consumer Reports Online
www.consumerreports.com/

Many features are free at this site, but subscribers have access to more information, such as "e-ratings" for online shopping sites and customized reports for new cars, which you can have delivered by fax or mail.

Dialog
www.dialog.com/

This site gives access to roughly 50,000 publications and has portals for business, science, and technology. Although Dialog is traditionally aimed at information professionals, a new service, Open Access, allows you to buy access to selected information using a credit card. To find out what's available, visit the sites listed under *Portals* in the selection window.

Electric Library
www.elibrary.com/

This is a comprehensive general reference with content from a range of sources. The Electric Library is a full-text service, meaning that entire magazine and newspaper articles and encyclopedia entries are displayed onscreen. You simply type in a keyword, and the screen

The InvisibleWeb Catalog provides access to over 10,000 databases, archives, and specialty information sources that are not easily found using traditional search engines. The Catalog is located at:
www.invisibleweb.com/

FIGURE 4-5

The Electric Library's
subscribers have access
to newspapers and maga-
zines.

displays up to thirty items containing that word. Beside each entry
is an icon showing whether the item is from a magazine, newspaper,
book, newswire service, or TV or radio transcript. There are also
photos available online. Click on the title to display the whole text.
It's free to search the library, which gives you the periodical name
and date of publication — so you can find it at your local public
library. Subscribers can download text at a monthly cost of $9.95
U.S. for unlimited access. You can choose a free two-week trial.

Hoover's Online
www.hoovers.com/

This is a well-established source for information about companies.
Some of the information is free, but if you sign up for a membership
you can get in-depth company profiles and financial information. A
free trial offer is available.

Lexis-Nexis
www.lexis-nexis.com/

A well-established database service used for research in newsrooms
and university libraries. In the past, many researchers have found
the subscription costs prohibitive. More recently, short-term credit
card access is available.

Media Stream's News Library
www.newslibrary.com/

This is a full-text news library archive. Download full-text versions of over 16 million stories for $1.95 per story. Search for free and pay per viewing.

Northern Light
www.northernlight.com/
Northern Light offers Web searching along with the option to search its special collection of more than four million articles that were originally published in print. Northern Light is relatively inexpensive. Summaries are provided after an initial search, followed by the option to view complete articles for a cost ranging from $1.00 to $4.00 for each article you select to view. The Special Collection covers Arts, Education, Government, Heath, and Medicine, and the collection includes hundreds of popular and special-interest publications.

WinStar Telebase
www.telebase.com/
This resource offers telnet and Web access to hundreds of commercial databases, including Dialog, DataStar, Dun & Bradstreet, and NewsNet. There is a cost, but much of the information is not available elsewhere. Professional researchers will appreciate the fact that this highly specialized information is made available from a single source.

Media on the Web

> "What was once a trickle of international source material available in full text is now almost a rapid stream. The scenario is parallel to what literary historian Patrick Parrinder described happening around the turn of the nineteenth century, when an explosion of published books resulted in proto-information overload. 'The stream of books is felt as at once a promise and a threat,' he wrote. 'There is the promise of intellectual progress and cultural improvement ... by keeping up with the new. But there is also the threat of losing one's bearings, of being carried along in the cultural torrent with no sense of fixed standards.'"
>
> — *"Browsing the Global Newsstand,"* Database Magazine, *October 1994.*

The Internet is transforming traditional media sources. There are now hundreds of newspapers, magazines, and books available on the Internet. Currently, access to many of these is free.

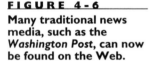
The advantage in using the Web for culling news stories is that you can access articles quickly and from many different sources. Further, online sources provide up-to-the-minute coverage, background information, feedback, and sometimes forums for public discussion.

Newspapers on the Web include specialized news sources such as **UniSci** (**http://unisci.com/**), a science news publication, and weeklies, such as the **Village Voice** (**www.villagevoice.com/**), along with hundreds of dailies. Magazine sources include traditional general-interest publications and trade journals, as well as "e-zines."

E-zines are online magazines, often the work of one individual. They cover a wide range of topics, from science fiction and fantasy to politics. While it is easy to dismiss e-zines as a variation on the "vanity presses" of an earlier era, some enjoy wide readership and are published by writers who are well informed about their topic. E-zines are an excellent source for story ideas for journalists and writers.

Hard-copy consumer magazines are understandably reluctant to put every article from every issue on the Web: they'd lose subscriptions. But many magazines have enough content online to justify visiting their sites. Academic journals are more likely to have full-text, complete issues online — although even some of these provide only abstracts, as a teaser to get you to subscribe or to order back issues.

Newswire services on the Net are an additional source of news. These services publish full-text bulletins, articles, and even scripts of

FIGURE 4-6

Many traditional news media, such as the *Washington Post*, can now be found on the Web.

speeches and debates online. Reuters, Associated Press, and United Press International all provide hourly updates on world events.

Journalists and researchers preparing background reports can tap into these online resources for in-depth coverage of an issue that may comprise different perspectives. Online articles often include an electronic mail address for the author. If you're a journalist writing an article and find an academic paper on your topic, you might contact the expert author for an interview.

The best way to find out about newspapers online is to sample what's available. The following sites make good starting points. Additional media resources are included in Appendix A.

AJR NewsLink
www.newslink.org/
This is a massive set of links to news sources. The site is sponsored by the *American Journalism Review*. Broadcast news sources are included.

Alternative Press Center
www.altpress.org/
This resource has links to an excellent collection of publications considered to represent an alternative view of the news. Many of the sites included offer sample articles from current issues, and some include archives of past issues. In addition to providing gateway access to a number of alternative press sites, this site also has developed a set of links to 350 alternative online resources where you can access "the other side of the story" on topics ranging from Sustainable Development to New Age Politics.

Broadcast.com
www.broadcast.com/
A classified list of broadcast events on the Net, including archived radio and news broadcasts.

INFOnugget

The annual Media in Cyberspace Study (www.middleberg.com/) reports on how journalists are using the Net. In the latest study, CNN Interactive and the *New York Times* are named as favorite news sites for journalists. Here are their top picks:

- CNN.com and NYTimes.com were mentioned more than 50 times
- MSNBC.com got 28 mentions
- WashingtonPost.com received 23 mentions
- USAToday.com received 19 mentions

- Regional newspaper Web sites, including those of the *Chicago Tribune* and the *San Francisco Chronicle*, SFGate, also received mentions as favorites
- Among non-newspaper Web sites, Matt Drudge's controversial Web site received 8 mentions as a favorite Web site and 2 as an "obnoxious" one.

— From WebTrends
www.mediainfo.com:80/ephome/news/ newshtm/webnews/wt110399.htm#1

CIC Electronic Journals Collection
http://ejournals.cic.net/
This site aims to be an "authoritative source of electronic research and academic serial publications." Here you will find links to many freely distributed electronic journals.

CMPA Reading Room
www.cmpa.ca/maghome.html
Sponsored by the Canadian Magazine Publishers Association, this is an important site for links to Canadian magazines online.

Editor and Publisher Media Links
www.mediainfo.com/emedia/
With links to more than 1,500 online newspapers, this resource is one of the most comprehensive. A good source for journalists.

InfoJump
www.infojump.com/
InfoJump offers a large depository of information collected from newspapers, magazines, newsletters, journals, and e-zines. You can limit your search to published articles in selected categories. For example, you can search for articles on genetically altered foods that have appeared in science publications, or for articles on learning disabilities that may have appeared in education magazines.

Moreover
www.moreover.com/
A tool for journalists. You can search for headlines in 200 categories of news.

My Virtual Newspaper
www.refdesk.com/paper.html
This site offers up-to-date links to newspapers around the world.

NewsDirectory
http://ecola.com/
This is another mega-site that provides separate indexes for English-language newspapers, magazines, and computer publications. Here you can also search for a publication by name.

News Index
www.newsindex.com/
This is a news-only search engine that lets you search for current news stories. You can have the results of five queries sent daily to your e-mail account.

Newsroom
www.auburn.edu/~vestmon/news.html
The focus here is on the best sources for today's news.

TOP NEWS SOURCES ON THE WEB

ABCNews.com
http://abcnews.go.com/
Good source for national and international news. A Reference section provides background information on the people, places, and issues behind the news stories. You can also subscribe to a free notification service for breaking news.

BBC Online
www.bbc.co.uk/home/today/index.shtml
Up-to-the-minute news coverage. Articles include audio clips, links to related stories, background reports, and relevant Internet links.

CANOE/Canadian Online Explorer
www.canoe.ca/Canoe/home.html
First-rate Canadian source for news.

Chicago Sun–Times
www.suntimes.com/
Includes a searchable database of Roger Ebert movie reviews.

Christian Science Monitor
www.csmonitor.com/
Well-established and respected online news source. Includes Special Features, Discussion Forums, and a Links Library.

CNN
www.cnn.com/index.html
Top stories and program transcripts from CNN.

The Globe and Mail
www.theglobeandmail.com/
Many articles from each section of Canada's national newspaper.

The New York Times
www.nytimes.com/
Full-text articles from the last 365 days of the newspaper are available from the online archives. Some recent articles are free, but most can be purchased for $2.50 per article.

Newsweek
www.newsweek.com/
Weekly coverage of news events. Includes breaking headlines from WashingtonPost.com and backgrounder articles from Britannica Online. The Artscope section provides capsule reviews of books, films, videos, and CDs.

Time Daily
www.pathfinder.com/time/daily/
Top stories and a news search for additional information.

The Times
www.the-times.co.uk
Several full-text articles from the daily edition are available for free, as is the complete text from the London-based *Sunday Times*.

USA Today
www.usatoday.com/
Regularly updated news, plus a number of useful archives for research.

U.S. News Online
www.usnews.com/usnews
Breaking news and background stories developed by *U.S. News*. "News You Can Use" reports on popular topics — health, computers, travel — and provides links to useful sources on the Net.

Washington Post
www.washingtonpost.com/
Value-added service with its Search the World database. Lists resources for news, reference materials, and Internet sites for more than 220 countries and territories.

Omnivore
http://way.net/omnivore/index.html
Global coverage of today's news. Use this source for access to current stories from world sources.

On-line Journals List
http://bioc02.uthscsa.edu/journal/journal.html
Compiled by the University of Texas Health Science Center, this list

links you to online sites of journals publishing in science, news, business, art, and entertainment. The science list, for example, includes the *Journal of Molecular Biology* and *Physics World*.

Ultimate Collection of Newslinks
http://pppp.net/links/news/
Here you can browse through more than 3,700 links to newspapers around the world. The directory is organized geographically. Clicking on a link to a particular newspaper opens a new browser window with that paper's home page. This allows the user either to continue searching from the Ultimate Newslinks site, or to read the highlighted newspaper.

Government information on the Net

Knowing how to access government information is a vital skill for any researcher or journalist, and this is an area where the Internet is playing a major role. Access to government information is increasingly streamlined; you can now retrieve documents in a fraction of the time it would once have taken. Most national and many regional governments have established a presence on the Web, and you can contact them by e-mail.

As well, the Web is an important communication vehicle for political parties of every stripe. This means that the proverbial man-or-woman-in-the-street is less dependent upon the traditional news media for information about politics: with very little effort, anyone can now obtain information on party platforms, policy statements, and campaign contributions. Jesse Ventura, the former pro wrestler, was the first politician to conduct a successful, low-budget campaign on the Web when he captured office as Governor of Minnesota.

The vast range of government material available via the Internet includes bureaucratic and legislative information, guidelines and applications for grants, and consumer publications far too numerous to list here. Through the Congressional Record (the official record of what goes on in the U.S. Congress), researchers can get full-text newspaper articles related to current bills (when the articles are read into the record as addenda called "Extensions to Remarks"). Because governments play a significant role in fostering social and economic development, you will find useful government publications dealing with the environment, education, health care, and small business.

The *Washington Post* publishes **Federal Internet Guide**, which includes links to popular U.S. government sources, including the Departments of Education; Energy; Health and Human Services; and Housing and Urban Development. The Guide highlights the most popular offerings, such as NIH's Consumer Health Information. Access the Guide at:

www.washingtonpost.com/wp-srv/politics/govt/fedguide/fedguide.htm

Check under the Net Guide Archives for Spotlights reviews of selected government-related Web sites.

One of the best ways to start hunting for government information on the Internet is to use one of the guides available from the Argus Clearinghouse. Here are three good ones:

LSU Libraries' U.S. Federal Government Agencies Page compiled by David Atkins
www.lib.lsu.edu/gov/fedgov.html

Government Sources (Whitewater Anderson Library)
http://library.uww.edu/subject/govinfo.htm

Canadian Government Information on the Internet by Anita Cannon
http://dsp-psd.pwgsc.gc.ca/dsp-psd/Reference/cgii_index-e.html

For information on access to regional, European, and other non-North American governments, check the government listings at **Yahoo!** (www.yahoo.com/) or the International Governments resources that you will find listed at the **Librarian's Index to the Internet** (http://sunsite.berkeley.edu/InternetIndex/).

If your research requires access to government information, spend time exploring each of these resources, as well as the additional sources included in Appendix A of this book.

GOVERNMENT INFORMATION SOURCES ON THE WEB

CIA World Fact Book
www.cia.gov/cia/publications/factbook/index.html
This resource provides factual information for all the countries of the world. Here you can locate data on population, transportation, languages spoken, religions, GNPs, maps, diplomatic contact information, and much more.

Federal Web Locator
www.infoctr.edu/fwl/
Operated by the Center for Information Law and Policy, this site aims "to be the one-stop shopping point for [U.S.] federal government information on the World Wide Web." It offers well-organized links to home pages for government branches, agencies, departments, and corporations. You can also type in a keyword to find a link to a specific agency or organization.

FedStats
www.fedstats.gov/
This resource links to seventy-plus U.S. federal government agencies that produce statistics of interest to the public. MapStats provides profiles of states and counties.

FedWorld
www.fedworld.gov/index.html
Pull-down menus provide quick access to government information, documents, and files. From this site you can also find and order recent U.S. Government Reports.

Government of Canada
http://canada.gc.ca/
This is the Canadian government's official central site. Click on "About Canada" for geographical facts, a list of prime ministers, and more. The Federal Institutions section links Web sites of dozens of ministries, departments, agencies, and Crown corporations.

▶

Government Resources on the Web
www.lib.umich.edu/libhome/ Documents.center/
Developed at the University of Michigan, this is another comprehensive and well-organized reference site for U.S. government information. It includes pointers to international organizations and governments around the world.

GPO Access
www.access.gpo.gov/#info
This site is a gateway to many full-text databases of U.S. government information. Databases currently available include the Federal Register, the Congressional Record, the Budget of the United States, and the Economic Report of the President. The GPO also links to GILS (Government Information Locator Service), which identifies and describes publicly available federal information resources, including electronic information.

Infomine
http://infomine.ucr.edu/
From the main screen, select Government Information. This site is a comprehensive collection of government information on the Internet. It can be browsed using the alphabetical list of subjects in the Table of Contents. You can also search for a resource by subject, keyword, or title.

Intergovernmental Online Information Kiosk
www.intergov.gc.ca/
This searches all online information from federal and provincial government departments in Canada and allows you to download full-text documents. The site is also an excellent gateway to U.S. and international government information.

Library of Congress: Federal Government: General Information Resources
http://lcweb.loc.gov/rr/news/ extgovd.html
The LOC is a gateway to much U.S. government information, including facts and figures, speeches, reports, news releases, and legislative documents. From the Library of Congress you can also access a Z39.50 gateway specifically devoted to federal or to regional government sources.

Parliament of Canada
www.parl.gc.ca/
Current information about the Canadian Parliament's activities and a useful collection of background papers. Here you will also find a list of Canadian senators and members of the House of Commons.

Thomas Legislative Information
http://thomas.loc.gov/
Named after former U.S. President Thomas Jefferson, this site summarizes recent U.S. government activities: major bills (arranged by topic, title, and number), the Congressional Record, committee information, historical documents (such as the Declaration of Independence), and much more. There is even a primer describing how a bill becomes law.

United Nations Web Site Locator
www.unsystem.org/
Navigating the quagmire of U.N. information can be a researcher's nightmare. This site makes your search systematic. It links home pages of U.N. departments and agencies, indexing them according to subject. Documents from the World Trade Organization, UNICEF, World Health Organization, and others are at your fingertips. Check the listing of other international organizations.

The White House
www.whitehouse.gov/
As the name implies, this site features information from the executive branch of the U.S. government. An Interactive Citizens' Handbook offers press releases, speeches, and full text from presidential press conferences.

A last word

When you need specialized information such as government statistics, an all-purpose search engine may not yield the best results. This chapter has highlighted library, database, media, and government sources on the Web. Knowing some of the specialized databases now available on the Internet will help you to refine your

FIGURE 4-7

Welcome to the White House!

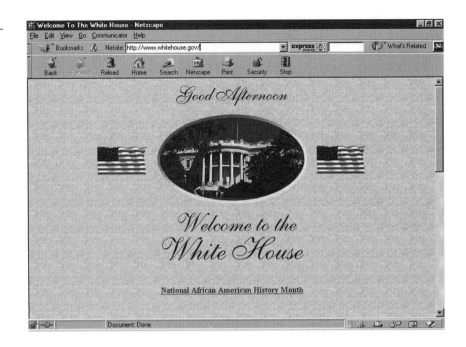

search techniques and increase your efficiency online. If you invest a little time exploring the resources introduced in this chapter, you'll find you have many new and valuable research tools at your fingertips.

Further reading

"Databases" (Canada and U.S.)
JournalismNet
www.journalismnet.com/data.htm

Directory of Database Services. St. Petersburg, FL: Poynter Institute for Media Studies.
www.poynter.org/car/cg_cardirec.htm

Gale Guide to Internet Databases. Detroit: Gale Research. (Annual.)

"Internet Research — McFarlin Library Research Guide"
www.lib.utulsa.edu/guides/rsrch.htm

Maxwell, Bruce. *How to Access the Federal Government on the Internet.* Available from *Congressional Quarterly*, 1414—22nd Street NW, Washington, DC 20037; (tel.) 202 887-8500.

Megasources (a database of links from the School of Journalism, Ryerson Polytechnic University)
www.acs.ryerson.ca/~journal/megasources.html

Beyond the Web: E-Mail; Finding Sources; Listservs, Newsgroups, and FAQs

"Journalists can use e-mail to communicate with their colleagues and with sources ... to check facts and quotes ... to gather ideas and insights not available in other ways. ... They can also use e-mail to subscribe to discussion lists in which like-minded people communicate about specific topics. During the next few years, e-mail may become as important as the telephone as a means of communicating for journalists."
— RANDY REDDICK AND ELLIOT KING, *THE ONLINE JOURNALIST*. SECOND EDITION. ORLANDO, FL: HARCOURT BRACE, 1997, P. 38.

The Internet's value to writers, researchers, editors, and journalists goes well beyond the information available on the World Wide Web. There are many other online resources, beyond the Web, that are useful for finding ordinary people, as well as expert sources (along with their phone numbers or e-mail addresses!).

In addition, there are resources beyond the Web to help you find information in every conceivable field. For example, online mailing lists or discussion groups are great places to find interesting people sharing opinions and knowledge. Here you can pick up tips, locate experts, and make other contacts for breaking news and original story ideas. There are also online groups that allow you to network with other writers and researchers.

This chapter takes you beyond the Web to explore other electronic resources that are especially valuable to writers, researchers, editors, and journalists.

CHAPTER HIGHLIGHTS

- Electronic mail as a research tool
- Finding people and experts on the Net
- Listservs and newsgroups
- Conducting interviews online
- Getting the FAQs

Electronic mail as a research tool

Electronic mail is the most widely used feature of the Internet. It's estimated that more than a hundred million people worldwide use e-mail, and the number grows every day. E-mail is usually the means by which people are introduced to cyberspace. It's a good way to get comfortable online, because you can start by using it to contact friends and family members around the world. But it is also a tool you can use as a writer, researcher, or journalist to:

- introduce yourself and request information or an interview
- verify quotes and information with someone you have interviewed
- check out simple facts with a source
- keep in touch with sources
- reach experts and other contacts relevant to issues you are researching
- make direct contact with someone who is hard to reach
- contact a Webmaster to check something published on a Web site
- receive updates, alerts, and news releases
- conduct interviews.

There are advantages to using electronic mail over the old-fashioned ways of contacting people:

- Sending messages is generally free; or at least, with most Internet service providers you don't pay for individual messages the way you would long-distance telephone calls.
- You can reach people around the world with ease.
- You can send a message when it is convenient for you, knowing the people to whom you send it will read it only when it is convenient for them.
- It's more efficient than playing telephone tag with hard-to-reach individuals, or trying to catch people during business hours in a different time zone.
- It can be a way to get directly to the person you want to reach, who may have an assistant screening phone calls and "snail mail."
- It allows you to send a single message to many people at the same time. For example, you could send a simple request for information about a topic you are researching to a discussion group devoted to that topic, and get lots of replies.

There are disadvantages to using electronic mail for research, too. Just because e-mail arrives with a name attached to it doesn't mean that's the name of the person who wrote the message. Lots of people use other people's e-mail accounts to send messages; others use pseudonyms; still others may be playing a hoax. If you plan to

quote an e-mail message, you should contact the sender directly to confirm authorship and to verify his or her credentials. The other thing to consider, these days, is that busy people are often drowning in e-mail, and sending messages may not be the best way to reach someone quickly.

Like a postal address, an e-mail address directs computers on the network to deliver the message to the right mail slot. An e-mail address consists of four parts, and you can often determine something about a person's e-mail account by following the clues in the address. For example, let's break down the e-mail address:

jsmith@harvard.edu

- **jsmith** is the *user name*. The first letter is probably the initial of the person's first name; "Smith" is probably the account holder's last name.
- **@** is the symbol for "at," which separates the user name from the rest of the address.
- **harvard** is the name of the *host computer*, where the user has an e-mail box.
- **edu** is the *domain name*, which identifies the type of institution where the address is located.

The final two or three letters in an address indicate the top-level domain. For U.S. sites, the letters identify the type of institution where the address is located:

Domain	Type
.edu	Educational institution
.com	Commercial organization
.mil	Military site
.gov	Government department or agency
.net	An Internet resource, such as a service provider
.org	Noncommercial organization

For non-U.S. sites, an Internet address will end with a two-letter designation for the country where the site is located:

Domain	Country
.au	Australia
.ca	Canada
.de	Germany
.il	Israel
.jp	Japan
.ru	Russia
.uk	United Kingdom

While traditionally, U.S. sites have not included a country code designation at the end, slowly that is beginning to change, and some sites are appearing that end with *.us*.

Domain

A comparison of e-mail programs

All e-mail programs allow you to receive messages, display them, reply to them, compose and send new messages, and store messages. The ease with which you can do each of these things depends on the particular electronic mail package you are using.

In a Windows or Macintosh environment, you can choose among several user-friendly mail programs, such as Eudora Mail or Pegasus.

If you are using a Web browser such as Netscape or Internet Explorer, you can also choose the browser's built-in mail program to avoid having to use a separate one.

You should read your program's Help menu to ensure you know how to use its basic features and to become familiar with its more advanced features. Most mail programs offer the following advanced features.

Address books. Most mail programs allow you to add e-mail addresses easily to a list of addresses, along with other contact information you may find helpful. The mail program should provide an easy way to look the entries up, even when the list becomes very long. It should also let you set up group mail addresses, so you can send a single message to a group of people easily.

Nicknames. Nicknames spare you having to type in a complete address each time you send a message. Instead, you can simply type the recipient's nickname, and the program will fill in the correct address. It's a bit like using the speed-dial button on your phone.

Signature files. Signature files, which can be automatically appended to outgoing messages, lend a personal touch to your e-mail. Many people use humorous or thought-provoking quotes as part of their signatures. Some people also provide their phone number, address, and fax number.

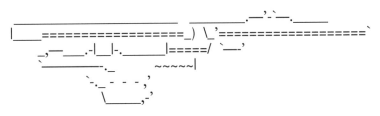

Steve Singh, PEng (ssingh@aol.com)
Boldly going where no one has gone before

FIGURE 5-1

Signatures lend a distinctive touch to messages and tell something about the sender.

FIGURE 5-2

Mail filter feature in
Eudora Pro

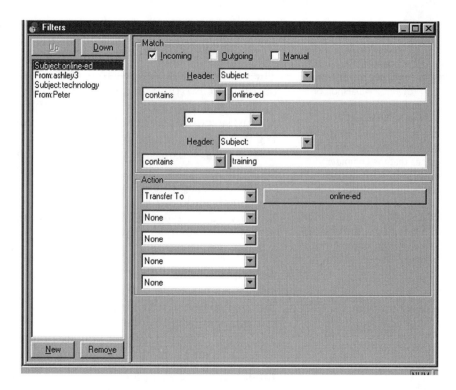

Folders. Most mail programs allow you to set up folders for filing messages that you may want to remove from your inbox yet keep. Your program should also offer an easy way to find messages once you have filed them.

Mail filters. Most mail programs now allow you to set up filters that essentially sort your mail for you. For example, you can set up a filter to send all the mail that comes in from your gardening list-serv directly to the mail folder labeled "Gardening." That way, you can open that folder only when you have time, and all those gardening messages won't clutter up your inbox. (See Chapter 6 for more on using mail filters to avoid e-mail overload.)

Sending and receiving attachments. This feature enables you to send and receive files that have been prepared earlier with a word processor. The files are sent as attachments to an e-mail message. However, if the people to whom you are sending the file do not use the same word processing software as you do, they may not be able to open the attachment.

> "E-mail is faster than faxes, usually arriving in a matter of moments, while faxes often get caught up on busy phone lines, jammed and backed-up fax machines, or machines out of paper. E-mail is cheaper than faxes, costing only the monthly Internet connection fees in contrast to the long-distance telephone charges and paper for fax machines. E-mail is more reliable than faxes, landing

tech.ease

If you are not sure which word processing program your recipient uses, save your file as a text or ASCII file (bearing the file extension .txt) by looking under the **File | Save** or **Save As** options and choosing **Text**. Then, create your message, click the **Attach** button, choose the text file you want to attach, and send the message in the usual way.

PRODUCT	FEATURES	AVAILABILITY
Eudora Lite	Very popular shareware package. Offers all the basic e-mail features with an easy interface.	Qualcomm Inc. (www.eudora.com/)
Eudora Pro	Offers advanced mail filter feature and supports multiple e-mail accounts.	Qualcomm Inc. (www.eudora.com/)
Netscape Messenger	Basic mail functions along with newer features such as the ability to filter and search messages.	Bundled with Netscape's latest browser, Netscape Communicator (www.netscape.com/)
Outlook Express	Supports multiple accounts and will filter messages to a specific account.	Bundled with Internet Explorer 4.0 (www.microsoft.com/)
Pegasus	Well-designed e-mail freeware that supports mail filters.	Pegasus (www.pegasus.usa.com/)

FIGURE 5-3
Popular electronic mail programs

fyi For more on managing your mail with some of the most popular mail programs, check out *PC World Online*, December 1999 for an article full of useful tips. You'll find it at:
www.pcworld.com/
heres_how/article/
0,1400,13480,00.html

fyi If you use America Online's mail program, you may find useful an article in the August 1999 issue of *PC World Online* called America Online Tips and Tricks. It's located at:
www.pcworld.com/
heres_how/article/
0,1400,12452,00.html

directly in a person's electronic mail system instead of arriving on a fax machine likely shared by an entire office. And, e-mail holds more potential as an innovative reporting tool."

— *Chris Callahan*, A Journalist's Guide to the Internet.
New York: Allyn & Bacon, 1999, p. 75.

A word of warning about e-mail

E-mail is not as private as many people think. Even if you send a single message to one friend, that message winds up on at least four computers — your own, your company's (or Internet service provider's) server, your friend's computer, and his or her company's server. Those messages can stay on those servers a long time, and as Oliver North and Monica Lewinsky discovered, they can be retrieved years later and used against you. What's more, your friend could pass your message on to another friend, who could pass it on to someone else. Without your knowledge, your "private" message could be on dozens of computers for years.

There are two lessons in this for researchers and reporters: (1) Don't treat e-mail as casually as you might treat a private conversation, and (2) don't put anything in a message that you wouldn't be willing to have published or broadcast.

E-mail messages sent to online discussion groups are, of course, not usually considered private. But they may be a lot more public than most people think. They can be archived, searched, and found by people years later who can simply use your e-mail address to track what kind of messages you may be posting where. We will discuss how to use search tools to track people's online behavior later in this chapter.

Finding people and experts on the Net

There are lots of resources online to help you find people's e-mail addresses, phone numbers, addresses — even their neighbors — if you know their name, or maybe just the name of the street on which they live. There are also resources to help you track down and find the names of experts and other possible sources for your stories or research.

Before you can contact someone via electronic mail, you have to get his or her e-mail address. The best way to do that used to be to phone and ask for it, assuming you knew the person's phone number or how to find it. But several new resources on the Web are making it easier to find e-mail addresses, as well as people's phone numbers, online.

There are now electronic databases of millions of e-mail addresses. There are also electronic versions of most of the world's phone books — White Pages, Yellow Pages, and even fax directories. Some give you more information than you can get from most directory assistance operators. For example, many online phone directories also give you a person's postal ("snail mail") address, including zip code or postal code. As well, they may include the names of anyone else listed in the phone book at that number. Some also let you search by city and category. For example, you can look up all the take-out restaurants in the city of your choice.

But while the e-mail and phone databases are massive, they are still far from comprehensive, and some of the listings may be out of date. For example, e-mail directories often list several old e-mail addresses for someone, and you can't be sure which ones are current. So, while databases are useful, it may still be more efficient to track down someone's phone number the old-fashioned way, then phone to ask for the e-mail address. If that's not possible or desirable, but you know where someone works, try going to that organization's Web site first and looking for a directory of employees, which might list e-mail addresses. Failing that, you can try one of the Internet directories described below to find e-mail addresses, phone numbers, or both.

Finding e-mail addresses

Anywho
www.anywho.com/
For e-mail addresses in the United States, this is an extensive directory with lots of additional features, such as maps. Anywho allows you to choose an exact match for the name you type, or only a "begins with" match.

Bigfoot
www.bigfoot.com/
One of the largest e-mail directories on the Web.

Infospace
www.infospace.com/info/email1.htm
One of the most useful directories on the Net; use it to search for people, businesses, Yellow Pages, or fax directories worldwide. A link to the City Guide from the main page also allows you to search any city in North America for lists of everything from art galleries to video stores. Infospace has a large e-mail directory, searchable by names or by e-mail addresses. It also provides addresses and telephone numbers, and even allows you to view the location on a street map!

The Internet Address Finder
www.iaf.net/
This popular directory is used primarily for searching e-mail addresses around the world. Like Infospace, it allows you to search using e-mail addresses or names.

The Ultimate E-Mail Directory
www.theultimates.com/email/
This tool allows you to search several e-mail directories at once.

Whowhere
www.whowhere.com/
Another well-organized database that allows you to search for e-mail addresses worldwide.

The World E-Mail Directory
www.worldemail.com/
Especially good for international addresses, this directory claims to have 18 million e-mail addresses worldwide.

Yahoo People Search
www.people.yahoo.com/
A vast directory that allows you to search for e-mail addresses and more.

Since none of these databases is comprehensive, it's best to try several rather than just one. It's also a good idea to try variations on people's names. If your first attempts are unsuccessful, modify your search by using only the person's first initial. For example, some Internet directories will return only exact matches — so if "Mary McGuire" is listed as "M. McGuire" in a directory or phone book, some online directories will not find a match unless you type in only "M. McGuire."

Finding phone numbers, addresses, and reverse directories
Phone books online offer features that make them far more useful to reporters and researchers than old-fashioned phone books. Both allow you to look up phone numbers according to someone's last name. But when you find someone's listing online, you get more than just the phone number. Often, you get the complete address

with zip code or postal code. You may also get the names of all the other people who are listed as having that phone number. So, you can find out the name of someone's husband, wife, or even their teenage children. Online, you can also access phone books from around the world easily.

Yellow Pages online allow you to search cities for categories of businesses, so you can get the names of all the car dealers, florists, funeral homes, etc. in a particular city.

For local reporters, the most exciting feature of online phone books is the ability to look up more than just someone's name in *reverse directories*, sometimes called *criss-cross directories*. Reverse directories allow you to type in a phone number, for example, and get the name of the person it belongs to. More important, they allow you to type in the name of a street and get a listing of all the people who live on that street, together with their addresses and phone numbers. So, if you hear about a hostage taking on a street in your city, or a major accident at a certain street corner, you can quickly find the names and phone numbers of all the people who may be eyewitnesses to the event.

Anywho
www.anywho.com/
In addition to the services described above, Anywho includes a limited reverse directory that allows you to look up entries by phone number, but not by address or street name. The reverse directory can be found at:
   www.anywho.com/telq.html

Canada 411
http://canada411.sympatico.ca/
For Canadian phone numbers, addresses, and reverse directories, Infospace is probably the best tool. But Canada 411 is an exclusively Canadian directory with listings from most, if not all, provinces for residential and business numbers.

555-1212.com
www.555-1212.com/
A useful directory that includes links to reverse directories.

Infospace
www.infospace.com/
In addition to the services described above, Infospace offers reverse directories for both the United States and Canada that you can use to search phone numbers, addresses, even just street names. The reverse directory for the United States can be found at:
   www.infospace.com/info/reverse.htm
The reverse directory for Canada can be found at:
   www.infospace.com/info/reverse_ca.htm

FIGURE 5-4A
Infospace's main page

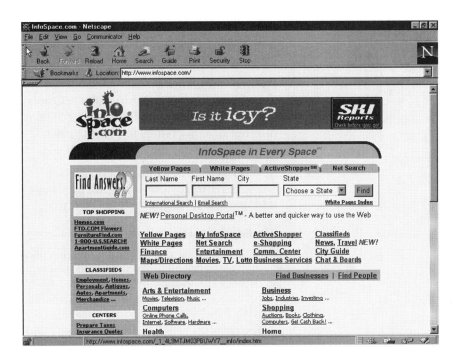

FIGURE 5-4B
Reverse directory at
Infospace

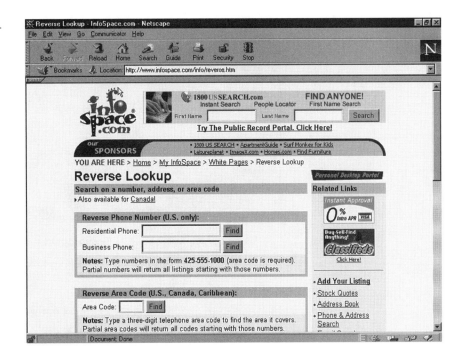

International Phone Books
www.whowhere.lycos.com/wwphone/world.html
Links to phone books from around the world.

Phonebook Gateway
www.uiuc.edu/cgi-bin/ph/lookup?Query=
Links to all sorts of phone directories online, including those to a number of universities in North America.

Switchboard
http://www2.switchboard.com/
Searches for residential and business phones as well as e-mail addresses, but has no reverse directory.

Finding experts online

"ProfNet is the global village's matchmaking service for academe and news organizations, and it has reporters and public information officers gushing about a new dialogue between the ivory tower and news media."

> — *Jonathan Rabinowitz*, The New York Times, *quoted at ProfNet*
> *www.profnet.com/repcomm.htm*

ProfNet
www.profnet.com/
One of the best resources for finding experts online is ProfNet. Instead of picking up the phone and trying to find an expert at your local university, you can ask ProfNet to search out the most knowl-

FIGURE 5-5
The home page at ProfNet

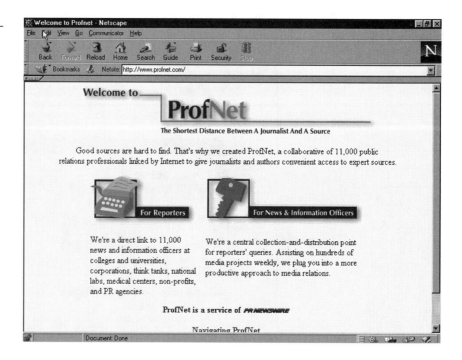

edgeable academics at universities, research institutes, think tanks, medical centers, and labs around the world.

ProfNet is an international cooperative of public information officers linked by the Internet to give journalists and authors convenient access to expert sources. Most of those experts are affiliated with colleges and universities, but some come from medical centers, nonprofit organizations, corporations, and government agencies.

Journalists are invited to send a query with information about the story or topic they are researching, their deadline, and the kind of expert they would like to interview. Queries are distributed to information officers at thousands of member organizations around the world several times a day. Appropriate experts are identified and asked to contact you, before your deadline, in whatever way you requested in your query — by phone, fax, or e-mail.

You can send queries by phone, fax, or e-mail, or by filling out the query form at the ProfNet Web site. You are even invited to send cloaked queries, if you are working on a particularly sensitive story, to keep the nature of the assignment private. Details about how to submit queries can be found at the ProfNet Web site.

For researchers other than journalists, and for people working on immediate deadlines, ProfNet also offers a small database of experts, identified as leaders in their fields by member organizations. The database can be searched by keyword at its Web site:

www.profnet.com/ped.html

The listings include all the information you need to contact the experts directly.

fyi For a more detailed list of expert resources, check out the links at JournalismNet: **www.journalismnet.com/ experts.htm** or at **PowerReporting: www.powerreporting.com/ category/People_finders/ Experts**

Other expert sources

Ask a Librarian
www.earl.org.uk/ask/index.html
A U.K. resource that allows you to send questions to a librarian and get answers quickly.

Directory of News Sources
http://npc.press.org/sources/
From the National Press Club in Washington, DC, a database of experts searchable by category, name, or keyword.

Experts.com
www.experts.com/
A searchable database of worldwide experts.

FACSNet's Reporters Cardfile
www.facsnet.org/sources_online/cardfile.htm
An address book of think tanks, advocacy groups, and special-interest organizations compiled by the Foundation for American Communications (FACS), an independent, nonprofit, educational

institution based in Los Angeles whose stated mission is to provide knowledge and resources to journalists.

FindLaw's Expert Witnesses Database
www.findlaw.com/13experts/witness.html
A U.S. database of prospective expert witnesses used by lawyers.

Sources Online
www.sources.com/
Canada's premier listing of organizations and experts, including an easy-to-search guide to foreign embassies in Canada.

U.S. Sources and Experts
http://metalab.unc.edu/slanews/internet/experts.html
A fabulous collection of links to expert resources compiled by Kitty Bennet, news researcher at the *St. Petersburg Times*.

West's Legal Directory
www.wld.com/direct/welcome.asp?form=names
Search for lawyers around the world by name or area of practice.

Listservs and newsgroups

Online discussion groups are another place to find expert sources, as well as ordinary folk you might want to interview for your stories or research. There are two kinds of electronic discussion groups: listservs (also called *listservers* or *mailing lists*) and Usenet newsgroups. Although they are similar, listservs are generally more valuable to reporters and researchers.

"Usenet" is short for "User Network" — an array of computer discussion groups that can be visited by anyone with Internet access. Don't let the term "newsgroups" fool you — these are not sources of breaking news. Newsgroups are the online equivalent of the call-in radio show, where anyone can call and share an opinion, no matter how uninformed. They could more accurately be called chat groups or even, sometimes, rant groups.

On the other hand, listservs are more like television panel discussions where experts are invited to share their views. The participants generally have some expertise in the subject under discussion. Sometimes, however, participants in a listserv may also be more opinionated than informed, as they often are in newsgroups.

While newsgroups and listservs are both online discussion groups, there are differences in the way you participate in them. For newsgroups, once you log on you must go to the newsgroup area, generally by clicking on your newsreader software. There you can read messages that are posted for all to see, just as you might browse at the bulletin board of a grocery store or community center. Listservs are less public. To read messages posted to them, you must subscribe to the list; then, the messages are sent directly to your e-mail box.

Serious researchers and journalists may not find much value in monitoring or participating in newsgroups. But many find listservs the most consistently valuable resource on the Net for finding information, making contacts, and seeking out experts. Let's take a closer look at both.

Listservs: Where experts share information

"The operative word in thinking about mailing lists is 'community.' Lists, much more so than Web-threaded discussions or Usenet newsgroups, create a deep sense of community among their members. I can attest to that with my own lists; on online-news and online-newspapers, many of us 'know' each 'other well through the online experience and meet for drinks or dinner when we show up at the same conferences."

— Steve Outing, "The Lowly Mailing List: A New Start?"
Editor and Publisher, *October 14, 1996.*

To participate in a listserv, or even just to monitor the list's discussions, you must subscribe. It's free, but you must send a specially composed message to the list owner's computer saying you wish to subscribe. If you have composed your message correctly, you will be automatically added to the list of subscribers and the computer will respond with a welcome message that confirms your subscription and outlines rules for membership. Thereafter, any and all messages posted by list members to the list will come directly to your e-mail box. You can read them and delete them, or respond — either by sending an e-mail message to the entire group, or by replying privately to the original sender.

Although anyone can subscribe to most listservs, the subscription process — not to mention the heavy volume of electronic mail these lists can generate — tends to weed out all but those with a genuine, ongoing interest in the subject. Instead of the noisy chatter you find in newsgroups, you get a higher quality of discussion on mailing lists. Also, unlike newsgroups, most listservs are moderated or screened by their owners or administrators and prohibit abusive language, hate mail, and spam (electronic junk mail).

Listservs can be very useful to researchers and journalists. For example, if you are asked to prepare a report or write a story about multiple sclerosis, you could search for and subscribe to a mailing list devoted to the disease. Many of the messages posted to the list will come from people who live with multiple sclerosis and use the online group to network with one another, compare symptoms and treatments, and share advice. Some messages may come from doctors or researchers interested in helping people with the disease.

After "lurking" (monitoring the discussion) for awhile, you might post a message asking for information or leads to experts in the field. Then, you might continue to correspond (perhaps via private e-mail) with people whom you meet in the group. When you have finished your report or story, you can unsubscribe — and perhaps go on to find another group more suited to your next assignment.

There are also some mailing lists that offer just a regular newsletter on a specific subject. For example, if you are interested in news from India (or some other countries that get little coverage in the North American media), you can subscribe to a mailing list that will send you a brief summary of news events in the country for that day or week.

Beat reporters or researchers on special topics should consider subscribing to at least one listserv on that topic to find out what the experts are saying, make contacts, and request information.

There are thousands of mailing lists on the Net. You will find out about them, often, as you research an issue and come across references to a list while doing background research on the Web. But there is also a search tool on the Net designed specifically to help you find mailing lists, called **Liszt**, at:

www.liszt.com/

When the Liszt welcome screen appears, you can just type in a single word that best describes the topic you're interested in, or browse its Yahoo!-like subject directory. For example, if you were

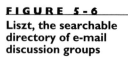

FIGURE 5-6
Liszt, the searchable directory of e-mail discussion groups

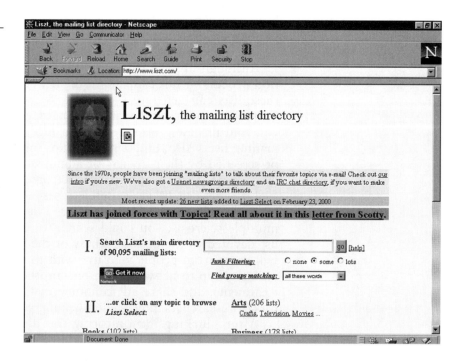

doing research on the Holocaust, you could type in *holocaust*. Liszt would respond with a list of at least eight groups, including one devoted to the children and grandchildren of survivors and another for historians of that period. But, like many search engines, Liszt will look only for exactly what you type. So, a search on "journalism" will not find one of the best lists for journalists, because it's called the Computer-Assisted Reporting and Research List and doesn't include the word journalism in its title.

You can subscribe to any listserv directly from the Liszt search results page. Just click on the link to that group, and follow the instructions. But be careful: you are sending a message to a robot computer — so you must fill in the information exactly as specified. Some commands require your name, others your e-mail address.

If you do it right, you should immediately get a reply confirming your subscription. *Be sure to keep that message.* It tells you how to post messages and, more importantly, how to unsubscribe when you need to do that. The most common and aggravating mistake people make on mailing lists is to post a message to everyone on the list asking how to unsubscribe. (People who do that tend to receive a lot of "flames" — angry e-mail messages — from other list members!)

Remember that every mailing list has two separate addresses. One is for sending messages to the group. That address generally starts with the name of the list, such as Writer-L for the writers' list, or NewsLib for the news librarians' list. The other address is for handling administrative matters, such as subscribing, searching the archives, or unsubscribing. It generally starts with the words "listserv," "listproc," or "majordomo." Don't confuse the two, or your experience with mailing lists may be an unpleasant one.

The welcome message usually explains such procedures as how to initiate a search of the list's archives of previous postings, and how to change your subscription options. For example, if you find the list generates too many messages each day that clutter up your mailbox, you can subscribe to a digest — one long message a day that includes the full text of all the messages posted that day. Or, you can simply request a daily index, which lists all the subject headings posted that day. If there are any that interest you, you can order them sent to your mailbox. Finally, the welcome message also explains how to suspend delivery of messages while you are on vacation, so that you don't come home to a mailbox overflowing with mail.

If you want to subscribe to a list without going to the Liszt page, you must send an e-mail message to the listserv's administrative address. Leave the subject line blank. In the body of the message, type:

subscribe (listname) (your first name) (your last name)
Don't include your signature.

Flame

For an extensive list of mailing lists and newsletters for people interested in the media, check out the site for **Syracuse University's Newhouse Net Lists** at: http://web.syr.edu/~bcfought/nnl.html

For other links to find mailing lists and an article on using listservs for research and reportage, check out **JournalismNet** at: www.journalismnet.com/listserv.htm#Best

For example, if Peter Jennings wants to subscribe to the list for people interested in Computer-Assisted Reporting and Research (CARR-L), he would send a message to the listserv address for that group saying only:

Subscribe CARR-L Peter Jennings

A welcome message outlining how to post messages, how to unsubscribe, and other important instructions should arrive in his mailbox shortly thereafter.

Another place (besides Liszt) to find scholarly and academic mailing lists is located at:

http://n2h2.com/KOVACS/

A third helpful site to find mailing lists by topic or country is at:

http://tile.net/lists/

Catalist, the official catalog of listserv lists, can be searched by subject and by country at:

www.lsoft.com/lists/listref.html

Listservs for networking

Listservs can be a great way to keep in touch with colleagues. Whether you are a writer, researcher, editor, or journalist, there is a special mailing list for others like you where you can share ideas, problems, solutions, and experiences. If you are a researcher or a journalist with a regular beat, such as science or high technology, it is also a great way to network with a community of sources and people who share your interest.

CAJ-L
This is a very active list for members of the Canadian Association of Journalists.

Here many of Canada's online journalists participate in wide-ranging discussions on everything from their frustrations with editors and publishers to tips on using software on the job.

> **Subscription address:**
> **majordomo@eagle.ca**

CARR-L (Computer-Assisted Reporting and Research List)
The best list around for journalists. Although its focus is computer-assisted research and reporting, it covers many journalism topics. The owner, Elliott Parker, an American university professor, feeds the

list with wonderful tips and posts about Internet resources for researchers and journalists. It's an active list, so expect lots of messages every day.

> **Subscription address:**
> **listserv@ulkyvm.louisville.edu**

COPYEDITING-L
A list for copy editors that includes lots of helpful tips on grammar and sentence construction, as well as Internet resources for copy editors.

> **Subscription address:**
> **listserv@listserv.indiana.edu**

CORREX-L

Foreign correspondents hang out here sharing contacts and ideas. The topics range from breaking news to the difficulties of reporting internationally.

Subscription address: majordomo@true.net

FOI-L

A list for journalists and others interested in freedom-of-information issues, access to meetings, and the public's right to know. A project of the National Freedom of Information Coalition, this discussion group operates from the S.I. Newhouse School at Syracuse University.

Subscription address: listserv@listserv.syr.edu

FREELANCE-JOURNALISTS

This list is for freelance journalists to share ideas and information.

Subscription address: majordomo@mlists.net

INTCAR-L

Here's where you'll find out all about investigative reporting internationally. Covers journalism and computer-assisted reporting outside the U.S. Run by Professor Chris Simpson at American University.

Subscription address: listserv@listserv. american.edu

IRE-L

A very active list for investigative reporters. Most posters are active members of the professional organization Investigative Reporters and Editors (IRE). A great resource for all reporters.

Subscription address: listproc@lists.missouri.edu

JOURNET

This is a must for journalism educators. It covers information and discussion about course content, resources, teaching strategies, ethics, and current news events. It's an active group run by Carleton University journalism professor, George Frajkor.

Subscription address: listserv@cmich.edu

NEWSLIB

All about researching news stories. Members of this list are predominantly news librarians, but some are journalists and researchers. It provides many helpful pointers to great sites on the Internet and tips on where to find information.

Subscription address: listproc@listserv.oit.unc. edu

NICAR-L

Information on computer-assisted reporting run by the National Institute for Computer-Assisted Reporting in Missouri. It is very helpful for trading detailed informa-

tion about CAR techniques and software programs.

Subscription address: listproc@missouri.edu

ONLINE-NEWS

This is a forum for writers, editors, and content producers working in the new media. It's run by Steve Outing, an online columnist and publishing consultant.

Subscription address: www.planetarynews.com/ online-news

ONLINE-WRITING

Another group run by Steve Outing (see above), along with Amy Gahran, a Web content developer. This group branched off Online-News to focus specifically on writing for online media, including the Web, e-mail publications, and intranets.

Subscription address: www.planetarynews.com/ online-writing

RTVJ-L

Radio and TV journalism and other issues of interest to professors and radio and television students. It's run by the Radio and Television Journalism Division of the Association of Educators in Journalism and Mass Communications, under the guidance of Prof. Bill Knowles of the University of Montana.

Subscription address: listproc@listserv.umt.edu

SPJ-L

An active list run by the Society of Professional Journalists, the oldest journalistic organization in the U.S. It covers a wide range of topics and current events.

> **Subscription address:**
> **listserv@psuvm.psu.edu**

SPJ-ETHICS

This is a forum for discussion of journalism ethics, run by the Society of Professional Journalists (SPJ).

> **Subscription address:**
> **majordomo@dworkin.**
> **wustl.edu**

WIW-L

The Washington Independent Writers (WIW) List is a professional organization in Washington, DC that includes writers, editors, and journalists. Topics include freelance writing, getting published, agents, copyright, writing for specialized markets, style manuals, and more.

> **Subscription address:**
> **listserv@cmuvm.csv.cmich.**
> **edu**

WRITER-L

Discussions of feature writing and explanatory, literary, and book journalism. Includes info on techniques, markets, jobs, agents, and editors. The list is moderated by Pulitzer-prize winner Jon Franklin, coordinator of the University of Oregon's creative nonfiction program. He requests that each subscriber send a short bio and contribute $20 to cover costs ($5 for students).

> **Subscription address:**
> **JonFrank@nicar.org**

To subscribe to a mailing list:

If the subscription address is a "listserv" or a "listproc" address — send a message to the address leaving the subject line blank. In the body of the message type:

> **Subscribe (listname) (your first name) (your last name)**

Do not include your signature.

If the subscription address is a "majordomo" address — send a message, leaving the subject line blank. In the body of the message type:

> **Subscribe (listname) (your e-mail address)**

Do not include your signature.

Save your welcome message for instructions about how to unsubscribe.

---

7 TIPS FOR USING LISTSERVS

- **Don't** send messages to a mailing list until you have "lurked" for awhile to get a feeling for the tone of the discussion on that list.
- **Don't** post questions before searching the group's archives to determine if the question has been asked and answered before.
- **Don't** post messages or questions that are not appropriate to the group's topic. Stick to the subject of the discussion list, or you risk being flamed.
- **Do** identify yourself. Sign your messages and include your e-mail address so that people can reach you privately, if necessary.
- **Do** choose your words carefully. Typing and sending a brief message may seem like the online equivalent of small talk. But your message can "live" for a long time in cyberspace, to be passed around or dug out by people searching the archives months, even years, later. You never know who might find it and read it long after you have forgotten it. So, post with caution.
- **Don't** ask for things you can easily find out elsewhere. People who ask about things they could easily look up at the library are often flamed for being lazy, or are simply ignored.
- **Don't** send messages to a mailing list asking how to unsubscribe. You will be flamed for not knowing basic list procedures.

tech.ease

For a list of listserv commands, just send a message containing the single word *help* to the listserv administrative address. In return you will get information on a number of useful listserv functions, including how to unsubscribe.

Newsgroups: Where people share opinions

Unlike listservs, newsgroups don't require you to subscribe. Many newsreader programs will ask you to "subscribe," but that simply means choosing which newsgroups you want to read on a regular basis.

To join a newsgroup, first find out how to access your newsreader program from your Internet provider. Then, once you log on, you can use your newsreader to select any one of thousands of newsgroups.

The newsgroup's messages will not come to your electronic mailbox. Instead, your newsreader allows you to get a list of subject headings for all recent messages posted to a given newsgroup. If you see a subject that interests you, you can select the message and read the full text. If you wish to reply, you can respond by posting a message to the whole group, or you can send a private e-mail message to the person who originally posted.

There are newsgroups on every topic imaginable, from *alt.sex* (the busiest newsgroup on the Internet) to *sci.zebrafish*. You could probably find a newsgroup on virtually any topic you might be researching.

The best place to search for newsgroups by subject is **Deja.com** (**www.deja.com/**). You just type a keyword for your topic into the Search box and hit **Enter**. You will get a list of the names of the newsgroups where that word has come up, followed by a list of the messages that have been posted to different newsgroups containing that word. You can click on any of the messages to read the full text of the message. From there, you can click to read other messages posted to that group.

While the quality of the discussion in newsgroups may not be as high as in listservs, newsgroups can be useful to writers, researchers, and journalists. For example, journalists might monitor newsgroups for new story ideas. They may also find newsgroups useful for locating people who are knowledgeable about a specific topic.

Spying on people online

A little-known feature of Deja.com allows people to track other folks' online behavior. Essentially, you can search on someone's e-mail address to get a list of all the messages they may ever have posted to newsgroups online.

From Deja.com's opening screen, click on the link for Power Searching. From that window, you can search all the newsgroup archives by topic, newsgroup, or even someone's e-mail address. It can be very revealing, if not a little embarrassing. Once reporters discover this tool and realize it could be used to uncover embarrassing postings, they often vow never to post to newsgroups again.

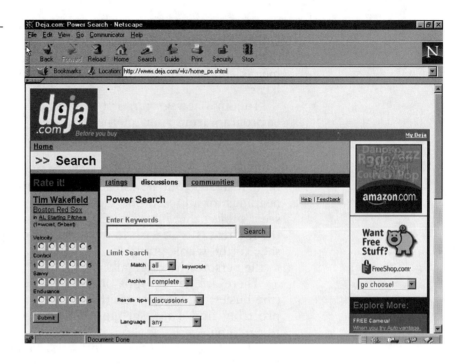

Conducting interviews online

It's easy to use e-mail, listservs, and newsgroups to request interviews, check facts, and verify quotes, or to determine whether someone is appropriate to interview. Some researchers and journalists even conduct interviews online, by sending a long list of questions to the interviewee.

This method may be necessary in some circumstances, but it poses some risks. Sending a list of questions via e-mail gives people a chance to polish their answers, perhaps with the aid of assistants or public relations experts who are never identified. In any case, their answers will not be the same as they would in a face-to-face interview, because very few people write the way they speak.

Online interviews also force interviewers to reveal their entire strategy up front. This makes it impossible, for example, for an interviewer to recover from a poor first question or an incorrect assumption, or to spring a tough question at the end. It also makes it impossible to ask questions that follow directly from the subject's answers.

In short, an online interview may get you a usable quote, but it's unlikely to produce a revealing interview. Most journalists will continue to prefer to do their interviews the old-fashioned way.

The rules are still being written on how writers and journalists can use information they find on the Net. Some news organizations have developed detailed and elaborate policies about how quotes from e-mail messages or postings to newsgroups can be used in published stories. Others have not yet come to terms with such issues.

In the absence of guidelines from your editors and publishers, it's important to use common sense if you want to use online resources.

- **Behave yourself as you would at a public meeting.** There's nothing private about the Internet — your messages and postings go out to hundreds or thousands of people. Messages can also "live" for a long time, be passed around among people, and even be retrieved from archives years after you wrote them.

- **Identify yourself just you would in person or over the phone.** Disclose who you are, something about why you are looking for comments, and the source of any information you are passing on.

- **Verify whatever you read in a newsgroup or mailing list.** Just as you wouldn't put something you overheard on the street in print without verifying it, check anything you read online before publishing or broadcasting it.

For an example of one organization's policy on online newsgathering, see Appendix D.

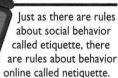

Just as there are rules about social behavior called etiquette, there are rules about behavior online called netiquette. A good guide to netiquette can be found at:
www.albion.com/netiquette /index.html

Getting the FAQs

FAQ is an acronym for *frequently asked questions*. These are compilations of questions (and, more importantly, answers) that are constantly being posted in a newsgroup or mailing list. Finding and reading FAQs can be a productive way to begin researching a topic.

One place you can search for FAQs by newsgroup or subject is at the **Internet FAQ Archive** at:
   www.faqs.org/
Another database of FAQs is the **FAQ Finder** at:
   http://ps.superb.net/FAQ/

A last word

Finding information at Web sites may be easy — but all you get is the information someone chooses to give you. For researchers and journalists, finding people and groups on the Internet who can answer specific questions is often more valuable. This takes more effort: you have to learn how to use e-mail programs, newsgroups, mailing lists, and one or more online directories.

We hope the advice in this chapter will help you get started. You will find the effort worth the results — because so much of what's valuable on the Internet lies beyond the Web.

Further reading

Paul, Nora. *Computer-Assisted Reporting: A Guide to Tapping Online Information.* 3rd edition. Poynter Institute for Media Studies, 1997.
www.poynter.org/car/cg_chome.htm

Sher, Julian. "Caught on the Net: Spying Gets Easier." *The Globe and Mail,* February 27, 1999.
www.journalismnet.com/globe.htm

Strom, David, and Rose, Marshall T. *Internet Messaging: From the Desktop to the Enterprise.* Englewood Cliffs, NJ: Prentice Hall, 1998.

C
H
A
P
T
E
R

Managing and Verifying Online Information

"People have to understand that the WWW is like a huge shopping mall; there are lots of stores and merchandise, but it's all in a size 5. There is a ton of 'stuff' out there, but so little actually fits one's needs."
— NANCY SCHAADT, FREELANCE WRITER, DALLAS, TEXAS

N ewbies to the Internet often feel like kids at Halloween: collecting all those goodies is so much fun, you don't want to stop. But eating them all can make you sick.

As you begin to find your way around the Net, you'll likely collect a great deal of information that is useful, interesting, or simply entertaining. Before you know it, your list of bookmarks will be overflowing, like a child's Halloween bag, with far more resources than you need. This is a problem for all Net users, but those most at risk are information junkies like writers, researchers, journalists, and editors. You need to develop special strategies to avoid being overwhelmed by the Internet's vast resources.

You also need to know how to sort the treasures from the junk. As too many people have learned the hard way, just because something is published on the Internet doesn't mean its true — but it may not be false, either. Often, it's hard to tell. To protect your credibility, you must find ways to assess and evaluate the information you find online.

This chapter explores some of the strategies that information professionals have developed to evaluate and manage online resources.

- ■ **Evaluating information resources**
- ■ **Managing information overload**
- ■ **How to organize a hotlist**
- ■ **Personalized news**
- ■ **Managing e-mail overload**
- ■ **Personal information managers**
- ■ **Keeping up to date**

Evaluating information resources

"It's becoming more difficult to distinguish 'official' sites from 'wanna-bes.' If you're looking for the text of the speech President Clinton made to a group of American veterans last week, you might find versions on half a dozen sites. Which can you trust? Which sites are corporate, government, or personal ones? Official-looking documents might still be bogus. [A few years ago] the Associated Press had to officially debunk a document circulating on the Net as an AP dispatch indicating Microsoft Corp. had bought the Roman Catholic Church. Incredible, but enough people believed it to create a problem."

— *James Derk, "Net Sites for Journalists,"* Online User, *1996.*

Evaluating the information you find on the Web can be the biggest challenge facing writers, researchers, and journalists who use the Internet for their work. All things may look equal on the Web but they're not any more reliable than the information you get from offline sources. Monica Lewinsky's version of her affair with President Clinton was, after all, quite different from Ken Starr's version.

When it comes to Web sites, it's probably wise to view them with the same degree of healthy skepticism as you would an infomercial. If you want to use information from a Web site in your story, you should first try to determine its credibility. You should also verify it with another source, just as you would information you received from offline sources.

Here are a few guidelines to apply when you're trying to determine the credibility of something you find online and want to use in your own work.

Check the authority of the person or institution that published the material. Who posted the information, anyway? It's important to find out, because the Web can be used as a soapbox by people who are biased about their subject.

There are a few ways to try to find out about the author of a Web site:

- Look for a phone number or an e-mail address on the Web page that you might use to verify who sponsored the site and their credentials.
- Look for clues in the Web site address. For example, if the address is *www.harvard.edu/library/~bmartin/*, then you know that the Web site is hosted on the server at Harvard University (*edu* stands for *educational institution*) in a directory called *library*. The tilde (~) generally means it is a personal page and, in this case, the author is bmartin — probably someone whose last name is Martin and whose first name begins with B. A personal Web page at a university could belong to a student, a researcher, or a faculty member. A call to the library at Harvard should help you determine something about the author, if that information is

missing from the page. If there is no contact information on the page itself, backtrack through the address by eliminating everything to the right of the / before the *~bmartin* and going to *www.harvard.edu/library/*, where you will probably find out how to contact the library. If the site is hosted or sponsored by an institution or organization, you should be able to verify the material through that organization, as well as get further information from their home page. In the case of personal home pages, it can be very difficult to determine an author's legitimacy. So, personal Web pages should probably be used only as a source of opinion, not a source of fact.

Check the owner of the Web site. Sometimes it is not easy to tell who sponsored the Web site from the address or the contact information at the site. In that case, you can try to find out who officially registered the site as the owner of the domain name, and get contact information for that person by using an Internet application called **Whois.**

- For non-military U.S. addresses, go to:
  www.networksolutions.com/cgi-bin/whois/whois/
  Type in the address of the site you are interested in, and you should get the name and contact information you need.
- For military sites, try:
  nic.ddn.mil

Check the accuracy of the material. Does the material appear to have been edited? Would the facts have been checked by someone other than the author?

The problem with the World Wide Web, for information professionals, is the same characteristic that makes it attractive to so many others — its egalitarianism. Anyone with access to a Web server can publish on the Web. Thus, the systems that exist at newspapers, magazines, and book publishers to ensure accuracy don't exist on the Web. If you find spelling, grammatical, and typographical errors, it is probably safe to assume the material has not been edited. You should take this as a clue that the information still needs to be verified. But even in the absence of any such mistakes, you must verify, verify, verify. Any reputable site should include links or references to other sources that you can use to corroborate the information on the page.

Check the currency of the material. Often, the problem is not so much that the information was inaccurate when it was published, but that it is now out of date. Many sites indicate the date when something was posted and even when it was last revised. But just because the site was updated yesterday doesn't mean the piece of information you need was updated. Again, the best thing to do is verify, verify, verify. If the site does not provide any date, do not assume the material is up to date. Many sites remain online and unattended for years.

Check the context of the material. Bear in mind that search engines locate Web pages out of context. When you find a page that looks interesting, try to link back to the site's home page to determine more about the source of the information and whether it is valid to your research. If there is no obvious link to take you back to a main page, then backtrack through the address by eliminating one level at a time, moving from right to left. Try to figure out why the Web page was created: is it meant to inform you, persuade you, or sell you something?

Check offline sources. All the information in the world is *not* on the Internet. While Net resources are growing quickly, there are millions of valuable reference books and other information sources that are not online. Sometimes you can check something by making a simple phone call. Other times you may need to use the library. A good library contains a lot of information more valuable than what you might find on the Net. A good librarian to help you find it is still a valuable resource.

Hacker

Check the links to and from the page. Try to determine if the links from the page take you to related sites that are credible themselves. You can also try to find out which sites link to the page you are interested in by using a search engine like AltaVista (search on *link:url* and fill in the Web site address for the URL). If credible sites link to the page, it is another sign that someone has decided the page is valuable.

Beware of hackers. Remember that Web pages can be altered deliberately by hackers, or even sometimes accidentally by users. This is just one more reason to verify, verify, verify.

Managing information overload

"As a person who is very thorough and wants to have all the information before making a decision, I'm finding that I'm spending more time collecting and organizing information than I am reading and using it. ... Some of the factors contributing to this include a compulsion about wanting to use the best resources available and make the best choices, and a fear of 'what if I need it and it isn't there?' ... I am attempting now to acquire only information that I can reasonably be certain I will use within the next few weeks."

— *Tracy Marks, software and Internet trainer, Cambridge Center for Adult Education*

The World Wide Web is a seductive place, especially for curious people. It's all too easy to follow one link after another, reading fascinating material from sources all over the world. But before you know it, hours have passed and either you still haven't found what you set out to find, or you haven't read everything you were able to find.

As an information professional, your time is at a premium. Make the most of it by acquiring a few simple strategies for online research.

- **Set goals and follow a map.** Before you go online, know exactly what you are looking for and stay focused. Always remember where you are going and why, and discipline yourself to resist distractions. Just as you wouldn't spend time at work reading a comic book, you must avoid doing the online equivalent just because you came across an amusing link.
- **Set time limits.** Know exactly how much time you are prepared to spend online trying to find what you're looking for. Taking the "scenic route" may be OK when you're on vacation. But when you're under the pressure of a deadline, you can't afford to get lost wandering among Web sites — even if they have spectacular graphics and live sound. You can always come back to explore when you have more time. Sometimes the information you want may be online, but finding it the old-fashioned way is simply faster. Other times, you just have to know when to give up. If you spend more than half an hour looking for something, chances are you're losing sight of your goal and are allowing yourself to be distracted.
- **Know when enough is enough.** Just because the Internet gives you access to more information than ever before doesn't mean you can actually process it all. Until someone figures out how to increase the hard disk space and processing speed of the human brain, there are limits to what you can digest about any given subject. You have to accept that you can't read everything there is to read on any subject. You have to learn when to stop researching and start writing.
- **Bookmark with care.** If you bookmark everything you think might be useful someday, your bookmark list will quickly become unmanageable. (In the next section, we give some tips for organizing a bookmark list.) Bookmark only those sites you know you'll return to over and over again. Beyond that, be selective. Learn to use search tools to find the rest as you require. Search tools like Yahoo!, Google, and AltaVista should be at the top of your bookmark list.
- **Don't waste hard disk space.** Be selective about what you keep. Much of the information you need is only a few clicks away on the World Wide Web. Just as you wouldn't collect and store the phone numbers of everyone you've ever met in your life, don't try to collect and store all the interesting information you find online. The phone book will always be there where you need it; so will the search engines.

fyi

Neil Postman, a well-known media critic and author of *Amusing Ourselves to Death*, gave a speech in 1990 about information overload, much of which is still relevant today. It's called "Informing Ourselves to Death" and can be found at: **http://world.std.com/~jimf/informing.html**

How to organize a hotlist

"I used to carefully catalog useful or nifty sites, and even organized them into a Web launcher, but I gave it up in a fit of common sense. The Web was just growing too fast. Now I treat the Net as any other information resource. I keep a short list of key addresses — sort of like my phone Rolodex — that will lead me either to sites I visit repeatedly or to broader sources of information. Search engines, led by AltaVista, are vital."

— *Mike Christenson, defense and foreign policy editor of* Congressional Quarterly; *former Washington correspondent for the* Atlanta Journal and Constitution

A hotlist is the online equivalent of a journalist's notebook of contacts. It's your personal collection of important Web addresses — ones you have found useful and may want to use again. But there's no need to keep a separate notebook for writing down all those long URLs. Instead, you can simply add them to your list of bookmarks in Netscape or your list of favorites in Internet Explorer. Then, when you want to return to those sites, you need only call up your bookmark or favorites list and click on the address you want. That's the easy part. The challenge is what to do when your list of bookmarks or favorites becomes so long you can no longer find things easily.

If you are using Netscape, when you first start making bookmarks, you will probably just select **Bookmarks | Add Bookmark**, and the Web address for the page you are viewing will automatically be added to the bottom of your bookmark list. Similarly, if you are using Internet Explorer, you will probably just click on **Favorites | Add Favorites**. As long as you have only a few bookmarks, that method will work well. But as the number of items begins to grow, you'll need to take steps to ensure that your hotlist stays useful. For example, you may want to alphabetize your bookmarks. Or, you may wish to organize them in folders, by subject.

Using Netscape

The way in which you organize your bookmark list will vary slightly, depending on which version you're using. If you are using Netscape 4.6, the following guidelines apply. If you're not using that version, it's worth upgrading to the newest version of Netscape because it offers many improved features.

To find a bookmark quickly in a long list

- Click on **Bookmarks** at the top of the Netscape screen.
- Choose **Edit Bookmarks**.
- Click on **Edit** at the top of the screen.
- Choose **Find** in Bookmarks.
- Type in the word or words you are looking for.
- Click **OK**.
- The bookmark you wanted should be highlighted. If not, select **Edit | Find Again**.

To give a bookmark a meaningful name — one you might remember

- Click on **Bookmarks** at the top of the Netscape screen.
- Choose **Edit Bookmarks**.
- Click on the bookmark you wish to rename.
- Click on **Edit** at the top of the screen.
- Choose **Bookmark Properties**.
- Replace the name of the bookmark in the appropriate box with a more appropriate name.

To insert a bookmark at a specific point on your list

- Select **Bookmarks | Edit Bookmarks**.
- Click on the bookmark you want to move.
- Drag it until a line appears above the bookmark where you want it to go.
- Release the mouse button, and the bookmark should appear where you wanted it to go.

To create folders for related bookmarks

- Select **Bookmarks | Edit Bookmarks**.
- Select **File | New Folder**.
- Type in a new name for the folder and click **OK**.
- You can drag and drop the folder to any point on the list the same you way insert bookmarks at specific points on the list, as described above.

To file bookmarks in the appropriate folders

- Add the bookmark to the bottom of your list and then drag and drop it into the right folder, as described above.

Or:

- When you find a Web site you want to save, click on **Bookmarks** at the top of the Netscape screen but choose **File Bookmark**, rather than **Add Bookmark**.
- An arrow beside **File** should point to all the folders you have created.
- Highlight the folder in which you want to place the bookmark.

To delete bookmarks

- Select **Bookmarks | Edit Bookmarks**.
- Highlight the bookmark you want to delete.
- Choose **Edit** at the top of the screen and click on **Delete**.

Using Internet Explorer
The following guidelines apply to Internet Explorer 5.0.

fyi

To use Netscape's **Drag and Drop** editing feature, place your cursor on the item you wish to move. Click and hold down the left mouse button as you drag the item wherever you want. You can reposition both bookmarks and folder entries this way. (If you drag and drop a folder, the items inside it will move as well.)

FIGURE 6-1

A bookmark list from
Netscape

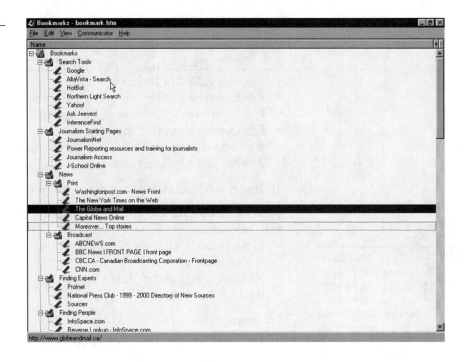

To give a favorite a meaningful name — one you might remember

- Click on **Favorites** at the top of the Explorer screen.
- Choose **Organize Favorites**.
- Click on the bookmark you wish to rename.
- Click on the box labeled **Rename**.
- Give the bookmark a new name.

To insert a favorite at a specific point on your list

- Click on **Favorites** at the top of the Explorer screen.
- Select **Organize Favorites**.
- Click on the favorite you want to move.
- Drag it to the point on the list where you want it to appear.
- Release the mouse button, and the bookmark should appear where you wanted it to go.

To create folders for filing related favorites

- Select **Favorites | Organize Favorites**.
- Click on the icon to **Create Folder**.
- Type in a name for the new folder and hit **Enter**.
- You can drag and drop the folder to any point on the list in the same you way that you insert favorites at specific points on the list, described above.

FIGURE 6-2

**A bookmark list from
Internet Explorer**

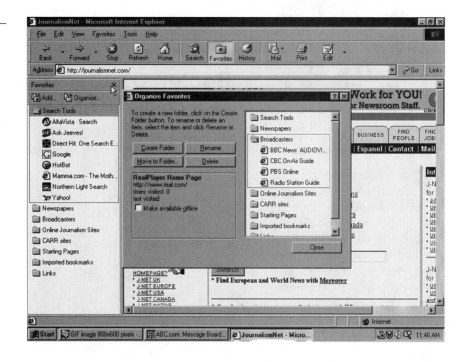

To file favorites in the appropriate folders

- When you find a Web site you want to save, select **Favorites |
  Organize Favorites.**
- A list of all your folders will appear. Select the folder in which
  you want to file the favorite. Then Click **OK.**

To delete favorites

- Select **Favorites | Organize Favorites.**
- Highlight the favorite you want to delete.
- Click on the box labeled **Delete.**

Each program offers many more sophisticated features to organize and manage your bookmarks. You can read through the Help
menus to find out more. Time spent reading Help menus may well
be time saved using your bookmark list.

Bookmark backups

It's a good idea to save backup copies of your bookmarks on a regular basis. Bookmarks can become corrupted or be deleted accidentally, and regenerating them can mean a lot of work.

To back up your bookmark file, go to your bookmark list and
choose **File | Save As.** Then, give your backup copy another name,
or save it to a floppy disk.

Bookmark organizers and Net search assistant software

Bookmark organizers

For people who want a little extra help organizing their bookmarks, or for people who want to be able to use their bookmarks with more than one browser (such as Netscape Navigator and Internet Explorer), there are some downloadable shareware programs and commercial products available to help you.

Clickmarks.com
www.clickmarks.com/
Allows you to upload, organize, and manage your bookmarks online and access them from anywhere in the world.

Columbine Bookmark Merge
www.clark.net/pub/garyc/
This program lets you merge Netscape, Internet Explorer, and Opera bookmark files. It eliminates duplicate bookmarks based on criteria you select. Other features include flags for recently visited sites and automatic backups.

Compass
www.softgauge.com/compass/
A sophisticated bookmarking system that you can use easily with Netscape, Internet Explorer, and the Opera browser. You can add bookmarks by dragging and dropping them from your browser. You can also sort, delete, edit, view, and search your bookmarks easily. Compass will also verify whether the bookmarks are still valid. This is an excellent program for cleaning up your bookmark files.

QuikLink Explorer Gold Edition
www.quiklinks.com/explorer/
This program helps you organize your bookmarks into a tree, with nested folders. You can import your existing Netscape and Internet Explorer bookmarks and send them to any of six popular browsers. You can add new bookmarks manually, or grab the URL from Netscape. Each link records the date created, last date visited, URL, an optional description, twelve user-defined fields, and more, all of which can be displayed by clicking on Tabs in QuikLink Explorer's right panel. Other features include an enhanced Find tool.

SyncIt
www.bookmarksync.com/
If you use more than one machine or are on the road a lot, this may be the program for you. It allows you to store your bookmarks on a server and use them from anywhere. Just install the client software on any computer that you use, and use your Internet connection with the SyncIt Web site to store your favorites. Then, you can make changes on any computer and have them reflected on your other machines, as well. SyncIt works with Netscape and Internet Explorer bookmarks. It also checks for dead links and duplicate entries.

WebTabs
www.rballance.com/products/
This advanced bookmark management tool also tracks your travels on the Web. You can drag and drop URLs into a bookmark window that allows deep nesting of multiple folders. You can also add notes to your bookmarks. The tracking mechanism makes creating new bookmarks easy. Each bookmark entry allows you to include private notes, password, date of visit, and more. The program also lets you search by keyword and date, and import bookmarks from Netscape and Explorer.

If you want to be able to access your bookmarks from any computer (and not just the one on which the bookmarks are saved), or if you want to make them accessible to other people, you can also make your bookmark list — which is simply an HTML file — a Web page. (We explain how to do this in Chapter 2.)

If you do set up your bookmark page as a Web page, you can then use it as your start-up page. From the main Netscape page, choose **Options | General Preferences**. Copy the URL of your Web page into the field that indicates where you want your browser to start.

Personalized news

If you want breaking news, but don't have time to read all the online news sources, there are services you can use to get the online equivalent of your own personalized clipping service.

NewsTracker
http://nt.excite.com/
One of the best general news services, courtesy of Excite. When you register, this site allows you to provide a list of topics you are interested in. Then, whenever you log onto that page in the future, you will get a list of stories on that topic from hundreds of news sources available at the NewsTracker Web site. You will find the instructions for using NewsTracker at:
www.excite.com/Info/newstr/quickstart.html

Other news services

MSNBC
www.msnbc.com/toolkit.asp
This site offers you various (free) personal services — including a

FIGURE 6-3
Excite's NewsTracker selects stories on topics of interest to you.

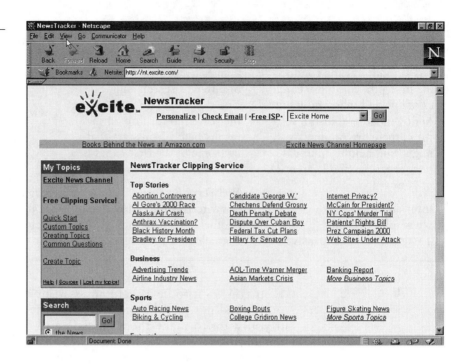

personalized front page with news that interests you, and even news alerts by e-mail.

My CNN
www.mycnn.com/
CNN has recently launched a Web site where you can get also get a personalized news service.

There are also *news tickers* available that update headlines across your computer screen all day long, so you don't have to stop what you are doing to know what's going on in the world. The British Broadcasting Corporation offers its **BBCTicker** at:
www.bbc.co.uk/inform/

Other online services will provide you with an e-mail message once a week summarizing the latest developments on a particular topic. You can find a list of such e-mail alert services at:
www.powerreporting.com/category/Alerts_by_E-mail

If you want to spend some money, there are *news filters* that will scan all the newsgroups or wire services on the Internet for messages on a specific topic. Each filter operates a little differently, but all allow you to specify topics of interest. The program stores your interest profile and checks for stories or messages that contain those topics. When it finds them, the news filter posts them to your e-mail box or provides them on a Web page, which you log onto with a special password.

For a list of all the all the resources available to help you filter news and information and develop personalized news services, try:
www.botspot.com/s-news. htm

Managing e-mail overload

"When I first got on the Internet, I was like a thirsty woman who hadn't had a drink in three days. Now I have to discipline myself and be very focused about what I'm looking for when I use this medium. I subscribe to only two or three select listservs that help me professionally, and even then I use the delete key a lot. I will scan the first one to two sentences of a message, and if it doesn't interest me, Zap! I also use the subject line as a filter. If I'm interested in a new listserv, I subject it to a 30-day trial period. During that time, it needs to meet specific criteria and filters."

— *Nancy Walsh, former editor/writer for The Research Foundation, State University of New York*

For most people, the novelty of having electronic mail faded in direct proportion to the expanding volume of mail that arrived each day. Now, most of us are at risk of drowning in e-mail messages. What's worse, we know the flood of e-mail is going to continue to grow while the time we have to deal with all those messages will remain the same, unless someone develops a cure for sleep.

If you want to avoid spending the rest of your life answering e-mail or sorting messages to answer on that slow day that never comes, try some of the following strategies for making the best use of your time.

- **Decide which messages have priority.** For example, you may want to consider messages from colleagues, friends, and family as the most important; then messages from professional mailing lists, such as those for writers and journalists; finally, those from lists about gardening, parenting, or other personal interests. Rather than read your mail in the order in which the messages are received, read only the most important. Save the other messages to read when you have more time. If you don't get to the others for three months or more, just select them all and delete them in one click!
- **Create folders for messages.** Establish a few clearly labeled folders for messages that you want to save. For example, you might create folders for each story or issue you are researching, one for personal mail, one for each mailing list you belong to, and one for tips about using the Internet. (Don't try to save and file everything — just those items you are likely to use in the future.) Once your folders begin to fill up, finding things in them may not be easy. Most e-mail systems offer some way to search for particular information through all the messages in a folder. Find out what that command is for your e-mail program.
- **Set automatic filters to sort your e-mail for you before you start reading it.** Instead of going into your mailbox and manually sorting your messages into folders, there are programs that will do this for you automatically. The newer versions of most e-mail

FIGURE 6-4
Filtering e-mail with Netscape

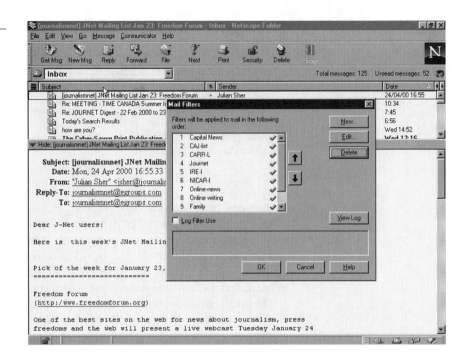

programs, including Netscape Mail, Microsoft Outlook, and Eudora allow you to set up filters so that, for example, all the messages you receive from one of your professional mailing lists go directly into a folder for that list. Then, the only messages that land directly in your inbox are those you have decided deserve highest priority. The rest will be in folders waiting for you when you get the chance to read them. You can even set up filters to send messages directly into the trash bin before you see them — for example, messages that have the word "sex" or "naked" in the subject line.

- **Be brutal with the delete key.** Don't read all your e-mail. Some of it is bound to be irrelevant junk. Before reading anything, scan the list of messages first to determine which ones deserve to be read right away. When you have time later, read the rest of the subject headings to decide which messages should be read, which can be filed away until later, and which can be deleted unread.
- **Don't leave your e-mail on all day, checking each message as it comes in.** You can waste a lot of time trying to ensure you don't miss anything. Every e-mail message is a potential distraction that will take you away from what you should be focused on. Set aside a limited amount of time each day to sort through your mail.
- **Read and reply to important e-mail every day.** In the long run, it saves time to attend to your mail regularly. This reduces the

number of times you end up "handling" each message. Of course, keep your replies short!

- **Request mail digests from mailing lists.** A digest is a collection of all the messages posted to the list that day (see the section on listservs in Chapter 5). This way, you get only one message a day from that list. It is much easier to scroll through one long message than it is to read and delete each message individually. The disadvantage, however, is that it is more difficult to reply to a single message from the digest, and it is easier to miss something.
- **Suspend your listserv subscriptions when you're away.** Whether you are going on vacation or simply need to avoid e-mail for a while, suspend your subscription. (The welcome message you received when you joined the list should tell you how to do this.) Otherwise, you'll return to a mailbox overflowing with mail.
- **Keep your messages short and simple.** Maybe others will learn to do the same!

Personal information managers

There are programs specifically designed to help you organize your personal information, and many of them are now Internet compatible. *Personal information managers* (PIMs) are essentially electronic day-timers: they include computerized address books, appointment calendars, to-do lists, autodialers, and notepads.

The newer PIMs also allow you to enter your contacts' e-mail addresses and Web sites on the address book entry form and make them live links. So, by clicking on your contact's URL from your address file, you automatically load Netscape and dial up your contact's Web site. Some PIMs also make it just as easy to send e-mail: by clicking on your contact's e-mail address, you are automatically presented with a mail form that has your contact's address and your return address already filled in.

As PIMs become more sophisticated they will not only help you keep in touch with others, but may also let others keep in contact with you. Some are being upgraded to allow users to post a daily schedule on the Web, so that colleagues can get in touch with you at critical times. They will also allow you to move your databases of names and phone numbers online so that others can use them, too. (However, considering how guarded some reporters are with their contact lists, this might not be a feature that journalists will use!)

Keeping up to date

> "If you are receiving too much e-mail and end up deleting half of your incoming messages before reading them, sign off from your least important e-mail discussion groups. If you can't keep up surfing around for the new, useful Web sites, then don't — let someone else do the work for you by reading 'best of the Web' magazines or visiting 'best of the Web' Web sites."
>
> — *Steve Cramer, Reference Librarian, Davenport College of Business, Holland, Michigan*

Keeping up to date with the phenomenal proliferation of Web sites and new software is a challenge. Rather than try to do it alone, it is sometimes best to rely on others to do it for you. There are several resources that offer tips and advice about sites you shouldn't miss.

One of the best resources for writers, researchers, and journalists is the mailing list for **Computer-Assisted Reporting and Research** (CARR-L; see Chapter 5 on listservs). The list owner regularly passes on messages of interest to those doing online research from other groups that monitor the Net for new Web sites and software.

Another is the **Scout Report**. It filters over 130 sources of new Internet sites and news stories each week and provides an annotated report offering the best new and newly discovered sites for people in the research and education community. "Surf smarter, not longer" is its slogan. You can subscribe to the Scout Report and receive it each week by e-mail, or you can access it and past editions on the Web at:

www.cs.wisc.edu/scout/

A last word

Managing information overload has become a bigger challenge than ever, thanks to the Internet. It's not a skill you can learn by taking a course but, instead, something you must learn the hard way, by trial and error.

This chapter has offered some tips and tricks from information professionals. As the Internet grows and becomes more sophisticated, it's a good idea to continue seeking the advice of experienced users. Online discussion groups and online publications for researchers are good sources of valuable advice, and will help you keep up to date with this ever-changing technology.

Further reading

Verifying online information

Alexander, Jan, and Tate, Marsha. "Teaching Critical Evaluation Skills for World Wide Web Resources." http://www2.widener.edu/Wolfgram-Memorial-Library/webeval.htm

Grassian, Esther. "Thinking Critically about World Wide Web Resources." www.library.ucla.edu/libraries/college/instruct/web/critical.htm

Managing information overload

Kerka, Sandra. "Information Management." www.ericacve.org/docs/mr00009.htm

Stone, Barbara. "Dealing with an Information Glut." http://info.berkeley.edu/~bstone/infoglut.html

Writing for the Web

"We can perhaps assume that the use of a medium of communication over a long period will to some extent determine the character of knowledge to be communicated … and that the advantages of a new medium will become such as to lead to the emergence of a new civilization.**"**

— HAROLD A. INNIS, *THE BIAS OF COMMUNICATION*. TORONTO: UNIVERSITY OF TORONTO PRESS, 1951, P. 34.

The Internet is changing communication, and so the future of work for writers, editors, journalists, researchers, and all other wordsmiths must change as well. This chapter explains how you can become a participant in — and not just a user of — this new medium.

You don't have to be a programmer or an artist to create Web pages. You probably don't even need any software that you don't already have. Word processing documents can easily be converted to Web pages.

Any writer can now put his or her work up on the Web for others to read. You can broadcast your résumé, start a newsletter, or just supply a list of your favorite online resources for others to share. There are no paper or printing costs, and the potential audience is in the millions.

This chapter introduces hypertext markup language (HTML), the foundation of all Web pages: what it is, and how to write it with a simple text editor. We'll give you enough of the "vocabulary" of this language to create your own Web pages — starting today. You'll see illustrated examples of HTML code and the actual Web pages it produces. If learning HTML isn't your cup of tea, you can use one of several software programs called HTML editors (described later in this chapter) that make a Web page as easy to craft as an ordinary business letter.

You'll also learn the basics of Web graphics, find recommended software to help you add visual elements to your Web pages, and discover the ground rules for designing Web content and how to write for this new medium.

All that's left is for you to put your Web pages online and publicize them. Further sources of information listed at the end of the chapter will enable you to build on the foundation skills you'll gain here.

What is HTML?

Changing a regular document into a Web page means using hypertext markup language. HTML gives us a simple way to format a document so that it can be viewed with any Web browser. Hypertext also makes it possible to link documents together.

HTML is not programming. It's more like a set of labels that identify the structure of a document. These labels are the HTML "tags." One kind of tag says, "Start a new paragraph here." Another kind of tag comes as a pair; the first tag says, "Start a heading here," and the second tag says, "End that heading over here." These tags are created by using combinations of familiar characters from your keyboard.

You can use a word processing program to put HTML tags into any plain text file, thereby turning it into a Web-ready document. It's only when you open the file with a Web browser that it looks like a Web page.

Figure 7-1 (page 136) shows one page of a newsletter as it might appear on the Web. Compare this with the text file that produced it (Figure 7-1A, page 137).

fyi You can turn any word processor document into a plain text file. Just open the document in your usual word processing program and select **Save As**... from the **File** menu. A dialog box will open, and near the bottom you'll see options for saving the file. Look for the option **Text Only**, **Plain Text**, or **ASCII Text**.

INFOnugget

Today, HTML allows all kinds of complex and wonderful things to happen on the World Wide Web. But its original purpose was very simple: in 1990, physicist Tim Berners-Lee wanted to enable scientists around the world to share their research papers quickly. He came up with a system that would make the papers readable on any kind of computer and that would allow the scientists to cite other research papers, not with a mere footnote but by actually connecting the papers to one another. These connections (called hypertext links) could cross borders and oceans in seconds via the Internet. So, this system of tags was created for writers and researchers — not for programmers!

To find out more about Tim Berners-Lee and the beginnings of the World Wide Web, visit:
www.w3.org/People/Berners-Lee/

FIGURE 7-1

A Web page from an online newsletter

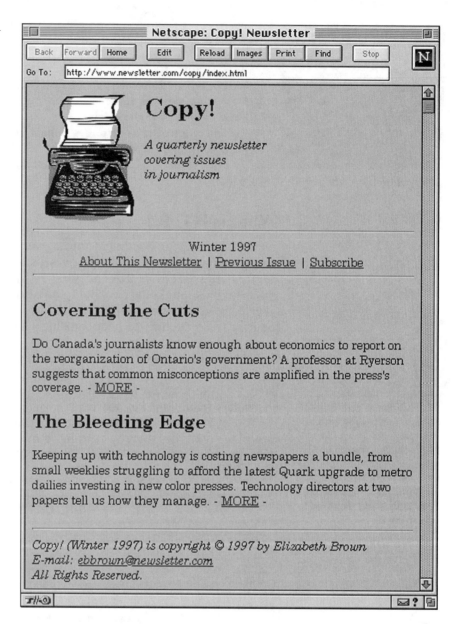

Some word processing programs (notably Microsoft Word) handle an HTML document differently from a plain text file. These programs may hide the HTML tags, acting somewhat like a Web browser instead of like a word processor. Automatic formatting can wreak havoc with the tags (which you can't see). It's not advisable to use these overly clever word processing programs for your own HTML editing (although some people find them satisfactory for quick-and-dirty conversions). Instead, you can use a low-end text editor such as Notepad (not WordPad) in Windows, or SimpleText on the Macintosh. (If you're using Notepad, remember to select **Word Wrap** on the **Edit** menu.) You might also acquire an HTML editor program (described later in this chapter).

The HTML tags, contained within angle brackets, cause headings, italics, boldface, and other formatting to be displayed in the Web browser window. The Web browser program (such as Netscape Communicator or Microsoft Internet Explorer) controls the typeface and size of the heading and the text — unless you explicitly specify them using <FONT> tags.

FIGURE 7-1A

HTML file for newsletter, as seen in a text editor

```
<HTML>
<HEAD>
<TITLE>Copy! Newsletter</TITLE>
</HEAD>
<BODY>

<IMG SRC="typewriter.gif" ALIGN=left>

<H1>Copy!</H1>

<I>A quarterly newsletter<BR>
covering issues<BR>
in journalism</I>

<BR CLEAR=left>

<DIV ALIGN=center>
<HR>
Winter 1997<BR>
<A HREF="about.html">About This Newsletter</A> |
<A HREF="96dec/">Previous Issue</A> |
<A HREF="subscribe.html">Subscribe</A>
<HR>
</DIV>

<H2>Covering the Cuts</H2>
<P>
Do Canada's journalists know enough about economics to
report on the reorganization of Ontario's government?
A professor at Ryerson suggests that common
misconceptions are amplified in the press's coverage.
- <A HREF="97jan/cuts.html">MORE</A> -

<H2>The Bleeding Edge</H2>
<P>
Keeping up with technology is costing newspapers a bundle,
from small weeklies struggling to afford the latest Quark
upgrade to metro dailies investing in new color presses.
Technology directors at two papers tell us how they manage.
- <A HREF="97jan/edge.html">MORE</A> -

<P>
<HR>

<ADDRESS>
Copy! (Winter 1997) is copyright  &copy;  1997 by
Elizabeth Brown<BR>
E-mail: <A HREF="mailto:ebbrown@newsletter.com">
ebbrown@newsletter.com</A><BR>
All Rights Reserved.
</ADDRESS>

</BODY>
</HTML>
```

tech.ease

The <DIV> tag as used in Figure 7-1A to center a block of text has been "deprecated" in the HTML 4.0 specification. Deprecated elements may become obsolete in future versions of HTML. There are other ways to center text with HTML, but all the simple methods have been deprecated. The 4.0 specification recommends that HTML *style sheets* be used for text alignment; a discussion of style sheets is outside the scope of this book. For more information, see the resources listed at the end of this chapter.

Basic HTML tags

You can see the HTML code for any Web page by using the **View** menu in your Web browser. Depending on your browser, the **View** menu will have an option labeled **Source**, **Page Source**, or **Document Source**. Click that option to see the code for the Web page currently open in your browser.

An excellent way to learn HTML is to print out Web pages you like (choose **File | Print** from the Web browser's menu), then print out the source code for those pages (first save each page to your hard drive as an *.htm* file, then open it in a text editing program such as Notepad or SimpleText, and print from there), and compare the two side by side to see exactly how the page was formatted.

HTML tags are always enclosed by angle brackets, which you can find on your keyboard above the comma and the period.

Many HTML tags come in pairs. The first tag in the pair goes just before the text you want to format, and the second tag in the pair goes immediately after that text. To format the phrase **Web browser** in boldface, frame the word between the `<B>` tag and the `</B>` tag:

```
<B>Web browser</B>
```

The key difference between the two tags in most pairs is that the second tag has a slash after the opening angle bracket. Note that the slash tilts to the right, unlike a DOS backslash. (Not all HTML tags come in pairs, as you'll see.)

Figure 7-2 shows a brief Web résumé. It uses no difficult coding or graphical elements, yet looks clean and attractive. The author has used hypertext links sparingly, probably because she hopes you will read the entire résumé!

Beginning below is the complete HTML document that produced the Web résumé shown in Figures 7-2 and 7-2A. Don't be put off by the tags! Look for the regular text (between the tags) and compare it with the Web pages in the two illustrations. You'll soon understand the direct relationship between the HTML and the final product.

```
<HTML>
<HEAD>
<TITLE>Elizabeth Brown / R&eacute;sum&eacute;</TITLE>
</HEAD>

<BODY BGCOLOR=#FFFFFF TEXT=#000000 LINK=#000099
VLINK=#660066 ALINK=#CCCCCC>
<H1>R&eacute;sum&eacute;</H1>
```

FIGURE 7-2

FIGURE 7-2A

To see the lower half of the résumé (Figure 7-2A), which is below the bottom edge of the Web browser, the user must scroll the page.

The lower half of the résumé. Additional sections could easily be included, such as "Personal," "Other Projects," or "Awards." However, if the Web page got much longer, the author might consider breaking some sections off onto separate Web pages.

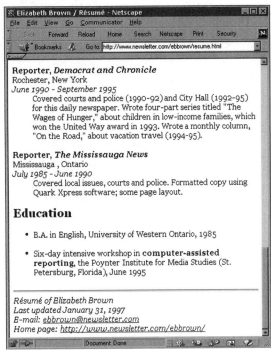

```
<H2>Elizabeth Brown, Journalist</H2>

<I>258 Queen Street West, Toronto, Ontario M5S 1Y2<BR>
Voice: (416) 555-1234 / Fax: (416) 555-5678<BR>
E-mail: <A HREF="mailto:ebbrown@newsletter.com">
ebbrown@newsletter.com</A></I><BR>
<HR>


<P>
<B>Summary:</B> As a journalist for 12 years, I have
worked for two newspapers and written freelance
articles for numerous magazines, often at the
request of editors familiar with the quality of
my work. Since 1995 I have published the quarterly
newsletter <A HREF="http://www.newsletter.com/copy/">
<CITE>Copy!</CITE></A>, which has more than 500 paid
subscribers via e-mail. In addition to my writing and
```

editing experience, I am well-versed in Quark Xpress,
MS Word, and all popular Internet applications.

<H2>Work Experience</H2>

<DL> <!-- begin definition list -->

<DT>
  <B>Freelance writer and newsletter publisher</B>
  Toronto, Ontario
  <I>September 1995 - present</I>
  <DD>
    My articles have appeared in <CITE>The Globe and
    Mail</CITE> (Toronto), <CITE>Travel & Leisure</CITE>
    magazine, and <CITE>Metropolitan Home</CITE>. See the
    <A HREF="publications.html">list of my publications</A>
    for details.
    My 16-page newsletter,
    <A HREF="http://www.newsletter.com/copy/">
    <CITE>Copy!</CITE></A>, which focuses on current issues
    in journalism, has been published quarterly since Fall
    1995. Most of its subscribers are media analysts and
    journalism educators.

<P><DT>
  <B>Reporter, <CITE>Democrat and Chronicle</CITE></B>
  Rochester, New York
  <I>June 1990 - September 1995</I>
  <DD>
    Covered courts and police (1990-92) and City Hall (1992-95)
    for this daily newspaper. Wrote four-part series titled
    "The Wages of Hunger," about children in low-income
    families, which won the United Way award in 1993. Wrote
    a monthly column, "On the Road," about vacation travel
    (1994-95).

<P><DT>
  <B>Reporter, <CITE>The Mississauga News</CITE></B>
  Mississauga , Ontario
  <I>July 1985 - June 1990</I>
  <DD>
    Covered local issues, courts and police. Formatted copy
    using Quark Xpress software; some page layout.
</DL> <!-- end definition list -->

<H2>Education</H2>
<UL> <!-- begin bulleted list -->

```
<LI>B.A. in English, University of Western Ontario, 1985

<P>
<LI>Six-day intensive workshop in <B>computer-assisted
reporting,</B> the Poynter Institute for Media Studies
(St. Petersburg, Florida), June 1995

</UL>  <!-- end bulleted list -->

<P>
<HR>

<ADDRESS>
R&eacute;sum&eacute; of Elizabeth Brown<BR>
Last updated January 31, 1997<BR>
E-mail: <A HREF="mailto:ebbrown@newsletter.com">
ebbrown@newsletter.com</A><BR>
Home page: <A HREF="http://www.newsletter.com/ebbrown/">
http://www.newsletter.com/ebbrown/</A>
</ADDRESS>

</BODY>
</HTML>
```

Feel free to copy this HTML formatting for your own online résumé. To add more sections, just copy and paste the formatting for Elizabeth's "Work Experience" or "Education" sections and write a different heading. (Note: Elizabeth Brown doesn't exist, and her résumé and newsletter are completely fictitious.)

The following guide is by no means a complete dictionary of HTML. However, you could create dozens of good Web pages without knowing any tags other than those described below. The aim here is to *keep things simple* so that you can get started. For more detailed information about HTML and other tags and options, see the resources listed at the end of this chapter.

Tags that should be in all HTML documents

```
<HTML> </HTML>
```

The first and last codes in your document; they frame the entire document.

```
<HEAD> </HEAD>
```

Frame the document's header, which includes the title, and which can also contain other information about the document that will not be displayed (such as <META> tags).

```
<TITLE> </TITLE>
```

Frame the actual title that will be searched on the Web and that users will see in the title bar of the browser window (or equivalent) and in the **Go** menu (**History** in Internet Explorer). This also shows up in the users' Bookmarks (Favorites). This is *not* a heading.

```
<BODY> </BODY>
```

Frame the body of the document — everything after the header (but before the closing `</HTML>` tag).

Let's look at a very simple example of a complete Web page:

```
<HTML>

<HEAD>
<TITLE>My Home Page</TITLE>
</HEAD>

<BODY>
<H1>Welcome!</H1>
This is the text of my home page. It is only
two sentences long.
</BODY>

</HTML>
```

Now compare the above text file with the Web page it produces (Figure 7-3). Notice where the title appears (in the bar at the top edge of the window). The Web browser program has determined the typeface and size of the heading and the text (because no `<FONT>` tags were used).

---

tech.ease

The HTML specification, which describes the HTML tags and how they work, is continually changing (typical of new technical specs). In practical terms, this means three things:

- New capabilities are always being added to HTML. If you feel an urgent need to be hip and snazzy, you will redesign your pages often. But this isn't necessary. Simple tags work fine, and they still convey your message.

- The dominant browsers support newer features in different ways. If you're trying something snazzy, you'd better test it with different browsers (and with different *versions* of those browsers) to make sure it really works. No time for testing? Then keep it simple and "by the book."
- Web browser software will change to keep up with the latest revisions to the HTML spec. If you use HTML tags

in unconventional ways to achieve certain design effects, the next generation of browser software may wreck your design. New versions of HTML try to stay compatible with earlier versions, but they cannot stay compatible with non-standard uses of the tags.

FIGURE 7-3
A Web page welcome

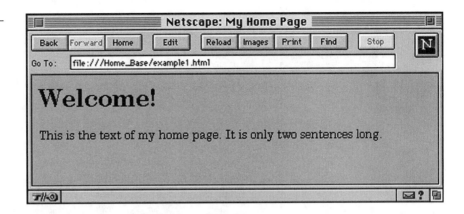

All HTML 3.2 and later documents should begin with a rather complex document type declaration in this format:

```
<!DOCTYPE HTML PUBLIC "-//W3C//DTD HTML 3.2//EN">
```

If you're using HTML 4.0 features, it gets more complicated (see **www.w3.org/TR/html4/struct/global.html#version-info**). This declaration tag always *precedes* the <HTML> tag.

Common text-formatting tags

1. Headings

<H1> </H1>	Frame the largest heading (or headline)
<H2> </H2>	Frame the second largest heading
<H6> </H6>	Frame the sixth largest heading

(There are six heading levels, including H3, H4, and H5.)

2. Text-breaking tags (no closing tag required for these)

<P>	Start paragraph (adds one line of space)
<HR>	Insert a horizontal rule (dividing line)
 	Break the line

3. Tags for emphasis

<B> </B>	Boldface
<I> </I>	Italics

4. Lists

<OL> </OL>	Frame an ordered (numbered) list
<UL> </UL>	Frame an unordered (bulleted) list
<LI>	Begin each new list item (no closing tag required)
<DL> </DL>	Frame a definition list; instead of <LI>, use <DT> to precede the term to be defined and

FIGURE 7-4
The Web browser inter-
prets the HTML codes
indicating a bulleted list.

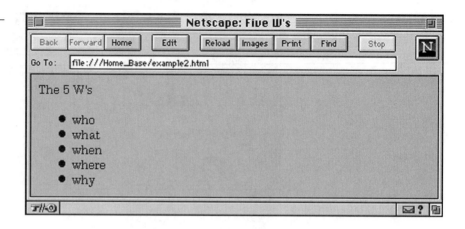

<DD> to precede the definition; no closing
tag is required with <DT> or <DD>.

Example:
```
The 5 W's
<UL>
 <LI>who  <LI>what <LI>when  <LI>where
 <LI>why
</UL>
```

The tag <LI> creates a bullet and also starts a new line, even if
your text document did not show a new line. In many browsers, a
list is automatically indented (see Figure 7-4).

Hypertext links

1. To a Web page on another server

```
<A HREF="http://www.someplace.com/">
```

Leave the present document and open one with the URL
http://www.someplace.com/

```
</A>
```

End the descriptive name (that is, the link text) — this is the second
tag in a pair.

Example 1a:

```
<A HREF="http://www.someplace.com/">The
Someplace Cafe</A>
```

Looks like this: <u>The Someplace Cafe</u>

Example 1b:

```
Come to the
<A HREF="http://www.books.com/writers/mystery.html">
Mystery Writers' Den</A> for a clue.
```

Looks like this: Come to the <u>Mystery Writers' Den</u> for a clue.

2. To a Web page on the same server

```
<A HREF="home.htm">
```

Leave this document and open one that is in the same directory on the same server and that has the filename *home.htm*. (Note that *http://* is not used for local documents; also note that some file-names use the extension *.htm* and others use *.html* — make sure you've used the one that matches the filename.)

```
</A>
```

End the descriptive name (the link text) — this is the second tag in a pair.

Example 2:

```
Come to <A HREF="home.htm">my home page</A>
today.
```

Looks like this: Come to <u>my home page</u> today.

3. To a place elsewhere on this same Web page

```
<A HREF="#hobbies">
```

Go to another part of this document where you have put the tag:

<A NAME="hobbies"> (see NAME anchor in Example 3b, on the next page).

tech.ease

If you have only a few Web pages and images, it's simplest to keep them all in one directory or folder. If you have more than a dozen Web pages, you should learn how to create new directories (folders) on the server where your pages are stored. Say that home.htm is in your main (or top-level) folder, and you also have a folder named *europe*. You have a page named *italy.htm* inside that folder. To put a working link to *italy.htm* on the page *home.htm*, you must include the name of the folder where *italy.htm* can be found:

```
<A HREF="europe/italy.htm">Italian Art</A>
```

```
</A>
```

End the descriptive name (the link text) — this is the second tag in a pair.

Example 3a:

```
There is <A HREF="#hobbies">a list of other things
I like</A> below.
```

Looks like this: There is <u>a list of other things I like</u> below.

Example 3b (the NAME anchor):

```
<A NAME="hobbies">My Other Interests</A>
```

Looks like this: My Other Interests

(This text will not be underlined or highlighted; the tags create an anchor location, not an active link.)

The NAME anchor marks a destination to which the HREF link above will take you. The text between the tags ("My Other Interests") could be *any text at all*, including a heading — or even an image. Alternatively, you could set up the two tags with only a space between them, and the anchor would also work:

```
<A NAME="hobbies"> </A>
```

Note the special function of the pound sign (#) in these anchor links: use it with HREF, but do not use it with NAME.

This kind of in-document link works best on a Web page divided into sections. You can provide a compact preview of all the sections at the top of the page by creating a small table of contents, with each section name linked to the start of a section below. For examples, look at how **Lonely Planet Online** formats its pages on individual countries (go to **www.lonelyplanet.com/** and look up any country you like; use **View | Source** to see the HTML code).

Example 3c:

```
<A HREF="#current">My Current Project</A>
<A HREF="#history">Work History</A>
<A HREF="#edu">Education</A>
```

Farther down the page we would find `<A NAME="history"> </A>` followed, no doubt, by a list of jobs this person has held, and `<A NAME="edu"> </A>` followed by a list of degrees earned and schools attended.

Adding images to Web pages

```
<IMG SRC="globe.gif" ALIGN=top ALT="">
```

Insert an image (in this case, one that is contained in a file named *globe.gif*). There is no closing tag.

Obtaining images and using file formats are discussed later in this chapter.

IMG tag attributes

There are many options (attributes) that can be included within the `<IMG>` tag; they are too numerous to list here, so we will look at only two. To learn more, consult the online graphics resources listed at the end of this chapter.

```
ALIGN=top
```

The options for the `ALIGN` attribute include *bottom*, *middle*, *left*, and *right*. These affect how the *text* before and after the image will be aligned, relative to the image.

```
ALT=""
```

The `ALT` attribute spares text-only users from seeing an unhelpful label, such as [IMAGE] or [INLINE] (see Figure 7-5B, page 153). More important, it can be used to provide information that substitutes for the graphic — for visually impaired users, and for the *many* Web users with slower Internet connections who surf with graphics turned off. To do so, put useful text between the quotes. For example, if you have an art banner that says *Welcome*, you might use `ALT="Welcome"` so that the word "Welcome" would be printed for people who will not see the banner.

You can leave out the `ALIGN` and `ALT` attributes. This is an example of the simplest form of the `<IMG>` tag:

```
<IMG SRC="globe.gif">
```

Using an image as a link

When text is used as a link, it is framed by the two parts of the `<A>` tag; that is, it is preceded by `<A HREF="filename.html">` and followed by `</A>` (see "Hypertext Links," above). An image is handled the same way, but instead of framing a word or phrase with a pair of `<A>` tags, the complete `<IMG>` tag is framed.

Example:

```
<A HREF="home.html"><IMG SRC="globe.gif"></A>
```

This would show the *globe.gif* image, and the image would act as a link to the Web page *home.html*.

Most Web browsers will automatically draw a rectangular border around a linked image. If you don't like the border, turn it off by adding BOR-DER=0 within the `<IMG>` tag:

```
<IMG SRC="globe.gif"
BORDER=0 ALT="">
```

You could also make the border thicker by specifying, for example, BORDER=5.

Other tags and codes

Comments

```
<!-- an invisible comment -->
```

To note comments within your HTML code that will be visible when anyone views the source code but that will not appear on the Web page itself, frame the notation with `<!--` and `-->` (this can be useful for pages that will require maintenance).

E-mail links

```
<A HREF="mailto:mmcadams@well.com">
```

The e-mail link above enables users to send an e-mail message to this address: *mmcadams@well.com*

```
</A>
```

End the description (the link text) of the e-mail destination — this is the second tag in a pair.

Example 1:

```
<A HREF="mailto:mmcadams@well.com">Mindy
McAdams</A>
```

Looks like this: <u>Mindy McAdams</u>

Example 2:

It's better style to make the e-mail address visible:

```
<A HREF="mailto:mmcadams@well.com">
mmcadams@well.com</A>
```

Looks like this: <u>mmcadams@well.com</u>

Clicking either one of the links in the two examples above will cause an e-mail window to open so that someone can send a comment on the spot, without opening a separate e-mail program.

Symbols and accents

There are two ways to produce typographical symbols and accented letters, as illustrated below with the copyright symbol and the lowercase letter *e* with an acute accent (*é*). For a comprehensive reference, see the **Web Design Group's** "ISO 8859-1 Character Set Overview" (**www.htmlhelp.com/reference/charset/**).

Option 1. To produce a special character, find the ISO Latin 1 (ISO 8859-1) numeric entity for the symbol or letter you want (see the list at **www.w3.org/pub/WWW/MarkUp/Wilbur/latin1.gif**), precede it with an ampersand and a pound sign (&#), and follow it with a semicolon (;). The copyright symbol (©) is represented by *169* (©). An *e* with an acute accent (*é*) is represented by *233* (é).

Examples:

```
Copyright &#169; 1999
```

Looks like this: Copyright © 1999

```
r&#233;sum&#233;
```

Looks like this: résumé

Option 2. Many accented letters can be represented by a "character entity" instead. Find the character entity for the symbol or letter you want (see the list at **www.uni-passau.de/~ramsch/iso8859-1. html**), precede it with an ampersand, and follow it with a semicolon. The character entity for the copyright symbol is *copy* (©). For the acute-accented *e* the character entity is *eacute* (é).

Examples:

```
Copyright &copy; 1999
```

Looks like this: Copyright © 1999

```
r&eacute;sum&eacute;
```

Looks like this: résumé

Other HTML capabilities
HTML allows the creation of tables (both simple grids and complex layouts with cells of varying sizes). It also makes possible interactive forms, which enable users to type in information that can be e-mailed to you or entered automatically into a database, or that can be processed by the Web server to provide an immediate "personal" response. HTML forms require specific programming to work; the most common languages used are JavaScript and Perl. Other common methods for processing forms include Active Server Pages (ASPs), Cold Fusion, and Java (which is entirely different from JavaScript).

Multimedia content can be added to Web pages via numerous viewers, helper applications, and plug-ins (see Chapter 8).

Last but far from least, HTML 4.0 provides for the inclusion of style sheets, which let you specify fonts and font sizes, colors, and

(*continued on page 153*)

Making a Web page yourself

With what you have learned from this chapter so far, you can already make a fully functioning Web page with headings, paragraphs, lists, images, and hypertext links. For further guidance, compare the text document in Figure 7-5 to Figure 7-5A opposite it. Here's how to do it using software you already have on your computer:

1. Open a basic text editor program, such as Windows Notepad (not WordPad) or SimpleText on the Macintosh.
2. Open a plain text file in the text editor, or write a new one. (Keep it short for this first exercise.)
3. Type <HTML> at the very top of the document, before all other text.
4. Type </HTML> at the very bottom of the document, after all other text. (Note that the slash tilts to the right, unlike the DOS backslash.)

FIGURE 7-5

Notice the effects produced by the <P> **tags, the**
 tag, the two <HR> **tags, and by the extra spaces in the last paragraph. There are two hypertext links and one image in this example.**

```
<HTML>
<HEAD>
<TITLE>An HTML Example</TITLE>
</HEAD>

<BODY>

<H1>Hypertext Markup Language</H1>

<HR>

The text in an HTML document is plain text,
or ASCII.

<P>
Images are inserted <BR>
wherever there is a tag that gives the
filename <IMG SRC="monkey.gif"> of the image.

<P>
Hypertext links are also created with tags. The
filename of a local document or the complete URL
(Uniform Resource Locator) of an external document
precedes the link text, and a closing tag follows.
As an example of an external link, I offer
<A HREF="http://www.yahoo.com/">Yahoo!</A> As an
example of a local document, I offer
<A HREF="index.html">my home page</A>.

<P>
"Typographer's quotation marks" cannot be used in
HTML; neither can true dashes - or other marks that
do not appear on an old-style typewriter.

<P>
The number of spaces between                words
or
between lines



of text has no effect on formatting in HTML.

<HR>

</BODY>
</HTML>
```

5. Save your document by selecting **File | Save As...** . Make sure the new filename ends with the extension *.htm* — or *.html* on the Mac (example: *mystory.htm*). This extension enables the Web browser software to recognize the file as an HTML document. In Notepad, be sure not to save with the *.txt* extension. Windows 95 users should stick to eight-letter filenames for these files.

6. Open your Web browser. (You do not have to be connected to the Internet to do this.) Keep the text editor program open too.

7. Open your new document in the Web browser (it can be open in both programs at the same time, so long as you are using a basic text editor). To open it in Netscape, choose **File | Open File...** and then locate the file on your hard drive. To open it in Internet Explorer, choose **File | Open**, click the **Browse** button, and then locate the file on your hard drive. After

you select the file and click **OK**, you should see your document in your Web browser. It won't have any paragraphs or other formatting yet, but it will appear in the screen font that your Web browser uses.

8. Editing your document will be much easier if you can arrange your Web browser window and your text editor window in a way that lets you toggle (click back and forth)

between the two windows. Try dragging one window to the far left and the other window to the far right. Resize the two windows if necessary so that neither one entirely covers the other.

9. By clicking on the text editor window, go back to the editor program.

10. Just below the top tag `<HTML>`, type this:

    `<H1>My First Web Page</H1>`

    Be careful to get all the angle brackets and the slash correct. Also, be sure to type the numeral one after the two H's — do not type a lowercase L.

11. Save the document again. (Select **File | Save** from the menu in the text editor.) Do not change the filename.

12. By clicking on the Web browser window, go back to the Web browser.

13. Reload the Web page. In Netscape, click the button labeled **Reload**. In Internet Explorer, click the button labeled **Refresh**. (This button may be covered by the Address window. Slide the bar to the right to find it.)

14. You should see a large bold heading announcing your first Web page. Congratulations! You're ready to learn more HTML. Using this method, you can easily fine-tune your work and test it in your Web browser. Just remember to save the file in the text editor after you have made changes, and then reload in the browser.

FIGURE 7-5B

The text file show in Figure 7-5 was saved as *example.html* and then opened in Internet Explorer. The user of this copy of Internet Explorer has changed the default font (to Arial) and also has chosen to turn off the images. Compare with Figure 7-5A (previous page) to understand the effect of turning off images in a Web browser. Remember, you are seeing exactly the same file, simply shown as it appears in two different browsers.

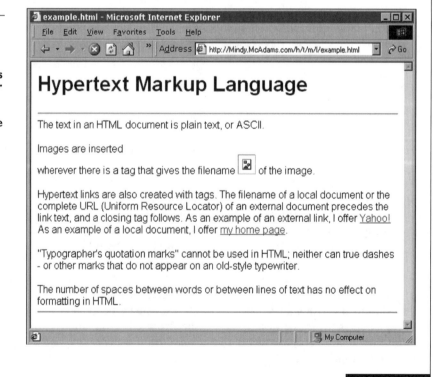

tech.ease

You can create a link to any site
on the Web, but you will have
to be connected to the Internet
to make those external links
work. If you want to test a link
without connecting, create
another Web page on your own
hard drive and link to it. For
example, create a text file
named *test.htm* and link to it this
way:

```
<A HREF="test.htm">my
test page</A>
```

even leading (line spacing) for an entire set of Web pages. The
major Web browsers support style sheets, but the results of using
them are not always predictable because many users still have older
browsers installed.

After you have created a few simple Web pages using the basic
tags, you can certainly go on to master any or all of the other features of HTML. The additional resources listed at the end of this
chapter ("More Resources on the Web," page 172) will tell you
everything you need to know to go further with HTML. The rest of
this chapter introduces you to additional aspects of creating and
publishing Web pages.

Web graphics

"If you really want to do some scientific testing, do the following: 1) Get a
group of volunteers who are all interested in a common subject (say, cats);
2) Show them ten cats Web sites. Make five of those sites highly graphical and
five highly informative; 3) 24 hours later, do a standard retention test and see
which sites they remember most. I'll bet that the content sites stay in their
minds better than the graphic-intensive sites. Ditto for people that are looking
for something specific, and searching all over the Net for it."

— *Mary Morris, "What Is Good Design?"*
www.sun.com/950801/columns/MaryMorris.col9508.html

It's not necessary to put images on a Web page, but they do look nice
— when used in moderation. There are two common ways to get
images to use on your Web pages: make them yourself, or use clip art
(ready-made images). You can also scan images from printed sources.

Clip art
It's very easy to copy images directly from a Web page:

1. Place your cursor on the image.
2. On the PC, click the right-hand mouse button once. On the
   Mac, hold down the mouse button. In either case, you will get a
   pop-up menu near your cursor.
3. Select the menu option **Save Image As...** (the wording may vary
   slightly depending on your browser).
4. You will get a dialog box that allows you to choose where (on
   your own hard drive) to save the image. Select a directory or
   folder (such as *temp*) and click the **Save** button. (You may want
   to create a separate directory just for Web images.)

Never copy and reuse an image from the Web unless you have
explicit permission from the person who created the image.
Otherwise, you would be violating copyright (see "Scanned
Images," below).

There are a number of Web sites that provide free clip art. Such
sites clearly identify themselves and plainly state that their images

may be freely copied. There's a directory at **Clipart.com** (**www. clipart.com/**). Here are some of the better sites:

Absolute Background Textures Archive
www.grsites.com/textures/
A treasure trove of more than 3,000 backgrounds.

Ender Design: Realm Graphics
www.ender-design.com/rg/
A big collection of nice backgrounds, bullets, buttons, icons, and lines.

Icon Bazaar
www.iconbazaar.com/
A vast site with hundreds of icons of all kinds.

Pixelsight
www.pixelsight.com/
An amazing array of beautiful graphics; not free (registration required), but well worth a look if you get serious about designing Web content. This service goes beyond letting you simply copy and paste — you can easily customize images and graphical text even if you have no artistic skill.

Your own original images

To create your own images for the Web, you must have a graphics program. Some of these cost hundreds of dollars (notably, Adobe's **Photoshop**); some cost less than $100. You can get very good effects with an inexpensive program. If you have no artistic skill, even the most expensive program won't help you. If that's the case, you should rely on clip art (or hire an artist). If you're very serious about creating original graphics and you have $649 U.S. to spare, then buy Photoshop (**www.adobe.com/**).

JASC Inc.'s **Paint Shop Pro** (**www.jasc.com/**) can do just about everything you will ever need. This full-featured Windows-only paint program saves in (and converts) many file formats, resizes beautifully, and has too many other features to name, for $99 U.S.

Adobe's **Photoshop Limited Edition** (**www.adobe.com/**) provides tools for manipulating photos. Available for Windows or Macintosh, it costs $95 U.S. Adobe's less expensive **PhotoDeluxe Home Edition** ($49 U.S.) runs only under Windows. If you buy a scanner, one of these programs (or a similar program from another publisher) will probably come with it.

ArtDabbler from **MetaCreations** (**www.metacreations.com/ products/dabbler/**), for both Windows and Mac, is a very nice paint program for $50 U.S., and it's fun to use. Its options for saving in different file formats are limited, though, so you would also need GIF/JPEG conversion software (see "Web Graphics File Formats," page 155).

Scanned images

If you have access to a scanner, you may be tempted to scan photographs and artwork to add to your Web pages. There are two important concerns: copyright and image file size.

Copyright. In most cases, you are within your legal rights *only* when you scan a photo you took or artwork you created. Even though no one may hold copyright on an ancient cave painting, the *photograph* of that painting is almost certainly copyrighted. The same is true of museum artworks, regardless of their age, and comic-strip characters. Even copyright-free clip art printed in a book may be protected from digital reproduction. If a permission statement regarding reproduction does not clearly include digital media, assume that they are excluded. (For more information on copyright, see Appendix D.)

Image file size. Scanned image files are usually large, often exceeding 100K. That is much too large a file for a Web page (details below).

Keeping image size in check

"Every day my modem seems to get slower. No, it's not broken. Rather, more and more sites ... use the latest and greatest fancy graphics with frames and images that flash and move repeatedly, and Java applets that make new things happen non-stop. There seems to be some law of human nature on the Internet that everyone needs to push the limits of the technology, using all the graphics and multimedia effects that they possibly can, to prove to themselves and to the world that they can do it. I ask myself — what are they communicating? What's the content?"

— *Richard Seltzer, "The Social Web," B&R Samizdat Express*
www.samizdat.com/lowtech.html

The most important thing to know about Web images is this: the smaller, the better. By "small," we mean the *file size*, not how big the image looks on the screen. There are various ways to see how large a file is; often your graphics program can tell you. Image files are reduced in size when they are saved in GIF or JPEG format (see below). You can further reduce the file size by saving the image with fewer colors.

Any image larger than 35K is questionable for use on the Web. Images larger than 50K can rarely be defended.

If you overtax a Web page with too many images that take too long to load, people visiting your page are likely to be annoyed. You may think it looks fantastic, but others will lose patience and go on to another, faster-loading page — without even reading yours.

Web graphics file formats

Images must be in a particular file format before a Web browser can display them.

A file format is a pattern for storing information. Word processing files, for example, can be stored in plain text format or in a special format such as the document formats used by MS Word or WordPerfect.

There are many different file formats for graphics files. Only two are commonly used for Web images: GIF and JPEG. As a rule of thumb, GIF is usually better for drawings, icons, and other simple images. JPEG is usually better for photographs, paintings, and other highly detailed images. If you copy an image from the Web, it will almost always be in one of these two formats.

If you have an image that is not in GIF or JPEG format, you must *convert* the image before you can display it on a Web page. To do so, open the image and then save it in the format you want. Many, but not all, graphics programs allow you to do this. (You get a list of file format options when you select **File | Save As...** within a graphics program.)

If your graphics program does not include these file formats, you can use graphics conversion software (see below) to open and save your file.

It's not always enough simply to save the file in the right format. Web browsers expect the filename of an image to have an extension (either *.gif* or *.jpg*). When you save a graphic as a GIF file in Windows, the filename will automatically end with *.gif* (and when you save a JPEG file, it will end with *.jpg*). Mac users may need to add the correct extension manually, depending on the graphics software they use.

A third graphics file format, *portable network graphics*, or PNG, is only imperfectly supported by the dominant Web browsers.

Recommended graphics software (shareware)
Below are some programs you may find useful for viewing, converting, or editing Web graphics.

Windows 95/98/NT

GIF Construction Set Professional
www.mindworkshop.com/alchemy/gifcon.html
A collection of tools for editing GIFs and creating animated GIFs and transparent backgrounds.

LView Pro
www.lview.com/
This full-featured image-editing program is excellent for creating transparent backgrounds. It also performs complex color-correction functions, simplifies building a Web "photo gallery," and saves in a variety of file formats.

Macintosh

GraphicConverter
www.lemkesoft.de/
Coverts to and from almost any graphics file format.

wwwART
www.microfrontier.com/
Convert file formats, create image maps, control the palette, paint, create 3D effects, and more.

Screen colors and Web browsers

Before you go wild with graphics on your Web pages, you should know that Web browsers can be trusted to display only 216 colors accurately. This can cause some very ugly effects if your computer is set to display millions of colors while you are creating images — what looks great on *your* screen may look appalling on someone else's. For a full explanation (and ways to compensate for this limited palette), see Lynda Weinman's page, **The Browser-Safe Color Palette (www.lynda.com/hex.html)**.

Adding color to text and backgrounds

Apart from adding images to your Web pages, you can make your text, links, and page background just about any color you like (within the limited palette, that is). This is done by adding codes within the <BODY> tag of the HTML document. The codes — actually, hexadecimal numbers — represent a value of red plus green plus blue (RGB; the color model used by your computer monitor) by using three pairs of characters: 00, 33, 66, 99, CC, or FF. Only those six pairs are "safe."

For example, 000000 is black, FFFFFF is white, FF0000 is bright red, 990099 is purple, and 00FF00 is a rather blinding shade of green. In the following example, the body tag sets the page colors to a black background with white text and red links; the followed links (VLINK) are purple, and the activated link (ALINK), which you see for only a moment as you press the mouse button, is blinding green:

```
<BODY BGCOLOR=#000000 TEXT=#FFFFFF LINK=#FF0000
VLINK=#990099 ALINK=#00FF00>
```

A note about being kind to readers: On a sunny afternoon on a very good screen, you may be able to read tiny dark-gray text on a

Palette Man is a Web site that lets you try out different color combinations and supplies the necessary codes for you to use on your own pages, making color selection very easy. You'll find it at:
www.paletteman.com/

black background, but always remember that your reader may be sitting in a windowless office with flickering fluorescent light, looking at an older screen with failing contrast.

To learn more about using graphics on the Web, including how to superimpose text on a background image on a Web page, see "More Resources on the Web" at the end of this chapter (page 172).

HTML editor software

Software can handle the HTML coding for you. Some HTML editor programs display the HTML tags; some hide them from you altogether. Most editors provide a WYSIWYG ("what you see is what you get") editing environment similar to that of word-processing programs.

The advantages of using an HTML editor program:

- You may never need to learn any HTML.
- Because you don't type the tags yourself, you won't make typographical errors that affect the appearance of the Web page.
- Changes in the name or location of Web files are updated automatically across all files created with that editor. (This is a huge advantage on sites consisting of many pages.)
- Uploading and downloading files (between your computer and the Web server) is simplified.

The drawbacks of using an HTML editor program:

- You must learn how to use the software (when you could be learning HTML directly instead).
- Your ability to control how your Web pages look is somewhat reduced.
- Your ability to compensate for odd behavior by the editor program depends on your knowledge of HTML. (When the code generated by the editor doesn't work properly, the only option is to fix the code manually. If you don't know even basic HTML, you will be stuck.)
- You'll have to wait for the next version of the HTML editor program before you can incorporate new HTML features developed after the editor program was released.

Our view is that it's still better to learn HTML, whether or not you choose to use an editor program. Many professional Web designers use an HTML editor to do the "first draft" or prototype of a Web page (or site) and then fine-tune the HTML using an ordinary text editor. Web professionals often rely on editor programs for doing updates and maintenance work on sites.

Using an editor program may make it easy to whip up a few decent-looking Web pages quickly, but none of these programs is a substitute for planning or design skill. Beginners are often too eager to start creating visual effects and using complex HTML structures such as frames. Lacking basic knowledge of HTML, however, their sites get out of hand — links don't work; images fail to appear; tables sprawl off the page for most users (making the content unreadable); strange fonts and clashing colors interfere with the message.

It takes time and effort to learn to build full-scale Web sites that work well. The editor program is nothing but a tool. Just because you bought a power saw doesn't mean you can build a house — or even a tool shed. So start small: build a birdhouse. Work up to the big stuff, and most important, learn the fundamentals as you go.

All the editor programs listed below include site-management tools unless otherwise noted; most also include templates (ready-made graphics and color schemes) for "instant" site design. Full specifications and feature descriptions are available at the manufacturers' Web sites. This list does not include every HTML editor on the market. It reflects an effort to highlight the best, the most popular, and the most-used programs available at a wide range of prices. Prices are manufacturers' list and may change.

If you're not ready to invest in one of the programs listed here, a good place to find "low-end," inexpensive or free editor programs is the **Tucows** site (**http://html.tucows.com/designer/software.html**). Click the link "Editors Beginner" under the heading for your operating system (Macintosh or Windows).

Both Windows and Mac OS

Dreamweaver 3.0 (Macromedia)
www.macromedia.com/software/dreamweaver/
The professionals' choice for clean, bug-free code, versatility, and ease of use. Cost: $300 U.S. Download a free thirty-day trial version.

GoLive 4.0 (Adobe)
www.adobe.com/products/golive/
High-end drag-and-drop functionality. Cost: $299 U.S. Download free "tryout" software.

Netscape Composer (Netscape)
www.netscape.com/computing/download/
The best thing about this is that it's free. Not a lot of features, but easy to use. If you have Netscape Communicator, you already have it. (On the **File** menu, go to **New** and select **Blank Page, Page From Template**, or **Page From Wizard**.) If you don't, it's a big download, but it's free.

PageMill 3.0 (Adobe)
www.adobe.com/products/pagemill/
Very popular with beginning Web authors; includes templates,

animations, Java applets; also includes Photoshop Limited Edition. Cost: $79 U.S. if downloaded from Adobe's Web site; otherwise, $99 U.S. Download free "tryout" software.

Windows 95/98/NT only

FrontPage 2000 (Microsoft)
www.microsoft.com/catalog/
Widely used; much improved over earlier versions. Similar to other Microsoft products such as Word. Cost: $149 U.S.

HotDog PageWiz (Sausage Software)
www.sausage.com/pagewiz/
Very simple for beginners; also includes an advanced "Editor Mode" for more experienced users. Cost: $70 U.S. Download a free thirty-day trial version. The company also offers the higher-end **HotDog Professional 5.5** for $130 U.S.

HoTMetaL Pro 6.0 (SoftQuad)
www.hotmetalpro.com/
Designed for professional use, but popular with beginning Web authors; offers a number of learning aids and templates. Cost: $129 U.S. Download a free thirty-day evaluation version.

Macintosh only

BBEdit 5.1.1 (Bare Bones Software)
www.barebones.com/products/bbedit/
A superior text editor; not WYSIWYG; lacks site-management tools; beloved by many Web developers. Cost: $119 U.S. Download **BBEdit Lite 4.6** free (not a trial version; does not "expire"); it may be the only editor you'll ever need.

Designing Web content

> "On today's Web, the most common mistake is to make everything too prominent: overuse of colors, animation, blinking, and graphics. Every element of the page screams 'look at me' (while all the other design elements scream 'no, look at me'). When everything is emphasized, nothing is emphasized. But it's just as bad to make everything equally bland."
>
> — *Jakob Nielsen, user advocate and principal, Nielsen Norman Group*
> *"Prioritize: Good Content Bubbles to the Top"*
> *www.useit.com/alertbox/991017.html*

Design means more than pictures. Every document, even a business letter, is designed, and Web pages are no exception.

A simple Web page may include no more than one heading and one short paragraph. The design of such a page is largely dictated by HTML. However, there are three things you should consider adding to *each one* of your pages:

- **Your e-mail address.** This is equivalent to signing your work on the Web, and it allows your online readers to contact you. People often send a Web author e-mail that corrects an error or suggests related sources, so listing your e-mail address on every page can bring benefits.
- **A link to your home page.** This is another way of signing your work. Anyone anywhere can link to any of your pages, so you should never assume that a reader will come to a page of yours via a link from another page of yours. If readers can find your home page, they should be able to find more of your work (more about that below).
- **The date your material was last revised.** Things go out of date quickly on the Web, and yet, because anything might have been updated five minutes ago, your readers don't know how current you are — unless you tell them.

These links usually appear at the bottom of a Web page. Without the first two, you may be mysteriously anonymous to many of your readers. Without the third, you may be dismissed as unreliable. If you are updating your material often, you may want to brag about that by posting the date at *the top of* your pages.

Page design

On the Web, people like to click much more than they like to scroll. That means if you really want people to hang out at your Web site instead of someone else's, you should try to keep your documents short.

How long is too long? Web-savvy writers and designers agree that the limit is about 1,000 words per page.

Admittedly, not all content lends itself to a short, click-happy format. Research reports often can be broken up into sections or chapters, but sometimes the sections themselves are lengthy and cannot be divided further.

As a rule, try to reformat, rewrite, and repurpose your work into 1,000-word chunks (or smaller). Follow these rules to try to hold readers' attention:

1. Keep your paragraphs short.
2. Use boldface and italics more than you would in print, to highlight key words and phrases that may catch a reader's attention.
3. Insert more headings than you would use in print (they scroll off the screen, so you don't need to worry about having too many).
4. Break out lists (bulleted or numbered) whenever you have more than two parallel phrases or clauses.

All these practices add variation to the text, make key words and phrases more noticeable, and increase the chances that readers who begin scrolling through your page at a fast clip (and they will, don't doubt it) will see something to make them stop and read closely.

Take care that no subheading clashes with or repeats any bold-face emphasis or hypertext links in the text below it. The point is to communicate clearly, not to create a typographical mess.

Navigation

So now you have a dozen little 500-word chunks and you don't know what to do with them?

Therein lies the beauty of hypertext. By creating links in HTML, you can easily connect all your Web pages to your home page. What's more, you can connect them to one another.

If you have a home page and only a few additional pages, you may be satisfied with a simple list of links on your home page and a single link back from each of the other pages. But once you have five or more pages, you should consider a more sophisticated scheme. When a list of links is long, it becomes a liability, just like a long Web page: readers lose interest before they get to the end.

Begin to group your pages into sets of related material. For example, if you're a freelance writer who specializes in travel and food subjects, split your material into two sections, such as "Places" and "Cuisine." Describe each section briefly on your home page, perhaps highlighting your most recent work (for example, a phrase such as "My journey through Tuscany taught me to love the region's wines" can take a reader to your article about traveling in that part of Italy, or to the section of your article specifically about the local wines). Don't worry about which section is a better "home" for the series you wrote on the cafés of the Mediterranean; you can link to that series (or parts of it) from *both* "Places" and "Cuisine."

For an even larger Web site, such as a newsletter with multiple issues online, be sure to consider the opportunities the Web provides that differ from those in libraries and other cataloging systems. You are not limited to listing issues only by number and by date (which is not very helpful at all to browsing readers). Articles on related topics can be linked together; links to something new can even be added to an older article. "Old" and "new" sometimes lose their distinction online; if you just started skiing, then a two-year-old article on how to ski is new — and valuable — to you.

Navigation is simply getting around. Make sure that anyone who finds any one of your pages can figure out how to get around to see your other pages.

If you're in charge of a Web site with changing content, the home page should reflect that. Readers are likely to bookmark the home page and check back to see what's new. Don't hide that information! Show off whatever's new, preferably near the top of the page.

A word about graphics

Pretty pictures deserve a lot of credit for making the Web popular and fun. But too many images on one page will make that page load very slowly, and people may not hang around to see what comes up.

When you have something to say, don't interfere with your message by scattering images all over your Web pages. Similarly, large background images and gaudy colors can get in the way.

You may be tempted to add a number of buttons, fancy borders, and three-dimensional titles just because you can. These things have their place, but think carefully about whether they really enhance what you're trying to get across.

A small, simple, original image repeated in a consistent manner can look very slick and professional, while a grab bag of mismatched clip art screams "Amateur!"

How to write for the Web

"Content creators who work in the Internet environment can think beyond traditional media venues — and *greatly expand their income potential*. The Internet has made it possible for content professionals to research, contact, and work with a wider variety of venues than would have been imaginable in the pre-digital age."

— *Steve Outing and Amy Gahran, "The Booming Business of Online Content"*
www.content-exchange.com/cx/html/essay.htm

The previous section probably got you thinking about reading from a screen and how it differs from reading a printed page. If the experience of reading is different on the computer screen (and it is), should your writing be different too?

You bet it should!

Before you make the argument that much of the written material on the Web looks just like it would in print, think about where that material comes from. Are you picturing the Web site of a major newspaper or magazine? Printed publications find economic advantages in copying articles directly from the printed page to the screen — but that doesn't mean the practice works well for *readers*.

How often have you printed out articles from the Web? Would you have printed them to read on paper if they had been written *for* the medium in which they appeared?

Online, your audience is impatient, addicted to movement (click-happy), and very, very likely to scan your prose at high speed.

INFOnugget

"Reading from computer screens is about 25% slower than reading from paper. ... As a result, people don't want to read a lot of text from computer screens: you should write 50% less text and not just 25% less since it's not only a matter of reading speed, but also a matter of feeling good."

— Jakob Nielsen, user advocate and principal, Nielsen Norman Group, "Be Succinct! (Writing for the Web)"
www.useit.com/alertbox/ 9703b.html

The **Content Exchange** site (**www.content-exchange.com/**) provides tips, resources, and job leads for "online content creators."

Whether readers are browsing to pass the time or actively searching for something in particular, they are not interested in extra words.

In Web usability studies conducted over several years, Jakob Nielsen found that 79% of test users always *scanned* a page the first time they saw it and "only 16% read word-by-word."

Journalists are well prepared to write for this demanding audience. Short sentences, active verbs, and clear, direct statements come naturally to most practiced journalists. Even better prepared are copy editors, who not only ruthlessly trim the fat from writers' copy but also write newspaper headlines — the ultimate example of concise communication. On the Web as in a headline, every single word should be doing *useful work*.

Style and tone

Text written for online publications and other Web sites tends to be less formal-sounding than text written for print, partly because Web writing often takes on a personal tone, even when it's not first-person (but often it is).

That doesn't mean it's sloppy, or filled with slang or jargon. Good online writing meets the requirements of all good writing; it's just tighter, leaner, more direct. Marketing slogans and unsupported claims come off as stuffy or stupid, similar to the worst junk-mail sales pitches.

An example of what you *shouldn't* do:

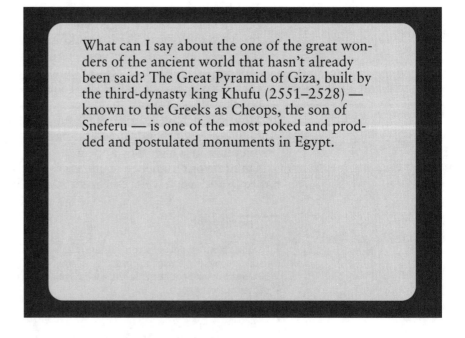

What can I say about the one of the great wonders of the ancient world that hasn't already been said? The Great Pyramid of Giza, built by the third-dynasty king Khufu (2551–2528) — known to the Greeks as Cheops, the son of Sneferu — is one of the most poked and prodded and postulated monuments in Egypt.

The first sentence is certainly informal, but it's also pointless. Here's a much better example from the same article (at *www. discovery.com/exp/pyramidquest/991020.html*):

> I ... found myself in a typical pyramid traffic jam, lined up with a group of tourists waiting to tackle the ascending passage, which opens the Grand Gallery to the King's Chamber. I managed to work up a pretty decent sweat struggling through this passage, lugging, as usual, too much camera gear — and fortunately, today, a bottle of water.

This could be tightened up without losing its personal tone:

> In a typical pyramid traffic jam, I lined up with a group of tourists waiting to tackle the ascending passage to the Grand Gallery and the King's Chamber. I worked up a decent sweat struggling through this passage, lugging, as usual, too much camera gear. Fortunately, today I had a bottle of water.

Because of readers' penchant to scan, and to click away to another Web site if you fail to hold their interest, online writing needs to be straightforward and fact-based. Focus on pure communication, not art. You don't have the time to warm up the audience; you must lay out the relevant facts immediately, drawing them in from the very first sentence on each and every page.

But don't stop there — you stand to lose these speed-demon readers at the end of every paragraph. As you go back to edit your copy a second and third time, check the first sentence of each paragraph. Does it clearly express the contents of that paragraph? If there's more than one idea in the paragraph, then break it into two. Remember "topic sentences" from your high school composition classes? That's the idea.

If your writing is highly organized and meaty but lean, you are far more likely to hold an online reader's attention.

Sometimes breaking information out into a table will aid this purpose. Compare:

"Akhet Khufu" — the horizon of Khufu, the original name for the monument — reaches a height of nearly 147 meters, making it the tallest pyramid in Egypt. Most of the limestone casing is gone; all the pyramids have served as quarries for modern building materials through the ages. The base measures over 230 meters, and the total volume of the structure is over 2.5 million cubic meters. It contains about 2,300,000 stones, with an average weight of 2.5 tons. It has a slope of almost 52 degrees and is almost perfectly square at the base. Remember — this was all done thousands of years ago, using simple tools and a lot of people over a few decades.

Use of a table within the text to present facts "at a glance":

"Akhet Khufu," the horizon of Khufu — the tallest pyramid in Egypt, almost perfectly square at the base — was built by many people using simple tools thousands of years ago. The work took a few decades. Most of the limestone casing is gone; all the pyramids have served as quarries for modern building materials through the ages.

Height	Nearly 147 meters
Base	Over 230 meters on each side
Total volume	Over 2.5 million cubic meters
Slope	Almost 52 degrees
Stones	About 2.3 million used
Average weight per stone	2.5 tons

Don't expect the "editor" at an online operation to trim and shape your copy for you. Online editors usually bear heavy production responsibilities that make it impossible for them to spend time cleaning up your prose. This sounds wonderful to writers who think that an editor butchers their copy, but in many cases, what you send in is exactly what goes online — warts and all, no second chances. So be careful about *accuracy* as well as brevity.

Consider the scope of your audience too — the Web is international. The audience may predictably be local, or at least within your own nation, but in many more cases, people from other countries will read your work. Consider their currencies (whose "dollar"?), systems of measurement (the metric measurements in the example above mean nothing to most people in the United States), knowledge of your geography, and familiarity with English idiom (phrases such as "treated like a guinea pig" or "fiddle with it" can easily confuse non-native English speakers, no matter how educated).

Exploding the pyramid
If you have taken even one journalism class, you'll remember the "inverted pyramid." No relation to the Great Pyramid of Giza

(except in shape), this equilateral triangle standing on its head illustrates how a typical news story packs all the most important information at the top (the beginning) and tapers off at the bottom (the end), where presumably the less important information hangs, ready to be hacked off if there's not enough space for it in the newspaper.

Writers who never studied journalism may gasp in horror to think that an editor might chop off the ending of their articles. Working journalists hate the idea too, but they're used to it.

No writer believes that any part of his or her work is expendable. If you've trimmed away all the fat and gristle, that may even be true. The good news about writing for the Web is that length is unlimited — there's never a need to "cut for space."

The bad news: Online readers will go somewhere else before they ever reach the end of your article, so no one will read it anyway.

That is, if you write as though you were writing for print.

But you don't have to write that way, as though your article were a sit-down dinner and every diner had to wait until you brought out the next course and the next. Instead, you can take the article apart and present a buffet of courses all at once to the reader. This allows some readers to go straight to the dessert table; imagine the desserts as those lovely endings that used to be thrown away by your heartless editor.

For successful examples of this kind of writing:

- Go to the Technology section of **CNN Interactive**'s online Cold War site (**http://cnn.com/SPECIALS/cold.war/experience/technology/**) and explore the article "Life Without the Cold War: An Exercise in Alternate History."
- Follow any collection of stories at **World News Megastories** (**www.megastories.com/**).
- Look at the **U.S. Environmental Protection Agency**'s global warming site (**www.epa.gov/globalwarming/**). Note the three distinct sections: "Climate System," "Impacts," and "Actions."

What all these sites have done is, first, to break up a collection of information into parts that are balanced (like courses at a formal dinner) but not necessarily equal in size (desserts may be smaller than entrées). Second, each site has a structure that gives the readers choices at the outset — like a buffet, this allows people to start wherever they like. The structure helps readers find what they're interested in.

One significant difference between a dinner buffet and a deep collection of online information: As readers reach each part of a Web story, they may discover that there are even *more* choices that weren't visible until they arrived there. On the EPA's global warming site, for example, in the "Impacts" section the reader finds a long list of choices such as "Health," "Water Resources," and

"Forests." One of those choices, "State by State Impacts," yields fifty *new* choices, each one leading to a complete report specific to the state selected. It's as if a single article about the impacts of global warming expanded into fifty distinct articles.

You won't usually be writing fifty articles for one freelance assignment, of course, and you may not have to plan the structure for an entire Web site. But as we discussed in "Designing Web Content" above, navigation and linking are important to individual articles as well as to entire Web sites. If your article is longer than 1,000 words, consider breaking off the lower parts of that inverted pyramid — or take the whole pyramid apart, if it's much longer, and rebuild it in a "buffet" shape better suited for the Web.

Linking it all together

A hypertext link (normally a different color from the rest of the text, and usually underlined) does more than simply connect one Web page to another. It *says something* about that page you will go to by clicking the link. So the text of the link should produce a reasonable expectation in the user. The phrase "click here" doesn't produce any expectation, so it's not effective link text.

When a link in an article about a headache remedy says "possible side effects," you have a clear idea of what to expect. If the link says "learn more," your idea is much less clear (and for that reason, maybe you won't click).

Using an active verb can make link text more specific. Instead of a link that says "membership form," write "Apply for membership today." Perk up the lifeless link "Our annual report is now online," by changing it to "Read our annual report."

Putting your own Web pages online

After you have created your Web pages, you must get them onto a Web server. The procedure for doing this differs depending on what kind of Internet account you have.

If your Web access is part of an account with a commercial online service such as America Online, or with a large Internet service provider such as Earthlink or Mindspring, contact the service provider to find out what procedure to use. You probably already have Web space that you can use immediately without paying any additional fees. With some full-service Internet accounts, you will transfer your files by using file transfer protocol (FTP). Some ISPs offer other methods (some of which may be simpler).

If you have Web access only through your job, you may not be permitted to put your own pages online. If that's so, you will need to sign up for a personal Internet account before you can "publish" on the Web.

Transferring your files via FTP will be easy if you use **Fetch** (Macintosh) or **CoffeeCup Free FTP** (Windows). You can download these free programs from: **www.dartmouth.edu/pages/ softdev/fetch.html** (for Fetch) **http://html.tucows.com/ webmaster/software/win95/ ftp95.html** (for CoffeeCup Free FTP)

If you're at a university, putting your Web pages online may be as easy as saving (or copying) your HTML files and images to a certain directory on the network. In other cases, you may have to contact someone who can set up a private directory on the university's computer for you. Contact the university computer services staff to find out what to do.

How to publicize your Web site

If you build it, will they come? Not unless they know about it. To let strangers know about your Web page, you will have to do some self-promotion.

The first step is to register your home page with the most popular search engines and directories on the Web. This will ensure that people looking for something like your page will be able to find it. You may want to register some individual pages in addition to your home page, but that isn't necessary on all search engines — most will automatically find all your pages after you register your home page.

From the search engine's or directory's home page, find the link for registering, adding, or listing a URL. Go to the appropriate page and follow the instructions there. Every site has different rules for adding your URL.

The more careful and specific you are when registering, the more people will be able to find your pages. For that reason, we don't recommend using a one-stop registration form such as **Submit It!** (**www.submit-it.com/**) — it's more like "one size fits all." Registering your site *carefully* at the top four or five search sites will serve you better than sloppy registration at two dozen or more search sites. Above all, don't make any typographical errors in your URLs! (It's safest to copy and paste the text of a URL to avoid mistakes.) Also, be sure to describe your site accurately and well when you have the opportunity. If there's a word limit, stay within it. For directories that allow you to register your page in a specific category, take some time to consider which category is best.

Optional HTML <META> tags can boost your pages' ranking with some (not all) search engines. See **Search Engine Watch**'s page "How to Use HTML Meta Tags" (**http://searchenginewatch.com/webmasters/meta.html**).

A great way to promote your Web site is to list it in the sig (signature file) that you attach to all your e-mail messages. That way, anyone who receives mail from you will know you have a Web page — including everyone on any mailing lists you belong to. If the topic of a mailing list is related to information on your Web pages, you can send a message to the list to announce your new pages (or later, to announce a significant update).

Have new business cards printed with your URL on them, and include your URL on all printed correspondence you send. If you advertise in print or broadcast media, include your URL in all your ads.

Consider using a mailing-list search engine (such as **Liszt**, at **www.liszt.com/**) to find a list suitable for announcing your pages (see Chapter 5 on listservers). The copy editors' list (Copyediting-L), for example, would be a fine place to publicize a page on grammar tips but a poor place to promote a page about photojournalism.

Under no circumstances should you announce your pages in an inappropriate place; that would only breed ill will toward you. Remember that there are now millions of Web pages on hundreds of thousands of sites, and yours will appeal only to specific groups of people. It's in your interest to seek out those groups and speak directly to them.

If your pages focus on a particular topic or subject area, consider joining (or starting) a WebRing to steer like-minded people toward your site (see **http://nav.webring.com/** for details; the "Directory" shows what rings already exist). WebRings provide an organized way to trade links with other sites closely related to yours — without any cost to you.

A last word

This chapter has given you all you need to know to get started publishing your work on the Web: a little HTML, how to put your pages on a Web server, and how to let people know your pages are out there. What are you waiting for?

After you have created several Web pages, you may want to learn more about HTML or other Web technologies than we have space to tell you here. Everything you could ever need is available free on the Web, so happy surfing!

"Call me young, call me foolish (just don't call me late for dinner), but I believe
you should use your Web site to make people (including yourself) happy. Don't
just aim for money. That leads nowhere. Aim for happiness."

— *Daniel Will-Harris, "The Once and Future Web," Will-Harris Wire*
http://news.i-us.com/wire/wire.htm

Further reading

Conner-Sax, Kiersten, and Ed Krol. *The Whole Internet: The Next
Generation.* Sebastopol, CA: O'Reilly & Associates, 1999.
www.ora.com/catalog/twi3/
Learn everything there is to know about the Internet, its history,
and how it works.

Lemay, Laura. *Sams Teach Yourself Web Publishing with HTML 4
in 21 Days* (2nd ed.). Indianapolis: Sams.Net Publishing, 1999.
$29.99.

Lemay, Laura. *Sams Teach Yourself Web Publishing with HTML 4
in 21 Days, Professional Reference Edition* (2nd ed.). Indianapolis:
Sams.Net Publishing, 2000. $49.99.

Weinman, Lynda. *Designing Web Graphics.3.* New Riders Publishing, 1999.
www.lynda.com/products/books/
This is the best printed guide to creating and optimizing images for use on the Web.

Williams, Robin, and John Tollett. *The Non-Designer's Web Book.* Berkeley, CA: Peachpit Press, 1998.
www.peachpit.com/books/nondesign.html
For the graphics-challenged: a very friendly introduction to Web design.

CHAPTER

Technology: Beyond the Basics

"... Many people, including some experienced Net riders, don't have a good grasp of what the Internet really is. [For them] it's sort of a virtual embodiment of Gertrude Stein's description of Oakland, California: there's no 'there' there. Strip away the peels of the Internet onion, and all you have are layers of technology — a bunch of rules for moving data around."
— STEVEN LEVY, *NEWSWEEK*, FEBRUARY 25, 1995, P. 22.

N ot very long ago, if you wanted to get online you had to know something about all those layers of technology tucked into the Internet onion (and you could expect to shed a few tears once you started peeling). Luckily, connecting to the Internet is now much easier. Where once you had to find your way through a confusing maze of options, today it is possible to buy software from a local computer vendor, or unpackage an AOL (America Online) CD that will have you connected in less than an hour.

While connecting to the Internet is much easier than it used to be, for many people, there are still technological hurdles to get over, particularly when you want to go beyond the basics. For example, if you've already connected to the Internet, should you be considering one of the new high-speed modem options? Where can you get software on the Net, and what should you do with a "zipped" file?

This chapter will explain a bit more about some of the technical aspects of using the Net.

CHAPTER HIGHLIGHTS

- Getting connected
- High-speed modems
- Client/server computing — the skinny
- Browser plug-ins
- Offline browsers
- Downloading software
- Compressed files
- Computer viruses

Getting connected

If you do not yet have a personal Internet account, the following section will help you get started.

Computers

You can have simple access to electronic mail even with an old computer and a slow modem. But for surfing the World Wide Web, you will quickly get frustrated if you have an out-of-date machine. Such attributes as the amount of available RAM (Random Access Memory) and the size and speed of the hard drive inevitably have an effect on your computer's performance on Internet tasks. The table that follows gives a breakdown of computer requirements for surfing the Net.

If you are a researcher, you will require a substantial hard drive, particularly if you are planning to run Windows 98/2000 or Windows NT. A one-gigabyte (or more) hard drive is increasingly standard fare. To access video and multimedia applications, you will require a video adapter card with one megabyte or more of video memory and an SVGA monitor. If these options are currently beyond your budget, you can still comfortably use the Internet for research without these expensive options.

Modems

The purpose of a modem is to change computer data signals into analog signals so that they can be sent over telephone lines. Most computers come with a built-in modem, but if you are purchasing

tech.ease

If you can't buy a new computer, consider upgrading your current system. You can add memory to your CPU and a second hard drive for less money than it would cost to buy a new computer. Your local dealer can inform you of the range of options for upgrading.

WHAT YOU'LL NEED FOR CRUISING THE INTERNET			
	Slow	Acceptable	Great performance
Computer PC Macintosh	486 PowerPC 603	Pentium PowerPC 604	Pentium III iMac G3 or PowerMac G4
Operating system PC Macintosh	Windows 95 7.5.3	Windows 95/98 Open Transport	Windows 98/2000 or Linux Mac OS 9 (includes Sherlock 2*)
Hard drive	810 MB	1–2 GB	4+ GB
RAM	16 MB	32 MB	64+ MB
Modem speed	28,800 bps	33,600 or faster	DSL or cable modem

*Sherlock 2 is a desktop Internet search tool that streamlines access to search engines, news, reference sources, and shopping, as well as to files on your own computer.

an older, used computer you may need to buy a modem separately — or get a faster modem. Here are several things to be aware of.

Speed. The speed of a modem is known as the *baud rate*. This tells you how many computer bits can be transmitted per second (bps). Because most Web pages now include a lot of large-image files that are painfully slow to download unless you have a fairly fast connection, you should have at least a 28,800 or 33,600 bps modem.

Modems are no longer expensive: most are in the range of $100 to $300 U.S. Very high-speed modems, such as cable modems or DSL, are increasingly popular. (We discuss a number of high-speed modem options in the next section.) In assessing the overall cost, consider that having a faster modem can help reduce your online costs.

Installation. Your modem comes with a detailed manual describing how to install and use the product. Frequently, a diskette is provided that walks you through the installation on your system. Newer operating systems, such as Windows 98/2000, provide communications services (like Internet access) as an integral part of the operating system, and this makes things even easier. Windows 98/2000 streamlines modem setup by including auto-configure utilities for installing many different kinds of modems.

Modems come with many standard settings already in place. Most of the time, the factory settings will work just fine, but if you run into difficulty, check to see if your modem manufacturer offers a 1-800 help desk service. You can also ask your dealer for help. Some computer dealers will even install the modem for you, though they may charge a small fee for this extra service.

Getting an Internet account

Although a number of resources on the Internet (such as **The List** at **http://thelist.com/**) provide information on service providers, you will have difficulty obtaining this information unless you already have some way to access the Internet. A better way to begin is to look for lists of service providers in computer magazines. *Boardwatch Magazine* publishes an annual directory of ISPs. You can also check business magazines, Internet books, phone or business directories, and newspapers.

QUICK REFERENCE GUIDE TO NORTH AMERICAN INTERNET PROVIDERS

Access in the United States

America Online	800-827-6364	www.aol.com/
CompuServe	800-848-8199	www.compuserv.com/
EarthLink	800-395-8425	www.earthlink.net/
MCI WorldCom	800-459-8892	www.mciworld.com/
Prodigy	800-PRODIGY	www.prodigy.com/
A+ Net	877-APLUS-NET	www.aplus.net/
Mindspring	800-777-9638	www.mindspring.net/
MSN Internet Access	800-FREE MSN	www.msn.com/

Access in Canada

Sympatico	1-800-773-2121	www1.sympatico.ca/
iStar	1-888-Go-iSTAR	www.istar.ca/
Internet Gateway Services	1-800-268-3715	www.igs.net/

Frequently, you can get leads on ISPs from your local computer store, or you can ask friends who already have a service provider for their recommendations. Free accounts are also available, if you don't mind being bombarded with advertisements. **FreeiNet** (**http://Freei.Net/**) offers free Internet accounts in the United States.

Ideally, you want a provider that offers reliable connectivity, easy set-up, and good support. Ask friends and colleagues how they feel about their ISPs, and go with a provider who comes highly recommended.

If you travel a lot, consider getting an account with a major national provider or one that offers "roaming" (which allows you to dial into your account from cities across the country using a local number) or Web mail (which allows you to check your mail through a Web browser).

If you are thinking of publishing your own Web pages, also consider such features as the space available with your account, the cost of additional server space, and what supports your provider offers for Web publishing. America Online, for example, makes available to their subscribers a Web authoring tool. You can also watch for free trial offers that allow you to sample a service. AOL is one of the most popular services offering a free trial period.

tech.ease

If you are a student or a faculty member at a university, you may get free Internet access from your institution's computing services, but it may not include graphical capability. This type of non-graphical account is sometimes called a *shell account*. With a shell account, you will not be able to use Windows or Mac software to interact with the network unless the university is also running a special Internet adapter program. You can find out about an adapter program called **SLiRP** at: **http://blitzen.canberra.edu. au/slirp/**

tech.ease

If you need to access your e-mail from more than one location (work, home, etc.), sign up for a Web-based mail service such as **Yahoo Mail** or **Hot Mail**. These services allow you to access and display messages from other accounts. This type of Web-based mail service requires that your regular ISP use a standard Post Office Protocol (POP3) server.

For detailed information about commercial providers and a comparative look at some of the U.S. national providers, visit **Jay Barker's Online Connection** at:
www.barkers.org/online/

High-speed modems

Most of us are still stuck in a world of sluggish 33-Kbps or even 28-Kbps connections. While these traditional access speeds have been OK in the past, they can be extremely frustrating when you want to go beyond basic text and graphics to the newer real-time communications and video applications. Speeding up your connections can be a significant time saver. High-speed connections can also give you a streamlined way to exchange large files with your clients and co-workers.

Two increasingly popular options for high-speed Internet access are the cable modem and the digital subscriber line (DSL). With either of these, Web pages pop up with astonishing speed, and downloads that used to take half an hour or more are loaded onto your desktop in minutes. In addition, with both options you are constantly connected to the Net, so you don't have to log in each time you want to check your e-mail or look up a fact. Finally, these high-speed connections do not require a separate phone line.

If you currently use a second phone line to access the Internet, you may find that switching to a high-speed access alternative can be cost effective. You do, however, need to consider an installation fee and cable rental costs in addition to the monthly access fee. Be aware that costs are coming down, and the availability of each of these high-speed options is increasing.

High-speed connections can be complex to install; most providers will send a technician to your home or office, though they may charge a fee for this additional service. Watch for special offers that include installation at minimal cost. If you're thinking about high-speed access, here are some current cost breakdowns (and other considerations) to help you decide.

Cable modems

Because these use local cable TV lines, you must be located within an area served by cablevision. A cable modem gives you unlimited Internet access — dialing in and busy signals are things of the past.

Access speed: Very fast (1.5 Mbps to 4 Mbps)
Installation: $100 (est.)
Typical monthly cost: $30 to $40

Pros: Speeds can be over fifty times faster than with 28.8-Kbps access. You get unlimited access for a flat monthly fee. Typically, cable modem services offer multiple e-mail accounts. You could, for example, use one account for business and another for personal e-mail.

Cons: Some areas do not yet have cable modem service. Also, you share your connection with others in your neighborhood. As a result, speeds can vary depending on the number of users online at any one time (though service will still be faster than with dial-up access). Security can be an issue, particularly for businesses. Finally, if you switch, you will have to get a new e-mail address (unless you choose to keep your existing account at a basic rate).

Find out more: Phone your local cablevision company, or visit **@Home** on the Internet (**www.home.com/**). An FAQ site for cable modem users is available from:

www.modemhelp.com/links/Cable_Modems/ and at:
www.cablemodemhelp.com/.

Digital subscriber lines (DSLs)

DSLs are high-speed telephone lines. Currently, your home must be located within three miles of your phone company's central switching office to get a DSL. DSL modems come in a variety of flavors (ADSL, SDLS, RADSL, etc.), and costs vary.

Access speed: Fast (512 Kbps to 1.5 Mbps)
Installation: $100 (est.)
Typical monthly cost: $30

tech.ease

A high-speed connection requires Windows 95/98/2000, a Pentium processor, and 32 MB of RAM. You will also need an estimated 125 MB of disk space. If you're a Power Macintosh user, consult your ISP for more information about basic hardware requirements.

Pros: A DSL is fifty-plus times as fast as a 28.8-Kbps connection and doesn't interfere with your phone or fax machine. A few computer manufacturers now offer PCs with a built-in DSL modem. Some providers offer discounts for their telephone long-distance subscribers.

Cons: Access can be affected by the quality of local phone lines and competing digital lines at the local junction box. Costs are higher for the higher speeds required for running an Internet server.

Find out more: DSL modems and service are available from telecommunications companies such as Bell, Sprint, and Sympatico. You can also consult **The List** at **http://thelist.internet.com/** to find out about ISPs in your area that offer DSL and other high-speed connectivity. An FAQ about DSL modems is available at **DSL-dslreports.com** (**www.dslreports.com/**).

tech.ease

Web accelerators are browser add-ons that speed up Web surfing by storing previously viewed pages on your hard drive and/or by pre-fetching Web links. Reports vary on their effectiveness. Decide for yourself by trying the freeware version of **NetSonic** (**www.web3000.com/**) or by downloading a Web accelerator from **Tucows** (**www.tucows.com/**).

If a cable modem or DSL are not possible, consider upgrading to a 56-Kbps modem. Many service providers offer 56-Kbps access, although old or poorly maintained phone lines may interfere with connection. Before spending money, check out "Five Rules for Buying a 56K Modem" at **www.56k.com/**. In particular, you will need to find out what type of 56-Kbps modem your ISP supports.

If you live in a rural area you might consider satellite access which, like the other high-speed options, is becoming more affordable. To find out more about satellite access, visit **DirecPC** (**www.direcpc.com/**).

Client/server computing — the skinny

The software that is used to access and navigate the Internet is based on *client/server* technology. Client/server is an important concept that explains the relationship between your computer and the Internet.

In the client/server relationship, two pieces of software work together as a team.

The *client* is responsible for:

- the user interface (what the software looks like on your desktop)
- initiating the communications process
- displaying information sent from the server.

The *server*:

- retains information (such as Web pages and related files)
- analyzes requests coming from the client
- responds to requests by sending information back to the client.

In a nutshell, the client is the program that you use locally, and the remote server does what the client says.

Client/server computing allows information to be passed back and forth over the Internet without the connections between computers having to remain open. It's common for newbies who have surfed, say, from a computer in New York to one in Brussels and then to another in Japan, to imagine that they have opened up connections around the world that remain open until the surfer backtracks or logs off. In fact, this is not the case.

With client/server technology, your connection to a remote computer, which could be located anywhere in the world, stays open only long enough to respond to your immediate request for a menu or file. You, in turn, read the item only after it has been sent to your (local) computer. Your phone connection to your access provider, though, will remain open until you actually log off.

An advantage to client/server computing is that you can select whatever client software (i.e., your browser; see Chapter 2) is most useful for you. You are not necessarily stuck with the software selection provided by your Internet service provider if you find something better or more up to date.

tech.ease

File formats requiring plug-ins are known as *MIME types*. MIME stands for *multimedia Internet mail extension*. The name derives from the fact that the types were originally developed to work with e-mail software. For example, the MIME type for a TIFF image file is "image/tiff" and the MIME type for a .PDF file is "application/pdf."

If you are installing a plug-in manually, you will be prompted to fill in a MIME type. If you are unsure of the MIME type, leave this prompt field blank.

Browser plug-ins

Sooner or later you will arrive at a site where valuable information is packaged in a file format that your browser doesn't know how to display. Software developers are always launching new browser applications and making them available via the Internet. For some of these applications you need special software called a *helper application*, *viewer*, or *plug-in*. For example, sound, video, and multimedia files require a helper application or plug-in.

Some plug-ins are automatically installed as part of your browser. For example, LiveAudio and QuickTime video are pre-installed with Netscape Communicator. You can add other plug-ins to your browser. Web sites that use applications requiring helper files usually alert you to the need for a plug-in and provide a link to a site where you can download it. Many plug-ins are available for free.

Netscape and Internet Explorer give you the option of downloading various plug-ins along with the latest version of the browser, though if your computer is not set up to handle applications such as Internet Phone, Live 3D, or video, you probably won't want to bother getting these.

To find out about some of the file types requiring viewers, and to get information about how they are currently configured in your browser, select **Edit** I **Preferences** I **Applications** in Netscape. If you

FIGURE 8-1
Adding helper applications in Netscape

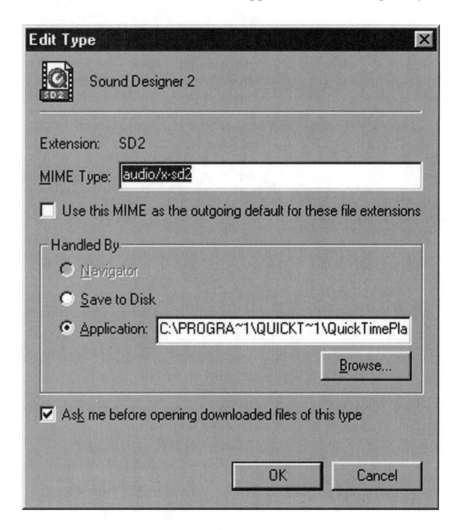

access a page requiring a particular plug-in that you do not currently have, Navigator takes you to Netscape's Plug-in Finder where you can download the plug-in you need. Internet Explorer will also alert you when a plug-in is required to view a file, prompt you to download the required program, and walk you through the installation.

If you are using an older browser, you may need to install plug-ins manually.

The kind of file you are dealing with can usually be identified by its *file extension*, or the letters following the filename. Here are a few of the most important file types you will find on the Web. The ones that may require special helper applications (particularly if you are using an older browser) are marked with an asterisk:

.html, .htm	HTML files — the basic file type for Web pages
.gif	GIF graphic; a picture file
.jpg, .jpeg, .jpe	JPEG graphic; another type of picture file
.au, .snd, .wav, .midi	Sound files*
.qt, .mov	QuickTime movie files*
.mpeg, .mpg	Another type of movie file*
.avi	Video in Windows*
.hqx	Macintosh encoded file
.ra, .ram	RealAudio; broadcast-type sound files*
.txt	Unformatted text (ASCII) files
.pdf	Portable document format*
.sit	StuffIt file; a Macintosh compressed file*
.zip	Zipped file; another type of compressed file*

Some plug-in files operate within the browser, while others, such as RealAudio, open up a separate window. Your browser's Help feature will provide details about how to deal with plug-ins. After you have downloaded the appropriate software, most plug-ins will install themselves, although you may be asked to select options during the installation process. Once you've learned to set up one helper program, it's easy to add new plug-ins for other types of files as your needs change.

Use these sources to learn more about browser plug-ins and helper applications.

Browserwatch Plug-in Plaza
http://browserwatch.internet.com/plug-in.html

Cnet.com Plug-ins and Add-ons
http://home.cnet.com/internet/0-3773.html

Netscape's Browser Plug-ins
http://home.netscape.com/plugins/index.html

tech.ease

Saving more than one or two
levels of a site can result in an
excessive number of links being
accessed and downloaded, and
many may not be relevant to
your purpose. Saving one level
at a time is a good policy.

Internet Explorer
version 5 has a feature
that will allow you to
save entire Web page
contents (including
graphics) with the **File | Save**
menu option.

Offline browsers

It can sometimes be useful to download Web pages and associated
graphics for viewing offline. With an offline browser you can surf
offline or run a Web demonstration without the need for an Internet
connection. In addition, offline browsers will let you organize, store,
and keep Web information up to date. You can also use an offline
browser to save sites that are of particular interest to you. Although
you can save Web pages using the **File | Save** option within your nor-
mal Web browser, the images on the page are not automatically
saved, and the individual pages must be saved one at a time.

Some offline browsers allow you to specify search terms and will
search for and download relevant pages. While this can be of value
if you have very specialized research requirements, most of the time
you will want to review pages before bothering to download them.

You can capture Web sites offline using any of the following
products. Offline browsers commonly cost between $40 and $60
U.S., though most products also offer a shareware trial period. Find
out about a range of offline browser options at **Tucows** (**www.
tucows.com/**).

FIGURE 8-2

**At i-us.com, you can
download desktop
publishing software,
fonts, and graphics.**

AnaWave WebSnake
www.anawave.com/websnake/
A good offline browser for Windows 95 that supports searching and retrieving files. This one includes a wizard that will walk you through the process and let you download your bookmarks.

Hot-off-the-Web
www.hotofftheweb.com/
Lets you grab Web pages, add your comments, and then e-mail, fax, print, or save the annotated page.

Web Devil
www.chaoticsoftware.com/
A tool for Macintosh computers for downloading Web pages and their associated images, textures, and links.

WebStripper
www.solentsoftware.com/webstripper
This one is free. It lets you browse the Web and download sites for viewing, and also allows you to select a text-only option.

Web Whacker 2000
www.bluesquirrel.com/
This popular offline browser lets you organize saved pages into categories.

WebZip
www.spidersoft.com/
Automatically compresses downloaded graphics and text files into a zip-compatible file. You can store a whole Web site on a floppy disk, or e-mail zipped copies to colleagues. WebZip also includes a built-in browser.

Downloading software

The Web is a great place to find free software and shareware. *Freeware* is a term used for programs that developers give away. *Shareware* refers to software that you can try before you buy. Frequently, trial versions of programs are usable for a limited period of time (usually 15 to 30 days). If you decide you want to continue using the software, you can register the program by paying the

ZDNet is the Web site for Ziff-Davis Publishing, which publishes such popular computer magazines as *MacWeek* and *PCWeek*. This site offers current magazine features that will keep you up to date about new Internet sites and products. **ZDNet** is located at:
www.zdnet.com/

required fee. Shareware programs are frequently inexpensive, and registration can often be done online.

Popular programs to download include Internet software (such as e-mail programs, MP3 players or offline browsers), games, educational software, desktop helps (such as personal organizers or database software), and utility software (such as programs that help you to download software or backup your computer files). You can also find great graphics, nifty screen savers, and funky fonts. Here are some of our favorite sites:

Clicked Shareware Gallery
www.clicked.com/shareware/
Includes a section offering the top twenty apps in six major categories.

DaveCentral
www.davecentral.com/
This site offers Windows and Linux software and includes office applications.

Download.com
www.download.com/
This site features up-to-date virus information, a step-by-step beginner's guide to downloading, and a collection of software utilities to help you manage downloading. There is also a great collection of downloadable software.

Info-Mac Hyperarchive
http://hyperarchive.lcs.mit.edu/HyperArchive/HyperArchive.html
From MIT, this is a mirror of the Info-Mac archive. You can search for software by keyword, or browse the directory. Each file in the archive includes an abstract that allows you to preview available shareware before downloading.

Jumbo
www.jumbo.com/
Plan to visit this site when you have time available to explore. It offers over 250,000 shareware programs and links, including business software, downloadable fonts, and pointers to downloadable electronic books.

MacDownload.com
www.zdnet.com/mac/download.html
Macintosh downloads from ZDNet, publishers of *MacWorld*. Subscribe to MustHaves for a weekly update on Macintosh shareware.

Shareware.com
http://shareware.cnet.com/
Search for shareware. The site includes software news and short reviews.

tech.ease

FTP stands for *file transfer protocol*. FTP software lets you upload or download programs. While your browser can easily handle most of your downloading jobs, and many servers are now set up to find and upload programs from your computer, you may occasionally need to transfer a file from one computer to another using an FTP program.

You can select and download FTP software from **Tucows**. FTP programs are not difficult to use if you keep in mind that the basic process is to transfer a file from one computer to another. You will need to specify the address of the computer that you are uploading to (e.g., ftp://ftp.microsoft.com); you may need a password to gain access to the computer, and you will need to find your way to the directory and subdirectory where you want to place the uploaded file.

Softseek
www.softseek.com/
Top downloads, new releases, and editors' picks from ZDNet, the publishers of *PC Magazine* and *Yahoo Internet Life*. The site offers a brief guide to downloading.

Stroud's Consummate Winsock Applications
http://cws.internet.com/top.html
To zero in on some of the best Internet software choices, check out Stroud's weekly and monthly lists of the top twenty-five downloads.

Tucows
www.tucows.com/
An excellent site for Internet software including browsers, audio players, electronic mail software, bookmark organizers, and more.

Also check the **Yahoo!** directory of software sites (**http://dir.yahoo. com/Computers_and_Internet/Software/**) or other portal site for a listing of sites featuring special-purpose software, such as desktop publishing or education software.

Compressed files

While it is relatively easy to download uncompressed text files, sooner or later you will need to deal with a compressed file. These are files that have been "shrunk" using a software program in order to save disk space or to speed up the time required for transfer.

There are many different programs that can be used to compress files. The key is to identify and obtain the particular type of software you need to decompress the type of file you have at hand.

One type of compressed file you will commonly see is *zipped* files. These have a .zip file extension. Sometimes zipped files are self-extracting — meaning they will automatically unzip when you click on the program name. In other instances, however, you will need a software utility to restore the compressed files to their normal size.

One of the most popular programs used to handle zipped files is **WinZip** (downloadable from **www.winzip.com/**). Versions for Windows 3.1, Windows 95/98 and Windows NT are available for a thirty-day free evaluation period. The latest version of WinZip can zip and unzip files, and create self-extracting files. For novices, a wizard walks you through the process for unzipping files.

Other programs for unzipping files include **PKZip** for Windows (**www.pkware.com/**) and **AutoZip** (available from **www.mfsoft. com/**).

E-MailZip Deluxe is a unique compression program designed specifically for mailing zipped files. After you have selected a .zip file, The program will prompt you for an e-mail address and a message, and the .zip file is sent as an attachment. The program will automatically unzip at the other end without requiring a separate program. This is a practical way to submit large files to publishers.

In the Macintosh world, compressed (.sit) files can be unpackaged using **StuffIt Expander** or **StuffIt Lite**. StuffIt can be found at **www.aladdinsys.com/**.

COMMON EXTENSIONS FOR COMPRESSED FILES

.exe	Executable file; performs a task when you double-click on it. Sometimes it will unpack other files
.uue	File that has been coded for transfer through e-mail
.hdx	BinHex; a Macintosh compressed file
.sit	StuffIt Macintosh compressed file
.sea	Macintosh compressed file that unpacks itself when you double-click on it
.arc	DOS compressed file
.zip	Zipped file
.tar	Unix file
.Z	Unix compressed file
.gz	Unix compressed file

You can locate a number of programs for decoding and decompressing files at **Tucows** (**www.tucows.com/**). An FAQ about file compression is available from:

www.faqs.org/faqs/compression-faq

Computer viruses

If you are on the Internet, it is critical that you be aware of the potential damage that can be caused by computer viruses. Viruses are computer programs that damage other programs by modifying them in some way. They can cause your computer and its programs to behave erratically, and can damage your files. For example, programs may take longer than normal to load, or a word processing program may refuse to save properly. When the programs that are affected are part of the system files that help your computer run, the damage caused by the virus can be considerable. Unfortunately, there are currently hundreds of known viruses — and more are on the way.

Computer viruses can infect your computer in several different ways. They can travel from one computer to another through a shared floppy disk. They can also be downloaded from the Internet if you download and run a program (even a screen saver can harbor a virus). However, most reputable sites scan for viruses before uploading software. You can also receive a virus with an e-mail attachment that contains an "executable" file such as a file with the extensions *.exe* or *.com* (a "command" file, i.e., a set of executable program commands).

The notorious Melissa virus, which affected thousands of Microsoft Outlook users in 1999, was hidden inside a Microsoft Word document attached to an e-mail message. Each time someone opened an infected document, the virus would cause fifty additional copies of the document to be sent as an attachment to the first fifty people listed in the victim's address book. Mail servers around the world were overwhelmed.

To protect yourself from computer viruses, you should have virus protection software on your computer. Such software is designed to detect viruses before they can damage your system. In many cases, it can clean or "disinfect" your files. Examples include

fyi *Back up your data!* This is the number one rule for protecting information on your computer. Even without a virus invasion, you can lose important files by accidentally overwriting them or having your hard drive fail.

You can store your data online with several Internet services, such as **Connected Online Backup** (**www. connected.com/**), **Safefguard Interactive** (**www.sgii.com/**) and **Driveway** (**www.driveway.com/**).

The Internet Handbook for Writers, Researchers, and Journalists

Norton AntiVirus (**www.symantec.com/nav/**), **McAfee Virusscan**, and **Panda Antivirus** (**www.pandasoftware.com/**). Further, you should keep your virus software up to date.

Popular virus protection software for both Windows and Macintosh computers can be downloaded from **Download.com** (**http://download.cnet.com/**).

Occasionally, it is necessary to reformat your hard drive to get rid of a virus. However, this is an extreme solution that will result in the loss of all of your existing data. You may want to get technical help before proceeding with this solution.

You can find out more about computer viruses by reading "**How Computer Viruses Work**" at:

www.howstuffworks.com/virus.htm

or by visiting IBM's **Antivirus Online** page at:

www.av.ibm.com/.

Further reading

"Cable vs. DSL." *PCComputing*, August 1999.

Keizer, Gregg. "Pluggin' Away at Plug-Ins."
www.zdnet.com/zdhelp/stories/main/0,5594,2308912,00.html

Prendergast, Richard A. *Learn to Use Your Modem in a Day*. (Popular Applications Series.) Plano, Texas: Wordware, 1995.

University of Chicago Campus Computer Stores. "Introduction to Modems."
www-ccs.uchicago.edu/technotes/misc/Modems.html

Epilogue

"Remember that the technology, in and of itself does nothing. Rather, it makes it possible for you to shape your own world-within-the-world."
— RICHARD SELTZER, "INTERNET ADVICE FOR NEWCOMERS"
WWW.SAMIZDAT.COM/NEWS20.HTML#NEWCOMERS

Learning to use the Internet efficiently and confidently is an accomplishment. But in the world of technology, the learning never stops.

The Internet is constantly surging ahead in new and often unexpected directions. New products, services, and technologies appear at such a breakneck pace that even high-tech professionals are hard pressed to keep abreast of the latest developments. One technology analyst recently claimed that a not-yet-released update of a popular Web browser had already been surpassed by a not-yet-released product from a competitor. For those who work at the leading edge of technology, it is a constant battle to remain in front.

We are regularly informed about developments — always just around the corner — that will transform the way we work and live:

- modems that will transmit data through radio waves, rather than through wires
- pocket computers that will run sophisticated applications such as videoconferencing
- miniature devices that will allow us to control our cars, home appliances, and office equipment via the Internet
- more — and more varied — electronic commerce.

Coping with all this change requires a continuing willingness to learn. We are still experimenting with the practical aspects of the Internet, and it is sometimes difficult not to be overwhelmed by the technology itself.

For writers, researchers, and journalists, the future of technology is not so much about smaller computer chips, faster modems, and the latest electronic gizmos, but rather about virtual offices and schools, online collaborations, and global communities — processes that are enabled by technology, but defined by people. Although technology will continue to move forward, people will embrace it only to the extent that it serves some practical human purpose.

Like other users of the Internet, information professionals can expect to have to continue learning. But — unlike the technicians who are bound by the rules of the technology marketplace — we have the luxury of selecting areas of learning that have practical and immediate value to our work.

If you are a writer, researcher, editor, or journalist, your most important Internet skill will be to gain confidence in finding and using the myriad resources on the Net. Once you've learned the basics of online navigation, there are no mandatory benchmarks for mastering more — though there will always be more to discover.

One of the greatest opportunities for information professionals today is the possibility of helping to shape this new cyber world, as content creators and experts. Your own interests and abilities will determine whether this challenge is for you.

The authors of this book like to think that using the Internet is a bit like owning a piece of real estate. If it suits you, you can build a mansion — say, dozens of skillfully developed Web pages featuring your work. Or, you can just settle for a meadow — in which you ramble contentedly among the unruly, exuberant growth.

The greatest delight of the Internet is that it offers so many possibilities.

Resources on the Web

The following selection of useful Internet links will be of particular interest to writers, researchers, journalists, editors, and students. Although the list is not comprehensive, it illustrates the range of resources on the Internet and, in many cases, may suggest starting points for research.

The list contains two sections: *Professional and Internet Resources* and *General Interest Resources*.

In *Part I: Professional and Internet Resources*, we have included sources that reflect the primary themes of this book. These include information about the Internet itself, as well as material directly relevant to information professionals. We have identified key reference areas — such as news sources, journalism links, and writing resources — and have developed these in some depth. Included in this section as well are sources pertinent to government, distance education, student information, and employment. The long list of Internet references will enable you to learn more about the technology and keep up with new developments.

In Part II: General Interest Resources, we have provided shorter lists of links to information on a broader range of subjects. Included here are topics that are frequently in the news; starting points for research in such areas as arts, sciences, and social sciences; and miscellaneous useful information resources.

These links are far from exhaustive; rather, they are highly selective. Deciding which general-interest topics and links to include was a major challenge. Our rule of thumb, if we had one, was to include the kinds of topics that we ourselves, as information professionals, want to know about.

Many of our favorite sources are highlighted in the chapters; for the most part, these are not duplicated here. We have assumed that, if you have taken time to explore the sites listed in the chapters, you will already have added your favorites to your personal hotlist. If not, be sure to refer back to the sites mentioned in the chapters, along with using this Appendix.

Contents

Part I: Professional and Internet Resources

1. General Reference
2. Internet and Computers

Part I: Professional and Internet Resources

1. General Reference

Acronyms

Acronym Dictionary. From AA (Alcoholics Anonymous) to ZT (Zone Time), this full-text dictionary lists acronyms as part of Carnegie Mellon University's English Server.

http://english-www.hss.cmu.edu/langs/acronym-dictionary.txt

Acronym Finder. A searchable database of meanings for more than 125,000 acronyms and abbreviations. All subjects, but focus is on computers, technology, telecommunications, and the military.
www.acronymfinder.com/

Atlases

MapQuest. Don't go on a trip before looking up your route on this interactive atlas showing the United States and major cities around the world. Zoom in and find a building on a certain street, or zoom out to find out how to get there using major highways.
http://mapquest.com/

National Atlas of Canada. Find out geographic and demographic information on Canada and its regions.
http://atlas.gc.ca/

National Geographic Map Machine. Searchable, free online maps from around the world, from *National Geographic* magazine.
http://plasma.nationalgeographic.com/mapmachine/

Perry-Castaneda Library Map Collection. From the University of Texas at Austin, this is a huge collection of maps from every corner of the world.
www.lib.utexas.edu/Libs/PCL/Map_collection/Map_collection.html

TIGER Mapping Service. TIGER (Topologically Integrated Geographic Encoding and Referencing) provides public data for generating detailed maps of anywhere in the United States. Includes a U.S. Gazetteer.
www.census.gov/geo/www/tiger/index.html

U.S. Gazetteer. The U.S. Census Bureau's official map service. Look up a place by name or zip code, then obtain census data for that location.
www.census.gov/cgi-bin/gazetteer

Citation style sheets

APA Style of Notation. Covers points of citation per the *Publication Manual of the American Psychological Association*, the preferred style guide in many social sciences.
www.uvm.edu/~xli/reference/apa.html

Beyond the MLA. Handbook for citations by Harnack & Kleppinger; includes models for documenting Internet sources.
http://english.ttu.edu/kairos/1.2/inbox/mla_archive.html

Columbia Guide to Online Style. Detailed guidelines for citing online references in humanities and scientific publications, from Columbia University Press.

www.columbia.edu/cu/cup/cgos/idx_basic.html

MLA Style of Citation. Uses the MLA style preferred by many university English departments.

www.uvm.edu/~xli/reference/mla.html

Online! A Reference Guide for Using Internet Sources. This Web site is based on the book by the same name that recommends four styles for citing online sources. Includes links to all the sites mentioned in the text.

www.bedfordstmartins.com/online/index.html

Databases
(See also references in Chapter 4)

Internets. Search thousands of free databases, including commercial sites, by category.

www.internets.com/

Lexis-Nexis. Billing itself as the "largest news and business online information service," this commercial site provides access to more than 10,000 international databases and 2.5 billion searchable documents, including company, country, and demographic reports, periodicals, and legislative and legal documents. You must subscribe for a whole day of searching and prices start at $24 U.S. per day.

www.lexis-nexis.com/lncc/

PacInfo Search Systems. Search more than 1,100 free public records databases in the U.S. and Canada, including historical archives and census information.

www.pac-info.com/

Webtaxi. Quick access to major search engines as well as access to hundreds of specialized databases in arts, business, health, and other categories.

www.webtaxi.com/

Dictionaries

Biographical Dictionary. Search entries for more than 28,000 notable men and women from ancient times to the present. Search by birth and death years, professions, positions held, and achievements.

http://s9.com/biography/

Dictionary of Phrase and Fable. The full text of E. Cobham Brewer's classic 1870 reference, which explains the origins of many English phrases and defines characters from myths and fables.

www.bibliomania.com/Reference/PhraseAndFable/index.html

FOLDOC: Free Online Dictionary of Computing. Definitions of computer terms are jargon-heavy but links will take you to further explanations.
www.nightflight.com/foldoc/index.html

One Look Dictionaries. Works like a search engine for more than 500 general and specialized dictionaries, including arts and humanities, business, computers, science and technology, and sports.
www.onelook.com/

Online Language Dictionaries and Translators. More than 130 languages are represented with links to dictionaries that translate to and from English and any number of other languages.
http://rivendel.com/~ric/resources/dictionary.html

Research-It. This is an all-purpose reference site. Search dictionaries, translators, financial, geographic, and other useful tools.
www.iTools.com/research-it/research-it.html

Semantic Rhyming Dictionary. Handy site for poets, writers, and editors alike.
www.link.cs.cmu.edu/dougb/rhyme-doc.html

Travlang's Translating Dictionaries. Easy-to-use, searchable free online dictionaries, translating to and from the major European languages.
http://dictionaries.travlang.com/

VoyCabulary. Online dictionary with a twist: it lets you type in a Web page address, and when you open it, click on any word in that page and the dictionary will give you its definition. Handy for reading technical texts online.
www.voycabulary.com/

A Web of Online Dictionaries. Search high-quality dictionaries in more than 200 languages, from Afrikaans to Zulu. Includes a Web of Online Grammars for many languages.
www.facstaff.bucknell.edu/rbeard/diction.html

WWWebster Dictionary. Search the Merriam-Webster's Collegiate Dictionary and Thesaurus.
www.m-w.com/netdict.htm

Encyclopedias

Encyclopedia Britannica. Billing itself as "the most trusted source of information, learning, and knowledge on the Internet," the encyclopedia is available free of charge online.
www.britannica.com/

Encyclopedia Mythica. Search for information and definitions on mythology, folklore, and legends.
www.pantheon.org/mythica/

World Factbook. Vital statistics on virtually every country in the world, compiled annually by the Central Intelligence Agency. Each country gets its own page with a map showing major cities and the capital, including statistics on geography, government, the people, economy, and the military.
www.odci.gov/cia/publications/factbook/index.html

Libraries and library resources

Beyond Bookmarks: Schemes for Organizing the Web. This clearinghouse for Web sites that use traditional library classification systems is compiled by a librarian at Iowa State University.
www.public.iastate.edu/~CYBERSTACKS/CTW.htm

Canadian Information by Subject. An extensive subject tree with links to Canadian sites, compiled by the National Library of Canada. Subjects are arranged by the Dewey Decimal classification system.
www.nlc-bnc.ca/caninfo/ecaninfo.htm

Electric Library. Search for full-text magazine and newspaper articles, and radio and TV transcripts, based on a natural-language or Boolean search. It's free to search the library, which gives you the periodical's name and date so that you can look it up in a real public library. But you have to pay to download the actual text.
www.elibrary.com/

ERIC/AE Full Text Internet Library. ERIC offers selected online resources for education. This site offers full-text books, reports, articles from journals, and newsletters. Browse by subject or search using a keyword.
http://ericae.net/ftlib.htm

Infomine. This is a virtual library built for university students, faculty, and researchers. It allows multiple database searching of more than 16,000 academic resources. Information from databases, electronic journals and books, bulletin boards, listservs, and library card catalogs is sorted according to disciplines, such as government information, social science and humanities, and physical science. It was created by librarians at the University of California and elsewhere.
http://infomine.ucr.edu/

Internet Public Library. Billed as the first online library, this is a collection of links to online resources, including magazines and periodicals, texts, and newspapers, arranged according to a subject tree compiled by the University of Michigan.

www.ipl.org/

Library of Congress Classification System. A California librarian has written an unofficial guide on how to understand the Library of Congress Classification System. Helps take the guesswork out of library research.

http://geography.miningco.com/library/congress/bllc.htm

Library Resource List. Hundreds of sources carefully selected by the Wisconsin Department of Public Instruction. Developed for professional librarians, but of interest for its lists of reference and government sources. Includes guides and evaluations of major search engines.

www.dpi.state.wi.us/dpi/dlcl/pld/lib_res.html

MELVYL. Library catalog of the University of California provides access to more than 9 million titles of U.C. library materials and a number of databases produced by libraries or organizations. Some of the resources are available for U.C. affiliates only.

www.melvyl.ucop.edu/

Ready Reference Using the Internet. Mainly full-text sources and data compiled by a librarian, using modified Library of Congress subject headings.

www.winsor.edu/library/rref.htm

Refdesk.com. One-stop shopping for finding quick facts and more in-depth research.

www.refdesk.com/

SJCPL's Public Library Servers. This page has a searchable database of more than 600 public libraries around the world that are online. You can also link directly to their home pages from a list of Web sites. Operated by the St. Joseph County Public Library in South Bend, Indiana.

http://sjcpl.lib.in.us/homepage/PublicLibraries/
PublicLibraryServers.html

UnCover. This online periodical article delivery service indexes nearly 18,000 English-language periodicals in its searchable database. You pay a fee to order articles, which are faxed to you. The articles go on the site the same day the publication hits the newsstands.

http://uncweb.carl.org/

Virtual Library. An easy-to-use catalog with links to quality Web sites on particular topics. Not comprehensive, but each list is maintained by a volunteer expert in that field.

www.vlib.org/

Virtual Technical Reports Center. Links to institutions that provide either full-text reports, or searchable extended abstracts of their technical reports on the Web: everything from the Agricultural Genome Information System to the Yucca Mountain Environmental Protection Agency.
www.lib.umd.edu/UMCP/ENGIN/TechReports/Virtual-TechReports.html

webCATS: Library Catalogs on the World Wide Web. Links to hundreds of online library catalogs around the world, arranged by region and library type.
www.lights.com/webcats/

Z39.50 Gateway. Search the Library of Congress catalog using simple or advanced search techniques. You can also search the catalogs of dozens of libraries around the world (including many universities). The search results display as bibliographic entries.
http://lcweb.loc.gov/z3950/gateway.html

Phone books

BigBook. U.S. addresses, including street maps. North American Yellow Pages, shopping guides, and classifieds.
www.bigbook.com/

BigFoot. Another people-finding source.
www.bigfoot.com/

Big Yellow. Find people, businesses, e-mail addresses, and more!
www.bigyellow.com/

Canada 411. Search more than 10 million Canadian business and residential phone listings, toll-free numbers and postal codes.
http://canada411.sympatico.ca/

Canada Yellow Pages. Search for businesses across Canada with the Yellow Pages.
www.canadayellowpages.com/

The Directory Organization. Phone, fax, and e-mail contact information for companies and individuals.
www.dir.org/

Infospace. Quickly find phone numbers and e-mail addresses.
www.infospaceinc.com/

Switchboard. Provides phone numbers for millions of residential and business listings in the United States.
www.switchboard.com/

Postal codes

Canada Post Postal Code Guide. This site works two ways: if you know the postal code, find out the address. If you know the address, find out the code. Fast and easy.
www.canadapost.ca/CPC2/addrm/pclookup/pclookup.shtml

United States Postal Service. Find a zip+4 code for an address, or find out what city belongs to a zip code.
www.usps.gov/ncsc/

Quotations

Bartlett's Familiar Quotations. Find classic quotes on many topics to spice up your writing. Search by author or keyword.
www.bartleby.com/99/index.html

Quotations Page. An eclectic collection of modern quotations. Receive a quote of the day via e-mail for inspiration.
www.starlingtech.com/quotes/

Style guides

Elements of Style. The writer's classic for decades, Strunk & White's bible of good usage and composition is online in its entirety.
www.bartleby.com/141/index.html

The Gazette (Montreal) Style. Online list of spellings used by *Montreal Gazette* reporters. Good source for Quebec English.
www.gazette.qc.ca/STYLE/

Style Book of the University of Queensland Department of Journalism. Some good pointers on Australian English, and hints for tightening journalistic style.
www.uq.edu.au/jrn/stylebook.htm

Style Guide for Editors and Proofreaders of IDRC Books. Geared toward staff of the International Development Research Centre, it's also useful for anyone working in scholarly and scientific publishing.
www.idrc.ca/books/edit/eindex.html#sguide

Wired Style. A style guide for the digital age with the same hip edge as its parent, *Wired* magazine.
http://hotwired.lycos.com/hardwired/wiredstyle/

Thesauruses

Roget's Thesaurus. Search by word or category to find your bon mots.
www.thesaurus.com/thesaurus/

WWWebster Thesaurus. Word search turns up related terms and contrasted words.
www.m-w.com/thesaurus.htm

Other reference

Biography.com. Biographies of more than 25,000 of the greatest lives from A&E Television.
www.biography.com/

Calculator.com. Easy-to-use, free online calculators for finance, business, science, cooking, hobbies, health — you name it.
www.calculator.com/

Classic 164 Currency Converter. Convert some common and not-so-common currencies, using current or past days' rates.
www.oanda.com/converter/classic

Convert It! Quickly do math and science conversions, such as to and from SI metric.
http://microimg.com/science/

The Phrase Finder. Database of more than 6,000 English phrases searchable three ways: as a thesaurus (to turn up phrases relating to certain words), a dictionary (explains the phrases' meanings), and as a reference to look up a phrase's origins.
www.shu.ac.uk/web-admin/phrases/go.html

The World Clock. Great resource for information about time zones. Look up the current local time in cities around the globe.
www.timeanddate.com/worldclock/

2. Internet and Computers

Electronic mail and related resources

Andrew Starr's Eudora Site. Good source of info for Eudora users. Also check out the official Qualcomm site.
www.e-mailman.com/eudora/

Beginner's Guide to Effective E-mail. How to write e-mails that communicate.
www.webfoot.com/advice/email.top.html

The Net: User Guidelines and Netiquette — Index. Introduction to etiquette on the Internet with lots of good tips on using electronic mail and discussion groups.
www.fau.edu/netiquette/net/

WebConferencing. Great resources on text-based Web conferencing.
http://thinkofit.com/webconf/

Whowhere? Find e-mail addresses worldwide and phone numbers in the United States.
www.whowhere.com

Internet facts

The Industry Standard. Subtitled, "Intelligence for the Internet Economy," *The Industry Standard* magazine presents in-depth reporting on the latest Internet trends and where the cyberindustry is heading.
www.thestandard.com/

The Internet Society. The home page of the international organization for global coordination and cooperation on the Internet has a gold mine of Internet facts, a history of the Internet, and lots more resources.
www.isoc.org/

The Open Market Internet Index. An occasional compilation of random, sometimes off-beat Internet facts and figures.
www.openmarket.com/intindex/index.cfm

Parallax Webdesign Internet Facts. A more serious look at Internet use and the demographics of those online.
www.parallaxweb.com/interfacts.html

Internet starting points, guides, and search engines
(See also references in Chapters 3 and 4)

About.com. A network of expert guides leads you through resources for popular subjects arranged A–Z.
www.about.com/

All-in-One-Search Page. Handy one-stop site with access to dozens of general and specialized search engines.
www.allonesearch.com/

AskJeeves. Type in a natural-language query, such as "How old is Bill Clinton?" and it will guide you to sites to find the answer.
www.askjeeves.com/

Beaucoup! Query 10 search engines at once or follow links to categories such as computers, reference, and general interest.
www.beaucoup.com/

Best Information on the Net. As compiled by librarians at St. Ambrose University in Davenport, Iowa. Includes links to sites listed by major, hot paper topics, and a reference desk.
http://vweb.sau.edu/bestinfo/index.htm

Direct Hit. Ranks search results based on site popularity. Good source when you need an overview of a general topic.
www.directhit.com/

Essential Links. Neatly organized links to search engines, other starting point directories, news sources, references, and cool Web sites.
www.el.com/

The Electric Monk. Ask the Electric Monk a question in plain English, and he will spit out a list of Web sites that are sure to (eventually) answer your query.
www.electricmonk.com/

Fast. Claims to be (and probably is) the world's biggest and fastest search engine.
www.alltheweb.com/

TheInfo.com. Use this resource for targeted searching, including news searches, music, movies, and recipes. Multiple databases can be searched at once.
www.theinfo.com/

List of International Search Engines. Localized engines listed by country and continent.
www.arnoldit.com/lists/intlsearch.asp

Pandia Search Central. A site dedicated to fast and efficient Net searching and a Web directory developed by volunteer indexers who sign up to add Web sites by interest area.
www.pandia.com/

Purely Academic. This site prides itself on going deeper than most Web guides, pointing academic researchers directly to the information itself. From the Dublin University Internet Society.
www.netsoc.tcd.ie/Background/

QuickFindit. Chat with live guides (during the day) to help point you to Internet resources on virtually any topic. Also offers a quick search of major search engines based on keywords.
www.quickfindit.com/

Search Engine Guide. Lists more than 3,000 search engines from around the world, from very general to highly specialized topics.
www.searchengineguide.com/

Starting Point. A concise subject tree with selective sites to weed out the redundancy in cyberspace.
www.stpt.com/

Subject Guides A–Z. An excellent resource list from the University of Delaware Library.
www2.lib.udel.edu/subj/

Top of the Web. Self-proclaimed professional Web surfer John December has put together a collection of his favorite sites. Browse for fun or type in keywords.
www.december.com/web/top.html

The Top 25 Most Useful Sites. Summaries and links to the most useful sites for everything from how to unclog your drain to how to search newsgroups, as chosen by ZDNet.
www.zdnet.com/yil/content/depts/useful/25mostuse.html

URLs for a Rainy Day. "Web sites recommended by users, to help you find anything and everything on the Net." Easy-to-use collection of places to start your research.
www.purefiction.com/pages/res2.htm

WebCentral. Calling itself "sanity amid the madness," Web Central has concise links to search tools, Web tutorials, e-commerce, and general-interest sites.
www.cio.com/central/

Internet tutorials

Best Information on the Net — Internet Training. University librarians have compiled useful links to beginner's guides on everything about the Internet: e-mail, browsers, troubleshooting, domain names, you name it.
www.sau.edu/CWIS/Internet/Wild/Internet/Training/trindex.htm

BKC2SKOL. A set of 30 lessons tells you almost all you need to know about the Net. It's designed for librarians but is useful for anyone.
http://web.csd.sc.edu/bck2skol/fall/fall.html

Computer-Mediated Communication Information Sources. Don't let the name fool you — we're talking about the Internet here. There are carefully selected links to the top Net resources: how to search, find people, join discussion groups, get software, and many other things.
www.december.com/cmc/info/

Internet Guides, Tutorials, and Training Information. The Library of Congress has compiled links to useful guides, many for beginners.
http://lcweb.loc.gov/global/internet/training.html

Learn the Net. An easy-to-use tutorial for beginners shows you through screen captures how to use the Net. A comprehensive guide to the Internet, including help with digging for data, using search

tools, mailing lists, and databases, exchanging files, and developing Web pages.
www.learnthenet.com/english/

Newbie Central. A guide for newcomers to the Internet, with definitions, explanations, and resources on searching, chat programs, Web site creation, MP3s, FTP, and more. Gives ratings for search engines, and lots of tips and tricks.
http://newbiecentral.cjb.net/

Internet updates

Eye on IT. A free, weekly, Belgium-based newsletter with trends, product announcements, and other news from the Information Technology and Internet world. Geared toward techies but written in easy-to-understand English.
www.itworks.be/EyeonIT/index.html

Netsurfer Digest. A weekly online magazine with the latest Internet news and hot Web sites. You can subscribe to the e-mail version.
www.netsurf.com/nsd/

Newsbytes. Commercial site with daily reviews of the best new sites on the Web. You must subscribe for $29 U.S. a month.
www.newsbytes.com/

Scout Report. A very trustworthy guide to what's new on the Web. Every week, surfers at the University of Wisconsin at Madison scout the Net and give honest reviews of new sites for value to researchers and educators. You can subscribe to a mailing list and receive the report, or you can read current and back issues on the Web site and follow the links directly.
www.cs.wisc.edu/scout/report/

What's Hot on the Internet This Week. Descriptions and links to new and updated sites with a focus on information resources, from the El Dorado County Library. Recent listings have included American cultural history and Microbe World. Highly recommended sites are flagged.
www.el-dorado.ca.us/~lib-pl/thisweek.htm

Yahoo! Internet Life. Reviews the latest sites — mostly for fun or personal interest — including the "Incredibly Useful Site of the Day."
www.zdnet.com/yil/welcome.html

Magazines

Internet World. Notable source for Internet information, from a

business and technical perspective. Geared to those who work in the industry.
www.iworld.com/

MacWorld. Visit the online digest of the Macintosh user's bible. Includes product reviews, tech tips, and breaking news from the world of Macs.
http://macworld.zdnet.com/

PC Computing. Online version of the hard-copy standby. Features include news and trends, downloads, and tech support.
www.zdnet.com/pccomp/

TidBITS. Weekly electronic publication covering topics related to the Mac and the Net. Subscribe by e-mail.
www.tidbits.com/

Top 100 Computer Magazines. Links to online magazines about the Web, the Internet, computers, and software.
www.internetvalley.com/top100mag.html

Wired News. The trendy *Wired* magazine covers news from cyberspace and examines cultural issues in the wide, wired world.
www.wired.com/

Mailing list information

CataList Listserv Lists. This is the official catalog of more than 27,000 listservs. Search for lists by country or subject, or browse alphabetically. The site claims to be always up to date since it generates the information automatically from its database.
www.lsoft.com/lists/listref.html

DaSilva's Mailing Lists. A searchable list of more than 7,000 publicly available mailing lists. An updated list is posted monthly. Claims to "personally guarantee that our listings are the most accurate."
www.neosoft.com/internet/paml/

Liszt Newsgroups and Mailing Lists. Search the comprehensive database of more than 90,000 mailing lists, or look up topics in the neatly organized subject tree. Includes a Usenet newsgroups directory and an IRC chat directory.
www.liszt.com/

Topica. All about e-mail lists, including how to start your own.
www.topica.com/

Vivian's List of Lists. A site developed around an original Internet resource for listservs called the "list of lists." The site also provides links to listserv software and mailing list providers.
http://catalog.com/vivian/interest-group-search.html

Software

Jumbo! Shareware. Its database of shareware and freeware programs just keeps growing, to more than 300,000 items. Find everything you need — for all operating systems — in terms of Web authoring tools, spreadsheets, audio, games, animation, screen savers, utilities, home business software, and more.
www.jumbo.com/

Tucows. Thousands of free or almost free software programs, all rated at least three out of five. Download everything you need to make your own Web page, as well as browser accessories, e-mail tools, and chat programs.
http://tucows.com/

ZDNet Software Library. Up-to-date reviews of the latest shareware and freeware programs. Not exhaustive, but everything is highly rated.
www.zdnet.com/swlib/index.html

Technical helps and troubleshooting

BrowserWatch — Plug-In Plaza! Download bells and whistles to make your browsers more productive — including plug-ins that help you download Internet files faster, and surf the Net with accents in other languages.
http://browserwatch.iworld.com/plug-in.html

Computer Viruses Information. Jeff Frentzen has developed this resource for the latest information on computer viruses.
www.pcweek.com/ir/0106/06jia.html

EZUser. Helpful info for beginners and pros on all aspects of the Net, including getting connected, surfing, using e-mail, and building your own Web pages. Send a question via e-mail to Ask the Surf Guru, who posts answers daily.
www.zdnet.com/yil/filters/surfjump.html

MacFixIt. Practical, easy-to-use solutions for technical problems. Updated three times a week with hints from Mac users who contribute quandaries and tips, even on the latest software and hardware. Topics are searchable by keyword.
www.macfixit.com/

Web page development

Bare Bones Guide to HTML. A handy reference to developing Web pages — in many formats and many languages. Includes all the HTML tags in common use.
http://werbach.com/barebones/

HTML Goodies. Lots of treats for HTML authors, with tutorials from beginners to advanced, regular tips and tricks, and even an HTML discussion group.
www.htmlgoodies.com/

HTML Writers Guild. The site of "the first international organization of World Wide Web page authors and Internet Publishing professionals." Geared toward getting new members, but includes links to HTML resources, such as writing HTML and design guidelines.
www.hwg.org/

The Icon Depot. Download free graphics for your home pages: icons, backgrounds, buttons, etc.
www.geocities.com/SiliconValley/6603

Suzanne's Computer Page. Excellent list of resources for developing Web pages, as well as graphics, fonts, multimedia, and shareware.
http://suzann.com/stuff/comp/computers2.htm

Webmaster's Reference Library. Recent articles with Web site design tips and tutorials, including how to use animated GIFs, pop-up menus, and maps.
www.webreference.com/

Other resources

AntiOnline. Regularly updated news and tips about computer security and hacking-related issues.
www.antionline.com/

B&R Samizdat Express. This fast-loading, no-graphics site promises lots of content. Its free electronic newsletter, *Internet-on-a-Disk*, offers Net trends and resources. The newsletter provides interesting commentary and insights on Internet trends. The site also offers links to a number of useful business, education, and disability information sources on the Web.
www.samizdat.com/

BotSpot. News and views on bots and agents, the little robot-like programs that search the Net for data. A bit technical, but very useful for refined, effective searches.
http://bots.internet.com/

CERT Coordination Center. Part of the Carnegie Mellon Software Engineering Institute, this site has virus alerts and other computer security information. Subscribe to its security alerts via e-mail.
www.cert.org/index.html

CNet. News and reviews with the latest from the computer world. Includes hardware and software product reviews, hot Web sites, tips, and how-tos to get the most from the Internet.
www.cnet.com/

Cookie Central. No, it's not a recipe archive — it's a site devoted to educating Net surfers about cookies, those little codes in Web pages that track user information.
www.cookiecentral.com/

December Communications. Excellent set of resources on computer communications, including the monthly *Computer-Mediated Communications* online magazine. Quite technical but very comprehensive.
www.december.com/

Electronic Frontier Foundation. News and views on Internet censorship, freedom of speech, privacy, and other electronic civil liberties.
www.eff.org/

The Informant. "Your personal search agent on the Internet" is a free service that saves your favourite Web sites and search engine queries and let you know via e-mail when there are new or updated pages.
http://informant.dartmouth.edu/

Internet Resources Newsletter. A free monthly newsletter of the latest Web resources for academics, students, engineers, scientists, and social scientists, published by Heriot-Watt University in Edinburgh. Back issues archive more than 5,000 links to journals, conferences, research, and more.
www.hw.ac.uk/libWWW/irn/irn.html

Odd de Presno Online World Resources Handbook. A practical guide to the online world, including tips on surfing smarter to get the most from your time.
http://login.eunet.no/~presno/index.html

Red RockEater. This mailing list, from Philip Agre, is filled with his personal insights on the social and political aspects of computing and networking.
http://dlis.gseis.ucla.edu/people/pagre/rre.html

ZDNet. Independent reviews of computer software, hardware, and games. Advice and how-tos from beginners to advanced.
http://www5.zdnet.com/

3. Government Information

(See also references in Chapter 4)

Canada

Canada Site (Government of Canada). Information on Canada and its government. The official government portal to dozens of federal departments, ministries, agencies, and Crown corporations. Includes telephone directory of federal government employees.
http://canada.gc.ca/

Canadian Parliament. Includes frequently asked questions about the House of Commons and Senate, visitor information, and a reference section.
www.parl.gc.ca/36/main-e.htm

Prime Minister's Office. Information direct from the top. Fact sheets, news releases, and speeches from the prime minister of Canada. (You can even e-mail the prime minister.)
http://pm.gc.ca/

Statistics Canada. Not only the definitive source for official numbers on Canada, but also an excellent place to look for trends to yield story and essay ideas. Free data tables and reports on the land, people, state, and economy. Includes full-text versions of *The Daily*, a daily newsletter of just-released statistics.
www.statcan.ca/start.html

University of Waterloo Electronic Library — Government Information. Well-organized links to government information in Canada, the United States, and other countries. Not always up to date, but easy to navigate.
www.lib.uwaterloo.ca/discipline/Government/

International

Address Directory — Politicians of the World. This directory (also available in downloadable, zipped-file format) contains the snail-mail address, fax/phone number, e-mail address, and Web page (where applicable) for leaders of 195 countries around the world.
www.trytel.com/~aberdeen/

Chiefs of State and Cabinet Members of Foreign Governments. The CIA has compiled lists of top-ranking government officials in hundreds of countries around the world.
www.odci.gov/cia/publications/chiefs/#N

Governments on the WWW. Links to government sites in more than 200 countries and territories. Includes date the link was last updated.
www.gksoft.com/govt/en/

International Information on the Internet. Links to international agencies such as the European Union, Asian Development Bank, and United Nations. More than 30 countries' parliamentary sites are linked.

www-libraries.colorado.edu/ps/gov/int/internat.htm

Organization of American States. Every country in the Americas (except Cuba) is a member of the OAS. The site includes news releases on OAS activities in the areas of democracy, business, human rights, the environment, and others. Information is available in English and Spanish.

www.oas.org/

United Nations Index. Official home pages of U.N. agencies are organized according to subject. Search the Depository Libraries Database for the United Nations System depository library nearest you.

www.unsystem.org/

United Nations Statistics Division. Contains selected data from member countries, compiled by the UN. Includes the Monthly Bulletin of Statistics, with numbers on economic activity, unemployment, consumer prices, and population from countries around the world.

www.un.org/Depts/unsd/mbsreg.htm

USA

American Fact Finder. Operated by the U.S. Census Bureau, this site lets you see community profiles, population and housing facts, and industry and business facts.

http://factfinder.census.gov/

Capitol Newswire. A free service, for journalists only, that e-mails daily news releases from Washington on topics you provide. Focus is on the political, government, and economic scene.

www.global-villages.com/capitolnewswire

Federal Government Information on the Internet. From the Government Publications collection at the University of Nevada Las Vegas library. This collection of links to U.S. government information is useful for anyone doing research in the field. Some sites contain information available only for a fee.

http://library.nevada.edu/govpub/index.html

Federal Information Center (FIC). Operated under contract to the U.S. General Services Administration, the FIC is a portal to federal government information, including links to the Web sites of hundreds of departments and agencies.

http://fic.info.gov/

FedStats. Central clearinghouse for the more than 70 U.S. federal agencies that compile statistics. Links organized A–Z by subject.
www.fedstats.gov/

Full-Text State Statutes and Legislation on the Internet. Links to official and non-official sites containing full-text state constitutions, statutes, legislation, and session laws (bills that have become laws).
www.prairienet.org/~scruffy/f.htm

GPO Pathway Services. The Federal Depository Library Program has developed this site to guide librarians and researchers to U.S. government information. Browse topics, electronic documents, or search federal Web sites by keyword. Includes MoCat, a searchable monthly catalog of U.S. government publications.
www.access.gpo.gov/su_docs/aces/aces760.html

The House of Representatives. News and background information on current House activities, the legislative process, how to contact members, a schedule of events, and links to other government information.
www.house.gov/

Official Federal Government Web Sites of the Executive Branch. Links to dozens of federal departments, agencies, and services, compiled by the Library of Congress.
http://lcweb.loc.gov/global/executive/fed.html

OSU Government Information Sharing Project. Information on U.S. demographics, education, and economics, from Oregon State University. Option for searching databases using selected categories.
http://govinfo.kerr.orst.edu/

The Senate. Information on members, committee activities, daily events, and legislative procedures.
www.senate.gov/

Stateline.org. Facts and information on all 50 states. Includes resources for reporters, such as news releases on important political developments, and contact information for experts willing to be interviewed on state issues.
www.stateline.org/stateglance.cfm

STAT-USA. A service of the U.S. Commerce Department, it provides authoritative information on business, the economy, and trade. Includes the National Trade Data Bank, the U.S. Government's most comprehensive source of international trade data and export promotion information. Most data are available only by paid subscription. For individuals, it costs $150 U.S. for one year, or $50 for 90 days. Some reports are available individually for modest fees.
www.stat-usa.gov/stat-usa.html

UMich Documents Center. Search or browse through this huge collection of sites on local, state, federal, foreign, and international government information. Includes resources for doing class assignments. *Documents in the News* is archived to 1995 with current events.

    www.lib.umich.edu/libhome/Documents.center/

U.S. Census Bureau. Official census demographical data such as population counts, housing statistics, and income figures. Includes a searchable database of its online publications and reports.

    www.census.gov/

U.S. Historical Census Data Browser. The site contains data from every census held between 1790 and 1970. Find out about the people and the economy for every state and county. Made available through the Interuniversity Consortium for Political and Social Research (ICPSR), in Ann Arbor, Michigan.

    http://fisher.lib.Virginia.EDU/census/

U.S. Legislative Information on the Net (Thomas). U.S. congressional information: the Congressional Record, bills, committee reports, current activities, etc. Search the current Congressional session for texts of bills.

    http://thomas.loc.gov/

Webgator — Investigative Resources on the Web. Especially useful for journalists digging for information on people and government programs, this research tool provides access to such investigative resources as courts, parole boards, databases, locators, records access (vital stats, motor vehicles, estates), adoptee resources, state licensing agencies, and more.

    www.inil.com/users/dguss/wgator.htm

The White House. News releases, plus info on presidents past and present. Includes historical information about the White House and the office of the president.

    www.whitehouse.gov

4. Writing Helps

Grammar, etc.

FOG Index. An established method to analyze written material to gauge how easy it is to read and understand.

    www.fpd.finop.umn.edu/groups/ppd/documents/information/
    writing_tips.cfm

An Online English Grammar. A comprehensive, easily indexed textbook-style document from a British educator.

    www.edunet.com/english/grammar/fram-gr.html

A Web of On-line Grammars. Links to reference, learning, and historical grammars for "as many languages as can be found on the Web."
www.facstaff.bucknell.edu/rbeard/grammars.html

Tutorials and guides

Paradigm Online Writing Assistant. Guides you through the essay-writing process, from coming up with ideas to revising your own writing. Covers several essay styles, from informal to academic.
www.powa.org/

Purdue Online Writing Laboratory. More than 130 instructional handouts from Purdue University's online tutorial helps you write anything — research papers, business reports, personal correspondence. Includes links to other university writing tutorials available on the Web and through e-mail.
http://owl.english.purdue.edu/writing.html

5. Media

(News services, broadcast sources, and related links; see also resources listed in Chapter 4)

AJR NewsLink. Operated by the *American Journalism Review*, this has 9,000 links to newspapers, magazines, broadcasters, and news services worldwide.
www.newslink.org/

Artigen World News. Top stories from many sources. Allows a quick scan of headline news arranged by categories: world, health, science, and computers.
www.artigen.com/newswire/world.html

Associated Press (AP). Up-to-the-minute newscasts from the AP wire. Stories go back only a few hours, and include headlines as well as full-text features and transcripts of speeches and debates. Includes video and audio from the day's top news story.
http://wire.ap.org/

Canadian Broadcasting Corporation (CBC). Program information, news items, and live broadcasts from English- and French-Canadian radio and television. Includes Newsworld and Radio Canada International.
www.cbc.ca/

CANOE (Canadian Online Explorer). News briefs from Canadian media. Links to the major Canadian daily newspapers.
www.canoe.com/

CNN (Cable News Network). Read the top stories from news, entertainment, sports, business, travel, and weather. Includes analysis and in-depth coverage. See video clips from the newscasts.
www.cnn.com/

Editor & Publisher Interactive. Browse this global collection of media links by continent, media category, name, and city.
http://emedia1.mediainfo.com/emedia/

EntryPoint. This free, downloadable toolbar stays on your screen and lets you personalize news, stocks, sports, weather, and other information. Formerly called PointCast.
www.entrypoint.com/

First Things First. Extensive list of news sources. Includes links to hundreds of news services, wire services, and features, arranged by state and country.
www.refdesk.com/first.html

Media Literacy Project. Provides information and pointers to Internet resources on issues related to electronic media.
http://interact.uoregon.edu/MediaLit/HomePage

The MIT List of Radio Stations on the Internet. Links to more than 9,000 radio stations around the globe that broadcast on the Internet.
http://wmbr.mit.edu/stations/list.html

MSNBC. A digest of what's on the NBC networks. Enter your zip code to get local news, sports, and weather.
www.msnbc.com/news/default.asp

National Public Radio. Transcripts from the day's top stories, plus analysis and special features. Listen to live newscasts on the hour.
www.npr.org/

News Resource. An eclectic list of links to worldwide news sources from individuals, companies, and organizations. Searchable by region or keyword.
http://newo.com/news/index.html

Pathfinder. Home to Time-Warner media such as *Time, Life, People, Money, Fortune, Sports Illustrated,* and CNN.
http://pathfinder.com/

Reuters. This respected news source puts out news and financial summaries and headlines.
www.reuters.com/news/

Southam News. Searchable links to home pages of members of the

Canadian news chain: newspapers, magazines, and trade publications.
www.southam.com/

6. Online Books

Association des Bibliophiles Universels (ABU). Its home page offers dozens of French-language texts in the public domain from more than 80 authors. Includes links to other services offering French texts.
http://cedric.cnam.fr/ABU/

Bartleby Library. Full-text versions of classics from the 19th and early 20th centuries, courtesy of Columbia University.
www.columbia.edu/acis/bartleby/

Berkeley Digital Library Sun SITE. A collection of digital material, including online books, photographs, archival documents, training materials, and other useful sources. Collections include medieval texts, aerial photography, and 19th-century literature.
http://sunsite.berkeley.edu/index.html

Bibliomania. Full texts of more than 60 classic novels, plus works of non-fiction and poetry.
www.bibliomania.com/

Books on the Internet. Links to many online book sources from universities and publishers, covering politics, history, law, classic fiction, and more.
www.lib.utexas.edu/Libs/PCL/Etext.html

Dial-a-Book Chapter One. This free service bills itself as the "number one provider of book-browsing content on the Internet." You can browse the first chapters, tables of contents, and other excerpts from hundreds of books and dozens of publishers before you buy.
www.dialabook.com/

The English Server. Carnegie Mellon University publishes more than 27,000 humanities texts in many disciplines, from art and architecture to Web design. Also has links to academic journals, libraries, and sites about the Internet.
http://english-server.hss.cmu.edu/

Electronic Literature Foundation. A small but growing collection of classic English texts, many beautifully illustrated.
http://elf.chaoscafe.com/

Free Computer and Internet Online Books. Links to hundreds of full-text computer- and Internet-related books. Some books are available only in summary form.
http://hoganbooks.com/freebook/webbooks.html

History of Economic Thought. McMaster University in Hamilton, Canada has full-text versions of classic economic books by such authors as Karl Marx, John Stuart Mill, and Adam Smith, as part of its syllabus.
http://socserv2.socsci.mcmaster.ca:80/~econ/ugcm/3ll3/index.html

Internetbookinfo.com. The latest book news, as well as an extensive guide to book-related sources on the Internet. Includes links to full-text books.
www.internetbookinfo.com/

Malaspina Great Books. Links to full-text versions of great books, plus citations occurring on the Web, compiled by Malaspina University-College in British Columbia, Canada. Books are arranged by title, author, period, and topic.
www.malaspina.com/

Online Book Initiative. If you access this site, you will find the complete text of many full-length books.
http://ftp.std.com/obi

On-line Books Page. Seachable links to more than 10,000 free full-length books.
http://digital.library.upenn.edu/books/lists.html

Project Gutenberg. One of the original electronic text projects, this is a good source for full-text literary works in the public domain.
http://sailor.gutenberg.org/

Scholarly Electronic Publishing Bibliography. References to online publishing of scholarly works, from the University of Houston.
http://info.lib.uh.edu/sepb/sepb.html

The Universal Library. Hosted by Carnegie Mellon University, the goal of this project is to start a worldwide movement to make all the written works of humankind accessible over the Internet. Includes links to full-text books, journals, and periodicals.
www.ul.cs.cmu.edu/

7. Online Newspapers and Magazines
(See also references in Chapter 4)

Arts and Letters Daily. "An updated report of news and reviews" on philosophy, ideas, culture, history, trends, and other intellectual pursuits. Good set of links to humanities and arts magazines.
www.cybereditions.com/aldaily/

Canadian Electronic Scholarly Network. Canadian electronic publishing resources, including a number of full-text publications and publishing sources.
www.schoolnet.ca/vp-pv/cesn/e/

The Globe and Mail. A seven-day archive of selected parts of this Canadian national newspaper.
www.globeandmail.ca/

HighWire Press. A number of academic journals from Stanford University Libraries, including *Science Magazine*.
http://highwire.stanford.edu/

The Los Angeles Times. Full-text news, entertainment, business, and sports articles. Includes Hunter, a customizable news agent.
www.latimes.com/

The National Post. Daily full-text articles plus archived features from the Canadian national newspaper.
www.nationalpost.com/

The New York Times. A valuable resource of full-text articles. You must register (for free) before accessing the articles.
www.nytimes.com/

Newsbot. Search major dailies by category or date for the latest news.
www.newsbot.com/

NewsDirectory.com. Formerly Ecola Newsstand, this mega-site offers separate indexes for newspapers, magazines, and computer publications, as well as links to thousands of electronic newspapers and magazines.
www.newsdirectory.com/

NewsHub. The latest headlines from several trusted online sources, plus a searchable directory.
http://web.newshub.com/

News Trawler. Simultaneously uses the search engines of major newspapers and magazines to retrieve full-text articles or indexes based on your query.
www.newstrawler.com

The Onion. This is a satirical, politically incorrect e-zine. Where else could you find out about the FBI's raid on a fridge?
www.theonion.com/

Online Journals List. Compiled by the University of Texas Health Science Center, this list links you to sites of journals publishing online in fields of science, news, business, art, and entertainment.
http://bioc02.uthscsa.edu/journal/journal.html

Palmer's Full Text Online. An archive of about one million articles from Britain's trusted *Times* newspaper is available from 1785 to 1870. This searchable database is available only by subscription.
www.chadwyck.co.uk/products/

PubList.com. Searchable links to more than 150,000 American and international print and electronic publications including magazines, journals, e-journals, newsletters, and monographs. Browse by title or subject.
www.publist.com/

Salon. Impressive, well-written e-zine about popular culture. Regular columns and news features about media, entertainment, health, travel, and literature.
www.salon.com/

Serials in Cyberspace. Annotated links to many electronic journals sources. Largely academic focus.
www.uvm.edu/~bmaclenn

Suck. Irreverent zine on pop culture.
www.suck.com/

The Toronto Star. Searchable articles from Canada's largest daily.
www.thestar.com/

The Ultimate Collection of News Links. Links to more than 10,000 newspapers and magazines around the world, grouped according to country and subject tree.
http://pppp.net/links/news/

University of Chicago Press. Offers several of its journals in online editions.
www.journals.uchicago.edu/

Utne Reader. A searchable online site for the print publication. Check out the Alternative Press Awards.
www.utne.com/

The Wall Street Journal. The full-text articles are available by subscription, but there are also links to free business-related sites.
www.wsj.com/

The Washington Post. This giant daily has searchable archives of articles.
www.washingtonpost.com

WebWombat. A simple design helps you easily navigate to thousands of newspapers available online around the globe, even community newspapers in whistle-stop towns. Truly a site to behold.
www.webwombat.com.au/intercom/newsprs/index.htm

8. Resources for Journalists

General

The Beat Page. From agriculture to transportation, common news-room beats are listed with links to sources for reporters covering the issues.

    www.reporter.org/beat/

Canada NewsWire. Get fresh news releases from hundreds of companies, governments, and organizations across Canada. Search the release archives for background, and subscribe to releases from sources you choose, which arrive via e-mail.

    www.newswire.ca/

Canadian Corporate News. Distributes free news releases from Canadian corporations and organizations to working journalists, who must register for a password. You can personalize the service by subscribing to releases from certain sources, which are sent by e-mail.

    www.cdn-news.com/

CAR/CARR Links Page. Links to dozens of sites supporting journalists engaged in computer-assisted reporting. Includes how-tos, story ideas, examples of CAR stories, computer technology news, and discussion groups.

    www.ryerson.ca/~dtudor/carcarr.htm

Columbia School of Journalism Library. Resources are geared to students, but are also useful for professional journalists. Includes copies of master's projects, Pulitzer prize-winning stories, and statistical resources for journalists.

    www.columbia.edu/acis/documentation/journ/journnew.html

ETD Green Pages for Journalists. Links to resources for journalists covering the environment.

    www.etd.ameslab.gov/etd/library/greenpages/Journalist.html

FACSNet. Resources for journalists, organized by the Foundation for American Communications (FACS). Includes a Reporters' Cardfile with contact information for think tanks, advocacy groups, and special-interest organizations, plus links to reporting tools, sources, and background on top issues.

    www.facsnet.org/

Finding Data on the Internet: A Journalist's Guide. Includes a writer's primer on using statistics, with links to data sources listed by subject.

    http://nilesonline.com/data/

Freedom of Information Act Request. The Reporters Committee for Freedom of the Press has an easy-to-fill out form with step-by-step instructions that will automatically generate a letter that you can use when making a freedom-of-information request to U.S. authorities.

www.rcfp.org/foi_lett.html

JournalismNet. It bills itself as "a working journalist's guide to the Net — 150 different Web pages with more than 3,000 links designed to help journalists (and anyone else) find useful information fast." Great starting point for reporters. Includes a hot pick of the week.

www.journalismnet.com/

National Institute for Computer-Assisted Reporting (NICAR). NICAR offers training seminars to teach journalists to use databases and other electronic sources. Includes more than 15,000 resources of investigative stories, tipsheets, reporting guides, and beat sources.

http://nicar.org/

PR Newswire. Lists the latest news releases from U.S. companies and institutions. Free password for working journalists. Search the release archive.

www.prnewswire.com/

Student Press Law Center. This is "a nonprofit organization dedicated to providing legal help and information to the student media and journalism educators." Includes an online legal clinic with answers to FAQs about U.S. censorship, libel, copyright, and freedom of information (including getting access to public documents and meetings).

www.splc.org/

University Wire. College journalists have their own online wire service, with stories added daily. There are also writing pointers, job openings, and links to college newspapers and student journalism organizations.

www.universitywire.com/

U.S. Newswire. Distributes free news releases from U.S. governments, companies, and organizations.

www.usnewswire.com/

WebCentral Guide to Electronic and Print Resources for Journalists. A comprehensive guide to reference materials for journalists and other writers, including search tools, finding experts online, listservs, newsgroups, journalism associations and conferences, and print and online publications about the craft of writing.

www.cio.com/central/journalism.html

Finding experts

Experts.com. Search the database of thousands of experts and consultants, who pay to be listed. Listings include mailing addresses, phone numbers, and e-mail addresses.
www.experts.com/

MediaLink. Offers free online and phone help for journalists to find Canadian experts in every field. Sources pay to be listed in their directory of contacts.
www.medialin.com/

ProfNet. Search this online database of more than 2,500 experts at colleges and universities, corporations, think tanks, national labs, medical centres, and non-profit agencies. You can also send your research query to PR staff at these organizations and have them find you answers within a day or two.
www.profnet.com/

Sources. Search this online database of 5,000 media contacts from more than 1,000 mostly Canadian organizations and companies offering expertise and views on over 12,000 subjects.
www.sources.com/

Yearbook of Experts, Authorities & Spokespersons. Geared specifically to journalists, this is a searchable database of U.S. sources, indexed by subject keyword. People pay to be listed, and are available for interviews.
www.yearbooknews.com/

Media analysis

American Journalism Review/NewsLink. This is a joint venture between *American Journalism Review* magazine and NewsLink Associates, an online research and consulting firm. It includes weekly features from *AJR*, the worldwide online publication lists of NewsLink, and weekly original content created especially for online readers. Articles from back issues are archived.
www.newslink.org/ajrguide.html

The Columbia Journalism Review. Lots of free online content of current and back issues of the publication that critiques media coverage of current events and examines media ethics, technologies, and other issues.
www.cjr.org/

The Freedom Forum. Home of the non-partisan, international foundation dedicated to free press and free speech. Includes news stories on U.S. First Amendment rights, and analysis of free speech issues.
www.freedomforum.org/

Media and Communications Studies. Links to (mostly U.K.) Web resources for the academic study of media and communications. Developed by a professor at the University of Wales.
www.aber.ac.uk/~dgc/media.html

Poynter.org. Promising "Everything You Need to Be a Better Journalist," this site, operated by The Poynter Institute for Media Studies, is updated daily with information, tools, and suggestions. Includes Nelson, a specialized search engine for journalists that collects material from three databases and hundreds of online news sources.
www.poynter.org/

Project Censored. "The primary objective of Project Censored is to explore and publicize the extent of censorship in our society by locating stories about significant issues of which the public should be aware, but is not, for one reason or another." Maintained by Sonoma State University. Online files date back to 1989.
http://censored.sonoma.edu/ProjectCensored/

Associations

American Society of Journalists and Authors. ASJA members are independent non-fiction writers who must meet certain criteria. Site includes articles with tips on copyright, contracts, finding assignments, and other issues relevant to freelancers.
www.asja.org/

Canadian Association of Journalists. This site offers information on becoming a member of Canada's only national organization for professional journalists. Includes its own listservs, plus links to journalism-related sites, including Canadian freedom-of-information resources.
www.caj.ca/

Investigative Reporters and Editors Inc. This grassroots, non-profit organization was formed to help journalists tackle tough stories and issues, and improve the quality of investigative reporting. Search its Resource Centers collection of more than 15,000 investigative reporting stories, tip sheets, and other materials.
www.ire.org/

National Association of Black Journalists. Aimed at promoting and communicating the importance of diversity in newsrooms across the United States. Includes resources for journalists of colour.
www.nabj.org/

National Association of Hispanic Journalists. Includes a chat forum for members to discuss issues pertaining to Hispanic journalists.
www.nahj.org/

National Association of Science Writers. Helpful material for science writers, including freelancers and beginners. Includes discussion lists for non-members.
www.nasw.org/

National Press Club. The place where Washington journalists hang out (physically and cyberially). Lists club information, award winners, upcoming events such as guest speakers, and links to journalists' resources. It is a forum for discussing news, and is non-partisan.
http://npc.press.org/

National Writers' Union. "The union for freelance writers working in U.S. markets." Includes full text of NWU documents on everything from electronic rights to a sample standard journalism contract, plus reactions to media business events that could affect freelancers.
www.igc.apc.org/nwu/

Periodical Writers' Association of Canada. An organization for professional freelance writers, journalists, editors, and communications experts. Includes information on electronic copyright and Canadian publishers who allegedly mistreat freelancers.
www.writers.ca/

Society of Environmental Journalists. Operates the Environmental Journalism Home page, which includes a biweekly tip sheet and links to other sites useful to environmental journalists.
www.sej.org/

The Society for Professional Journalists. The largest professional organization for journalists in the United States. Site includes comprehensive resources on freedom of information.
http://spj.org/

9. Resources for Writers

General

About.com's Guide to Technical Writing. An overview of technical writing resources on the Internet, from expert Gary Conroy.
http://techwriting.miningco.com/

Inkspot. An all-around resource page for writers. Includes Inklings (a free biweekly e-mail newsletter), advice for beginning writers, and resources for children's writers.
www.inkspot.com/

io.Writing. Maintained by volunteers, this site guides writers to other sites for help with finding an agent or publisher; offers reference material and answers to questions on grammar. Includes links to mailing lists, newsgroups, newsletters, publishers, and Canadian resources.

www.deepsky.com/~writing/Overview.html

John Hewitt's Writer's Resource Center. A searchable collection of job listings for writers, editors, and reporters, plus feature articles on freelancing and honing your craft. Includes links to thousands of useful writing sites.

www.poewar.com/

Online Writery. "... An ever-evolving community of writers who offer a relaxing and open environment in which to discuss writing in any form." You can also post writing questions to "cybertutors" at the University of Missouri–Columbia.

http://web.missouri.edu/~writery/

On-Writing's Internet Resource Guide. This is an especially valuable source for information on Web stuff for writers. The publication includes notes on writing courses, classes, and projects, as well as info on publishing e-zines.

www.on-writing.com/ezines.html

Poets & Writers. Comprehensive resources for literary writers. Includes articles with advice, and links to professional development (workshops and conferences, university writing programs), publishers, writing organizations, and literary magazines.

www.pw.org/

Pure Fiction. For writers of contemporary fiction or those who simply love to read. Includes writing advice, and lists of U.K. and U.S. literary agents and publishers.

www.purefiction.com/

Resources for Writing Instructors. Includes links to online composition journals, links to sources for technical and business communications, and a section on writing for the Net.

www.devry-phx.edu/lrnresrc/dowsc/instres.htm

Society of Children's Book Writers & Illustrators. "SCBWI is the only professional organization dedicated to serving the people who write, illustrate, or share a vital interest in children's literature."

www.scbwi.org/

Teachers' & Writers' Collaborative. An organization to bring writers and teachers together to generate ideas and learning materials.

www.twc.org/tmmain.htm

Marketing and publishing

Directory of Literary Agents. Lists agents representing fiction writers (in genres from adventure to young adult) and non-fiction writers (in fields ranging from agriculture to women's issues). Part of the WritersNet site (see entry below).

www.writers.net/agents.html

Hollywood Screenwriters' Network. Sources for screenwriters, including a directory of agents and marketing information.

http://screenwriters.com/screennet.html

Inkspot: Market Info for Writers. Part of the Inkspot writing home page (see entry under "General," above), this includes free writers' classifieds to paying and non-paying markets, as well as tips and links to paying online markets, children's markets, and staff writing jobs.

www.inkspot.com/market/

WritersNet. An Internet resource for writers, editors, publishers, and agents. Includes the Internet Directory of Published Writers, a free, searchable directory of hundreds of published writers on the Net.

www.writers.net/

Associations

American Medical Writers Association. Offers professional development for writers, editors, and producers of medical information.

www.amwa.org/

Canadian Authors' Association. Information on CAA publications, conferences, writing awards, and links to similar resources. Offers advice on contracts for freelance writers.

www.islandnet.com/~caa/national.html

Society for Technical Communication. Members include writers, editors, publishers, and scientists. Includes information on conferences, competitions, seminars, and employment.

www.stc.org/

The Writers' Guild of America, West. Resources and tips for screenwriters. The WGAW is a labour organization representing writers in the motion picture, broadcast, cable, interactive, and new media industries.

www.wga.org

The Writers' Union of Canada. Members are published authors of fiction and non-fiction books. Includes information on membership, writing contests, book contracts, and literary agents.

www.swifty.com/twuc/

10. Resources for Editors

Editing tutorials

Copy Editor Workshops. This site is maintained by *Copy Editor*, a newsletter available by subscription in hard copy only. Courses are held by various groups in book, newspaper, and magazine copy editing; some are summer institutes or correspondence courses.
www.copyeditor.com/workshops.html

CP Copy Talk. This newsletter on the Canadian Press home page discusses Canadian English and views on the *Canadian Press Stylebook*.
www.canpress.ca/

The Editorial Eye. Home page for the commercial newsletter for editors (available in hard copy only, by subscription). Many how-to articles from back issues are free.
www.eei-alex.com/eye/

Magazine Copy Editing. Extensive syllabus from a course offered by magazine copy editor Mindy McAdams. The page includes links to a selection of Web sites related to editing and a reference to a mailing list for editors.
www.well.com/~mmcadams/copy.editing.html

The Slot: A Spot for Copy Editors. Operated by a U.S. copy editor, The Slot includes *The Curmudgeon's Stylebook*, with advice on spelling, style, usage, and grammar. Includes The Book Slot, a concise list of recommended editing reference books.
www.theslot.com/

Associations

American Society of Indexers. Includes links to indexing resources, information on courses and conferences, and reasons to hire a professional indexer.
www.asindexing.org/

Editors' Association of Canada. Information on membership, professional development seminars, and an annual award. Members include freelancers and in-house editors. Links to many editing-related sites.
www.editors.ca/

Freelance Editorial Association. This U.S. association of freelance editors lists members in an online Yellow Pages for potential employers to search.
www.tiac.net/users/freelanc/index.htm

Indexing and Abstracting Society of Canada. Information on membership, publications, and links to resources for indexers.
http://tornade.ere.umontreal.ca/~turner/iasc/home.html

11. Resources for Students

General

Braintrack University Index. Claiming links to more than 5,300 post-secondary institutions in 152 countries of the world, this site bills itself as "the world's most complete education index."
www.braintrack.com/

Campusaccess.com. An all-in-one site for Canadian students, with resources for academic, career, and social life. Includes reference and research links for writing those term papers.
www.campusaccess.com/

College Board Online. Access to SAT information and other useful tools, including a college cost calculator.
www.collegeboard.org/

CollegeNet. You can complete, file, and pay for your admissions applications to more than 350 U.S. colleges and universities, entirely through the Internet. Includes program information on hundreds more institutions.
www.collegenet.com/

Fastweb. Financial aid search throughout the Web. Free scholarship search.
http://web.studentservices.com/fastweb/

Peterson's Education Center. This "education supersite" offers information on North American colleges and universities, choosing a career, studying abroad, summer programs, distance learning, and many other areas.
www.petersons.com/

The Princeton Review. Information on top colleges and help with studying for tests such as the SAT and the LSAT.
www.review.com/

Professor Jones.com. The lighter side of Canadian post-secondary student life, with tips on being organized, socializing, and planning a career.
www.professorjones.com/

Studyabroad.com. Listings for thousands of study-abroad programs in more than 100 countries. Includes the full-text *Studyabroad.com Handbook*, a guide for travelling and studying abroad.
www.studyabroad.com

U.S. News.edu. Apply to U.S. colleges online, choose a grad school, find out about financing, and search top jobs for graduates.
    www.usnews.com/usnews/edu/home.htm

Essays

Best Information on the Net. From affirmative action to welfare reform, links are included to dozens of paper topics, compiled by librarians at St. Ambrose University in Davenport, Iowa.
    www.sau.edu/bestinfo/Hot/hotindex.htm

Homeworkcentral.com. Incredibly comprehensive — more than 100,000 scholar-selected Internet resources for students from grade school to college and beyond, searchable by keyword or more than 10,000 subjects.
    www.homeworkcentral.com/

Researchpaper.com. Claims to be "the Web's largest collection of topics, ideas, and assistance for school-related research projects." Lists more than 4,000 searchable research topics in more than 100 fields. Its writing center provides tips and techniques for writing better papers.
    www.researchpaper.com/

Study help

The Virtual Prof. Physics and chemistry professors at the University of Texas at Arlington provide personalized e-mail help to high school and university students. Basic help (such as sample tests) is free, while one-on-one sessions have a fee.
    www.virtualprof.com/

The World Lecture Hall. This site links to pages from faculty around the globe who have class materials on the Web, such as lecture notes, exams, and course syllabi. Operated by the University of Texas at Austin.
    www.utexas.edu/world/lecture/index.html

Textbooks

Bigwords.com. Buy and sell used college textbooks online. Searchable by author, title, and ISBN.
    http://bigwords.com/

Textbooks.com. Commercial site, selling new and used college textbooks.
    www.textbooks.com/

University Textbooks. Site run by college graduates who wanted to offer discounts to students.
    www.utbooks.com/

Careers

Campus WorkLink and NGR. Formerly the National Graduate Register, this service matches students and graduates with employers across Canada. Operated by the Canadian Association of Career Educators and Employers, and Industry Canada.
http://ngr.schoolnet.ca/

CareerPlanit. Career planning help for college and university students from the National Association of Colleges and Employers, which is "America's bridge between higher education and the world of work."
www.careerplanit.com/

Enter Magazine. This is a neat online magazine for those just starting out on their own and entering the work world. Good resource for students.
www.entermag.com/

Mapping Your Future. Students get help choosing a career and post-secondary courses, and applying for a student loan. Maintained by the U.S. guaranty agencies that participate in the Federal Family Education Loan Program.
http://mapping-your-future.org/

12. Distance Learning

Distance Education Clearinghouse. Sponsored by the University of Wisconsin Extension, this is an award-winning site with wide-ranging information about distance education. The site includes news, course information, and pointers to professional resources.
www.uwex.edu/disted/home.html

Distance Learning on the Net. Includes an overview of distance education for those just getting started as well as numerous links to institutions offering distance education courses, chosen based on their quality and reputation.
www.hoyle.com/distance.htm

Distance Learning Resource Network. This resource, the dissemination project for the U.S. Department of Education Star Schools Program, provides access to information, articles, and programs, from kindergarten to college.
www.wested.org/tie/dlrn/

Globewide Network Academy. This is from an educational non-profit organization that helps with virtual and distance learning through its *Online Distance Education Catalog*, which lists more than 21,000 courses and 1,600 programs.
www.gnacademy.org/

HungryMinds. Extensive database of online courses (some free) ranging from personal interest to university-level.
www.hungryminds.com/

ICDL Database. Distance education database from the Commonwealth of Learning. Information on over 31,000 distance learning courses, more than 1,000 institutions teaching at a distance worldwide, and more than 11,000 references to publications relating to all aspects of distance education.
http://www-icdl.open.ac.uk/

NewPromise.com. Founded by professors at Harvard University and MIT, this site contains information on courses offered online by colleges, universities, and other institutions.
www.newpromise.com/

OnlineLearning.net. Hundreds of tuition-based online continuing higher education courses offered by UCLA. Includes courses in writing, business, computers, and education.
www.onlinelearning.net/

Peterson's Education and Career Center. Career info, studies abroad, and applications for colleges and universities online. Distance learning study tips are included here as well.
www.petersons.com/

Resources for Distance Education. A long list maintained by a professor at Capital Community-Technical College in Hartford, Connecticut, of links to technology, journals, and course providers.
http://webster.commnet.edu/HP/pages/darling/distance.htm

SAVIE Videoconferencing Atlas. "Your information resource on the use of videoconferencing in education." SAVIE stands for Support Action to facilitate the use of Videoconferencing In Education. Includes FAQs on videoconferencing, and links to major distance education resources.
www.savie.com/

SmartPlanet.com. Free trial. Inexpensive monthly or annual membership provides access to hundreds of courses on computers, finance, hobbies, and more.
www.smartplanet.com/

United States Distance Learning Association. Serving pre-kindergarten through grade 12, post-secondary education, home school education, continuing education, corporate training, military and government training, and telemedicine. Includes useful links.
www.usdla.org/

Virtual University. Run by a non-profit group, this is an interesting

selection of free distance education courses, including courses on the Internet and on writing.
    www.vu.org/campus.html

13. Job Resources

Job-hunting help

Career Resource Center. Contains thousands of links to jobs and employers, plus job-related bibliographies, job-hunting tips, software, publications, and event calendars.
    www.careers.org/

OK Info Job Assist Guide. Links and descriptions of the best Web resources for starting your job hunt.
    http://jobs.okinfo.net/

The Riley Guide. Good starting point to begin your job search on the Internet. Includes tips on preparing résumés for the Internet, and where to find job listings and career counseling online.
    www.rileyguide.com/

Job listings

Academic Employment Network. Online job classifieds for U.S. teachers from kindergarten to university, indexed by subject, geographic area, and level of position.
    www.academploy.com/

AJR Newslink JobLink. Claims to be "the world's largest, best-read active listing of journalistic jobs, online or in print." Receive newly posted ads by e-mail.
    http://ajr.newslink.org/joblink/index.html

CareerPath. Search job listings no more than two weeks old, at major U.S. newspapers. Also pulls up postings from employers' Web sites.
    http://new.careerpath.com/

Creative Freelancers' Online. A commercial site that has a database of freelancers with creative talents geared towards the book publishing industry. It's free to list in their directory. Registry includes ad copy writers, conceptual editors, copy editors, ghost writers, grant/proposal writers, indexers, interviewers, journalists, researchers, script writers, technical writers, and translators.
    www.freelancers.com/

Editor & Publisher Classifieds. Hundreds of job postings across the U.S. are available free to anyone looking for work in new media,

newspapers, and publishing, from reporters and editors to advertising executives.
http://epclassifieds.com/

ELance.com. Companies looking for freelancers in fields including writing, design, and photography post requests for proposals on projects. You submit your bid and see what happens.
www.elance.com/

Freelance Online. List your skills in publishing and advertising for $15 a year. Employers post contracts for jobs such as writing and editing, and browse the freelancers' directory for free.
www.freelanceonline.com/

Headhunter.net. Boasts more than 150,000 job listings in all fields and salary levels.
www.headhunter.net/

HRDC National Job Bank. Search jobs posted across Canada (by province and occupation) through regional employment centers. This site is operated by the Canadian government (Human Resources Development Canada).
http://jb-ge.hrdc-drhc.gc.ca/index.html

JobLink for Journalists. Part of the AJR NewsLink site (see entry under section 5, Media), this is a free, searchable listing of job openings in journalism. Includes entry-level and more advanced positions.
www.newslink.org/joblink.html

JobSAT. A Canadian-based service with a searchable database of jobs across North America in the private, public, and voluntary sectors. Claims to maintain the largest employment database in Canada.
www.jobsat.com/

The Monster Board. Based in the U.S., the leading global online career network boasts sister sites in Canada, the United Kingdom, the Netherlands, Belgium, Australia, and France. Search thousands of jobs by location and discipline. Get career advice, read profiles about potential employers, and build your online résumé.
www.monster.com/

Résumé writing

The Best Résumés on the NET. Free tips for writing résumés and covering letters, and handling the ever-important job interview.
http://tbrnet.com/

Curriculum Vitae Tips. Links to free and fee-based resources on

writing résumés, including hot cover letters and defining your skills.
www.cvtips.com/

Resumania! Résumé-writing tips, including funny bloopers from actual résumés, from Robert Half International, the job placement firm.
www.resumania.com/

WorkSearch. Links to the best-rated résumé-writing articles on the Web.
http://members.xoom.com/gwwork/reswri.htm

Part II: General-Interest Resources

1. Arts and Culture

Artsedge. The U.S. arts and education information network from the Kennedy Center and the National Endowment for the Arts. Includes arts education news, links, database, and curricula for the performing and visual arts.
http://artsedge.kennedy-center.org/

Canadian Arts, Culture, and Heritage Network. Gateway to selected Canadian heritage and arts resources.
http://cnet.unb.ca/achn/

Gateway to Art History. Well-organized links to sites chock-a-block with information on art through the ages.
www.harbrace.com/art/gardner/

Guide to Museums and Cultural Resources. This guide, compiled by the Natural History Museum of Los Angeles County, lists museums and other cultural institutions around the world, according to continent. Tour a virtual exhibit, or find out how to visit a museum while on vacation. Links include "cybermuseums" that exist only on the Web.
www.lam.mus.ca.us/webmuseums/

Internet Art Resources. The latest news, book reviews, and discussion forums on visual art galleries, artists, and museums.
www.artresources.com/

World Wide Arts Resources. Billing itself as "the definitive gateway to the arts on the Internet," this site lets you choose from hundreds of arts categories: galleries and museums, film, theater and dance, antiques and crafts, and more.
http://wwar.com/

The World-Wide Web Virtual Library: Architecture. Searchable database of architecture resources, compiled by the University of Toronto.

www.clr.toronto.edu:1080/VIRTUALLIB/arch.html

2. Business and Economics

Bloomberg News. Catch the latest stock quotes, market news, financial analysis, book reviews, and business deals from the Bloomberg News Service.

www.bloomberg.com/

Canadian Financial Network. Descriptive links to more than 6,000 Canadian and international, mostly free financial resources, from accountants to stocks.

www.canadianfinance.com/

Companies Online. Directory of more than 100,000 U.S. public and private companies, including sales figures, Web and street addresses, and number of employees.

www.companiesonline.com/

Company Sleuth. Promises "the inside scoop" on U.S. publicly traded companies, including stock quotes, insider trades, news, and patent registrations. Provides personalized daily updates via e-mail.

www.companysleuth.com/

The Economist. Selected articles from the current issue of the weekly newsmagazine. Search the archives after a free registration.

www.economist.com/

Hoover's Online. Access to Hoover's Masterlist database of more than 15,000 companies. More detailed information available by subscription.

www.hoovers.com/

Individual.com. This commercial site is a free, customizable daily business online news service. Information from more than 50,000 public and private companies.

www.individual.com/

Inflation Conversion Factors for Dollars 1800 to the Present. Handy calculator to determine U.S. prices in current or past dollars, adjusting for inflation.

www.orst.edu/dept/pol_sci/fac/sahr/sahr.htm

International Business Resources on the WWW. Well-chosen links to sites around the globe, compiled by Michigan State University.

http://ciber.bus.msu.edu/busres.htm

International Monetary Fund (IMF). Search the publications database

of this United Nations agency, and download full texts of some titles.
www.imf.org/external/

Scout Report for Business and Economics. Sites carefully chosen and reviewed by librarians and content specialists with the Internet Scout Project at the University of Wisconsin–Madison. Focus is on resources for students, faculty, and librarians in business and economics.
wwwscout.cs.wisc.edu/report/bus-econ/current/index.html

Sookoo! Specialized search engine and subject tree for business strategy.
www.sookoo.com/

Statistics Canada. Free government tabular data and analytical reports on Canada's economy and industrial sectors.
www.statcan.ca/

Strategis. The Canadian government's detailed, searchable information about Canadian industry: company information, business information by sector, technology, laws, regulations, and consumer information.
http://strategis.ic.gc.ca/

10K Wizard. Free full-text search of the latest U.S. Securities and Exchange Commission (SEC) filings, including corporate annual reports, of nearly 70,000 companies.
www.10Kwizard.com

U.S. Census Bureau Economic Indicators. The latest economic indicators and other economic data from the U.S. Census Bureau.
www.census.gov/econ/www/

VIBES—Virtual International Business and Economic Sources. More than 1,500 links to free international business information: full-text files of articles and research reports, graphs, and statistical tables from government and private sources on Web. Maintained by a business librarian at the University of North Carolina at Charlotte.
http://libweb.uncc.edu/ref-bus/vibehome.htm

WebEc. A compendium of academic economic resources on the Web, compiled by the University of Helsinki, Finland.
http://netec.wustl.edu/%7eadnetec/WebEc/WebEc.html#scm

World Bank (IBRD). Retrieve news releases, publications, and the annual report from the United Nations agency.
www.worldbank.org/

3. Disability Information

Council for Disability Rights. National American news affecting the disability community.

www.disabilityrights.org/

disABILITY Information and Resources. Comprehensive, searchable subject tree with links to disability information and issues.

www.eskimo.com/~jlubin/disabled.html

Disability Mailing Lists. Instructions on subscribing to about 25 mailing lists, including Disabled Student Services in Higher Education.

www.vicnet.net.au/vicnet/Adrian/dislist.htm

4. Education

AskERIC Service for Educators. An information service of the ERIC System (Educational Resources Information Center) based at Syracuse University. Ask questions about education via e-mail and receive a response within two business days. Also, download hundreds of lesson plans and info guides.

http://ericir.syr.edu/

Canadian Association of Learned Journals. Dozens of Canadian academic journals are accessible from this site: either their tables of contents, or full-text articles. Subjects include law, history, engineering, literature, public policy, and more.

www.ccsp.sfu.ca/calj/

Chronicle of Higher Education. Weekly news source for college and university faculty and administrators. There is a fee to access the full-text articles, but the links page to further Web resources is free.

http://chronicle.merit.edu/

Education Index. "Guide to best and most useful education-related sites on the Web," from prenatal to post-secondary.

www.educationindex.com/

Education Week Web Edition. The online edition of "America's Education Newspaper of Record." Full-text articles of education news, special reports, plus the monthly *Teacher Magazine*. Archived articles are searchable.

www.edweek.org/

Educause. Bills itself as "the most extensive collection of higher education information technology materials assembled on the Web."

www.educause.edu/

Electronic School. Focuses on instructional technology for K–12 teachers and administrators.
www.electronic-school.com/

From Now On: The Educational Technology Journal. Valuable publication with articles about technology and learning.
www.fno.org/

Global Campus. Educational institutions share resources on this database, with links grouped according to discipline. Maintained by California State University.
www.csulb.edu/gc/index.html

HighWire Press. Calling itself "one of the three largest free full-text science archives on Earth," with more than 120,000 free articles. This site has links to scientific journals compiled by Stanford University Libraries.
http://highwire.stanford.edu/

Kathy Schrock's Guide for Educators. This daily updated site is an Internet guide for classroom teachers, including links arranged by subject, and professional development.
http://school.discovery.com/schrockguide/

The Node.org. Resources for teaching with technology.
http://thenode.org/

OISE — Ontario Institute for Studies in Education/University of Toronto. Information on this graduate school of education, plus links to Canadian education on the Web.
www.oise.on.ca/

RAMS. Home to FEDIX, "the largest and most updated database of research and education funding opportunities." Its free e-mail service notifies subscribers of research and education grants from the U.S. government in their area of interest.
www.rams-fie.com/

SchoolNet. Comprehensive links to Canadian information related to education, including searchable links to more than 1,000 learning resources.
www.schoolnet.ca/

United Nations Educational, Scientific and Cultural Organization (UNESCO). News releases; information on UNESCO programs and publications; worldwide statistics on education, science, and culture.
www.unesco.org/

U.S. Department of Education. Includes education headlines, guides to the department, and reports and links to educational organizations and statistics.

www.ed.gov/

5. Entertainment

HollywoodNet. Extensive reference to help you find your way around Hollywood. Includes links for writers.

www.screenwriters.com/indexmain.html

The Hollywood Reporter. You must pay to subscribe to full-text articles of the entertainment trade magazine, but its Hollywood Hyperlink Web site directory has links to entertainment industry sites with free information.

www.hollywoodreporter.com/

Internet Movie Database. Free information on more than 200,000 movies and TV shows, 400,000 actors, and 40,000 directors.

http://us.imdb.com/

Rolling Stone. *Rolling Stone* magazine has a one-stop interactive shop for information on music genres, artists, books and magazines, even concerts.

www.rollingstone.tunes/com/

The Ultimate Band List. News and information on the latest from the music scene, including live online chats with hot bands.

www.ubl.com/

Ultimate TV. Your guide to the current shows airing on major American networks.

www.ultimatetv.com/

6. Environment

Amazing Environmental Organization Web Directory. Search engine and subject tree of resources from environmental organizations, mainly in the U.S. and Canada.

www.webdirectory.com/

CoVis Online Resources: Geosciences Resources. A neatly presented page of links to academic and other resources in the geosciences.

www.covis.nwu.edu/Geosciences/resources/environment.html

EcoPortal. "Full text searches of reviewed environmental Internet content." Includes topic-specific sites on biodiversity, forests, urban sprawl, oceans, and the ozone layer.

www.eco-portal.com/

EnviroLink. A beautifully designed site from the EnviroLink non-profit organization, aimed at providing the most comprehensive, up-to-date environmental news and resources available online.
http://envirolink.org/

Environment Canada's Green Lane. Environment Canada's Web site provides information about current issues and access to Canadian regional environmental sites. Free publications provide information on environmental legislation, educational resource guides, and fact sheets.
www.ec.gc.ca/

National Hurricane Center. Issues hurricane and tropical storm warnings in the U.S.; also has historical and general information.
www.nhc.noaa.gov/

The Right to Know Network. Provides information and databases on the environment, housing, and sustainable development.
www.rtk.net/

United Nations Environment Programme (UNEP). Search UNEP documents online, and follow links to other international environmental resources.
www.unep.org/

7. Health

Achoo. A good jumping-off point for finding health resources on the Net, geared to medical professionals and anyone with an interest in navigating through the mountain of online health material.
www.achoo.com/

AEGIS (AIDS Education). AIDS Education Global Information System bills itself as the "largest HIV/AIDS Web site in the world," updated hourly. Includes the HIV Daily Briefing with the latest news.
www.aegis.com/

American Medical Association. The AMA home page includes links to medical journals, plus a searchable database of more than 650,000 licensed U.S. physicians, according to name, specialty, and location.
www.ama-assn.org/

CancerNet. Cancer information from the U.S. government's National Cancer Institute. This is a comprehensive resource documenting the latest research. Includes pointers to related global sites.
wwwicic.nci.nih.gov/

Complete Home Medical Guide. Free, full-text guide from

Columbia University College of Physicians and Surgeons. Chapters include "Symptoms and Diagnoses" and "Treatment and Prevention of Disease."
    http://cpmcnet.columbia.edu/texts/guide/

Hardin Meta Directory of Health Sources. Metalist of medical and health sources on the Net, from the University of Iowa.
    www.lib.uiowa.edu/hardin/md/index.html

Health Canada. News releases and links to health resources arranged by topic.
    www.hc-sc.gc.ca/english/

Healthfinder. "A free gateway to reliable consumer health and human services information developed by the U.S. Department of Health and Human Services." Includes links to publications, databases, and self-help groups.
    www.healthfinder.gov/

Internet Mental Health. Free encyclopedia of mental health information.
    www.mentalhealth.com/

Medical Matrix. A valuable, well-organized free directory of medical sites evaluated by physicians and medical librarians. Lists only sites determined to be of high quality, with an emphasis on resources useful to health care professionsals.
    www.medmatrix.org/

Mediconsult. Independent information on chronic medical conditions, which "must pass a rigorous clinical review process" before being listed on the site.
    www.mediconsult.com/

Merck Manual. Look up medical ailments, their symptoms and treatments in the full-text, free online version of this tried-and-true guide. Written for medical practitioners, but also understandable by lay people.
    www.merck.com/pubs/mmanual/

National Food Safety Database. Topical information on U.S. food safety.
    www.foodsafety.org/

NetVet. A place to start for healthy pets, compiled by a veterinarian.
    http://netvet.wustl.edu/

Psychnet. From the American Psychological Association, this site offers resources for psychologists, the public, and students.
    www.apa.org/

QuitNet. Need to stop smoking? From the Massachusetts Department of Public Health, this site provides lots of help.
www.quitnet.org/

World Health Organization (WHO). Statistics, reports, health advisories, and other useful information from the United Nations agency. Includes links to other health care sites.
www.who.ch/

8. History

English Server: History and Historiography. Site for full-text historical documents. Historical works are mainly U.S.-based but diverse, including material ranging from Bodleian Library manuscripts to the 1947 testimony of Walt Disney before the House Committee on Un-American Activities.
http://eng.hss.cmu.edu/history/

The History Net. Featuring hundreds of articles from history magazines published by Cowles Enthusiast Media, such as *Historic Traveler, Civil War Times,* and *World War II* magazine.
www.thehistorynet.com/

Horus' Web Links to History Resources. Award-winning site of academic historical resources, from the University of California, Riverside.
www.ucr.edu/h-gig/horuslinks.html

HyperHistory. More than 1,800 files of timelines, events, graphics, and maps tell the story of 3,000 years of world history.
www.hyperhistory.com/

Internet Medieval Sourcebook. Extensive resource for medieval documents and information, from the Fordham University Center for Medieval Studies.
www.fordham.edu/halsall/sbook.html

The Smithsonian Museum. Check out their libraries and archives pages as portals to the museum's extensive collections.
www.si.edu/start.htm

WWW-VL History. The University of Kansas Department of History has links to hundreds of sites of interest to historians, as part of the WWW Virtual Library.
www.ukans.edu/history/VL/

9. Human Rights

AAAS Directory of Human Rights Resources on the Internet. Descriptions and links to hundreds of human rights organizations

around the globe, compiled by the American Association for the Advancement of Science.
   http://shr.aaas.org/dhr.htm

Country Reports on Human Rights Practices. The U.S. Department of State writes annual reports on almost every country, assessing how well each one adhered to United Nations human rights laws based on incidents that occurred in that year.
   www.state.gov/www/global/human_rights/hrp_reports_mainhp.html

Death Penalty Information Center. News, debate, and information on the U.S. death penalty.
   www.essential.org/dpic/

Human Rights Research and Education Centre. Resources compiled by the University of Ottawa. Includes the Human Rights Bibliography, a database of 18,000 Canadian and international documents, which requires a fee to access.
   www.uottawa.ca/hrrec/index.html

International Labour Organization (ILO). The site for this United Nations agency includes information on international labour standards and human rights.
   www.ilo.org/

United Nations High Commission for Refugees (UNHCR). Information about UNHCR and refugees, back issues of *Refugees* magazine, news releases on refugees' situations worldwide, and a teacher's guide to using the site in class.
   www.unhcr.ch/

10. Language

Center for the Advancement of Language Learning. Foreign language learning resources and links are collected for learners and teachers. Includes links to periodicals in popular and less common foreign languages.
   http://call.lingnet.org/

Dave's ESL Cafe. English as a second language: links for teachers and students, compiled by an ESL teacher.
   www.pacificnet.net/~sperling/eslcafe.html

The Human-Languages Page. "A comprehensive catalog of language-related Internet resources." Each one of dozens of languages has a collection of links to online translating dictionaries, tutorials to learn the language, newspapers and texts in that language, and schools that teach the language.
   www.june29.com/HLP/

Language Dictionaries and Translators. Resources for learning foreign languages, including online courses and software, plus sites devoted to etymology:.

http://rivendel.com/~ric/resources/dictionary.html

Web of Online Grammars. Links to online grammar resources for more than 20 languages. Here you will find Russian, English, Greek, Hebrew, and many more language learning helps.

www.facstaff.bucknell.edu/rbeard/grammars.html

WWW Links in Spanish. Resources for students of Spanish, including links to Spanish-speaking countries around the world, from Grand Valley State University.

http://www2.it.gvsu.edu/~fernandr/spnlnks.htm

WWW Resources for French as a Second Language Learning. Learn to conjugate verbs, test your French grammar, and find other resources for learning French.

www.uottawa.ca/~weinberg/french.html

11. Law

General

Decisions of the International Court of Justice. Information on the United Nations' World Court is presented by the Cornell University Law School. There are full texts of some decisions, plus information on the court, its judges, and the U.N. Charter.

www.law.cornell.edu/icj/

Federal Bureau of Investigation. Home page for the FBI includes a library of reports, and updates on its Ten Most-Wanted fugitives list.

www.fbi.gov/homepage.htm

FedLaw. Comprehensive source for legal research links. This site includes links to a number of legal information documents and sources, such as *Roberts' Rules of Order* and help in finding missing persons.

www.legal.gsa.gov/

FindLaw. A legal-based search engine, with U.S. legal resources arranged under broad categories such as legal subject index, law firms and lawyers, cases and codes, and foreign and international law.

www.findlaw.com/

International Centre for Criminal Law Reform and Criminal Justice Policy. This Vancouver-based non-profit institute is affiliated with the United Nations. The site contains its publications and reports, an events listing, an online forum, and links to partners around the world.

> www.icclr.law.ubc.ca/

Law.com. "A single, comprehensive destination for legal information and e-law services on the Web." Designed for legal professionals and students, this commercial site also has breaking legal news and resources of interest to journalists, writers, researchers, and editors.

> www.law.com/

LegalDocs. This is a source for U.S. legal documents such as contracts and wills. Includes assistance in completing the forms; many are free but some have a fee.

> http://legaldocs.com/

Oyez Oyez Oyez. From the U.S. Supreme Court, information about major constitutional cases.

> http://oyez.at.nwu.edu/oyez.html

Supreme Court of Canada. Searchable full-text judgments dating back to 1989.

> www.droit.umontreal.ca/doc/csc-scc/en/index.html

Virtual Canadian Law Library. Includes links to national and international legislation, Canadian law libraries, firms, faculties, publishers, directories, and conferences.

> www.droit.umontreal.ca/doc/biblio

Copyright
(See also Appendix C)

Canadian Copyright Law. Copyright lawyer Lesley Ellen Harris answers questions about Canadian copyright law: what users of copyright material should know, and how creators such as writers can protect themselves.

> www.mcgrawhill.ca/copyrightlaw

Copyright and Fair Use Site. Stanford University's resources on U.S. copyright, including statutes, guidelines, Web sites, and mailing lists.

> http://fairuse.stanford.edu/

The Copyright Website. Award-winning source of information on U.S. copyright, especially as it relates to the Internet.

> www.benedict.com/

Guide to Copyright. An online booklet explaining Canadian copyright laws, from the Canadian Intellectual Property Office.

> http://strategis.ic.gc.ca/sc_mrksv/cipo/cp/cp_guide-e.html

U.S. Copyright Office Home Page. Offering general information and publications on U.S. copyright, including online forms to register copyright for your writing.
http://lcweb.loc.gov/copyright/

12. Literature and Book Reviews

BookWire. Bills itself as "the book industry's most comprehensive and thorough online information source." Includes industry news, features, book reviews, author interviews, and links to thousands of book-related sites.
www.bookwire.com/

Children's Literature Web Guide. Outstanding children's literature source with many useful links for writers.
www.ucalgary.ca/~dkbrown

CM: Canadian Review of Materials. Reviews Canadian books, videos, and other materials for children and young adults, from the Manitoba Library Association.
www.umanitoba.ca/cm/

Internet Book Information Center. Myriad book resources, including the *Dear Fellow Book-Lovers (DFBL)* newsletter, which provides daily news and reviews about the world of books.
http://sunsite.unc.edu/ibic/

The Pulitzer Prizes. Information on winners of the journalism, letters, drama, and music awards. Includes an archive of the full-text works of the prize winners dating to 1995, including photos, editorial cartoons, and music clips.
www.pulitzer.org/navigation/index.html

SharpWeb. Society for the History of Authorship, Reading, and Publishing. Research source for those with an interest in the history of books.
www.indiana.edu/~sharp

TopBestsellers.com. Bestseller news, reviews, analysis, and trivia. A great resource for bibliophiles.
www.topbestsellers.com/

Online bookstores

Amazon Bookstore. Search millions of titles and order them by e-mail. The site is updated daily with reviews of the latest releases. A personalized service notifies you by e-mail when your favourite author releases a new title.
www.amazon.com/

Bibliofind. More than 10 million used, rare, and out-of-print books and periodicals for sale.
www.bibliofind.com/

BookWeb: Bookstore Directories. Search for storefront bookstores inside and outside the U.S. Lots of specialty bookstores.
www.bookweb.org/directory/

Chapters.ca. Buy thousands of books online from the Canadian bookstore chain Chapters.
www.chapters.ca/

13. Locations

Canadiana. Canadian publications online, exchange rates, travel, technology, and more.
www.cs.cmu.edu/Unofficial/Canadiana/

European Institute for the Media. An indispensable source of information for global journalists from this non-profit research organization. Includes full-text research reports for many Eastern European countries.
www.eim.org/

Famous Canadians Theme Page. Links to sites with information on noteworthy Canadians past and present.
www.cln.org/themes/famous.html

50states.com. Facts and stats on state geography, history, people, economy, and politics.
www.50states.com/

Hotzones. Information for journalists (and others) who might be travelling to hazardous zones, such as Bosnia and Chechnya. Information includes health and safety tips, plus contact telephone numbers gleaned from journalists familiar with the region.
http://moon.jrn.columbia.edu/NMW/hotzones/

Library of Congress Country Studies. Free book-length reports on 100 countries, written by social scientists. Looks at their history, politics, economics, society, and defense systems.
http://lcweb2.loc.gov/frd/cs/cshome.html

U.S. State Home Pages. Links to official U.S. state home pages.
www.globalcomputing.com/states.html

World Factbook. Data and facts on almost every country in the world, compiled annually by the Central Intelligence Agency.
www.odci.gov/cia/publications/factbook/index.html

Yahoo! Canada. Links to Canadian-based sites.
www.yahoo.ca/

14. Mathematics

Hypatia. This directory of researchers in computer science and pure mathematics contains their published papers. Also has links to hundreds of university computer science and mathematics departments worldwide.

http://hypatia.dcs.qmw.ac.uk/

Math and Science Gateway. This Cornell Department of Education hotlist includes resources for maths and sciences, for teachers and students in grades 9–12.

www.tc.cornell.edu:80/Edu/MathSciGateway/

WWW Virtual Library Mathematics List. Links to general resources, specialized fields, math department Web servers, math software, and electronic journals.

http://euclid.math.fsu.edu/Science/math.html

15. Politics

CNN/Time AllPolitics. Political news and views, including poll results, special reports, and E-Wire, a free weekly e-mail update on U.S. politics.

http://allpolitics.com/

Doug Ingram's News and Politics Page. Links to sources on the left, the right, and various other ideologies.

www.shrubbery.com/ingram/politics.html

Mother Jones. Political news and views from the left.

www.mojones.com/

Political Information.com. A search engine for sites on U.S. politics and policy.

www.politicalinformation.com/

Richard Kimber's Political Science Resources. Source for international political information, political theory links, newsgroup archives, etc. Run by a former political lecturer at Keele University in England.

www.psr.keele.ac.uk/

World Political Database. Free access to public information on world leaders past and present.

http://personales.jet.es/ziaorarr/

16. Science and Technology

Biological Sciences World Wide Web Server. This site from

California State University attempts to "consolidate existing WWW biological science teaching and research resources."
http://arnica.csustan.edu/

Eisenhower National Clearinghouse Science. Intended as a teaching resource, this site is a good starting point for a wide range of science topics.
www.enc.org/

Frank Potter's Science Gems. A well-organized collection of links to more than 11,000 of the Web's best science resources, for students, teachers, and scientists.
www.sciencegems.com/

Inquirer's Guide to the Universe. An interactive online exhibit, with a helpful list of space science resources.
www.fi.edu/planets/planets.html

inScight. A daily information service with the latest science news. Includes an archive. Compiled in conjunction with Science, the weekly magazine published by the American Association for the Advancement of Science, and Academic Press.
www.apnet.com/inscight

The MAD Scientist Network. Scientists from around the world will field questions in different areas of science. Answers to previous questions are contained in a searchable database.
www.madsci.org/

Math and Science Gateway. Resources for science and math teachers and students in grades 9–12, from the Cornell Theory Center.
www.tc.cornell.edu:80/Edu/MathSciGateway/

New Scientist. Some full-text articles from *New Scientist* magazine are available free online.
www.newscientist.com/

Science in the Headlines. Science news headlines and background information from the National Academy of Sciences.
http://nationalacademies.org/headlines/

Smithsonian Institution. Information on the institution's exhibits, galleries, and research centres.
www.si.edu/start.htm

Telecommunications Act of 1996 Homepage (Benton Foundation). This site provides a hypertext version of the Act and various related documents, including a telecommunications glossary.
www.benton.org/Policy/96act/

Today at NASA. Daily updates of the space agency's activities,

including press releases and live Webcasts of current NASA missions.
www.hq.nasa.gov/office/pao/NewsRoom/today.html

Tree of Life Home Page. Resources about the diversity and history of Earth's organisms are linked together like a giant tree.
http://phylogeny.arizona.edu/tree/phylogeny.html

17. Social Sciences

ChildStats.gov. Easy access to U.S. federal and state statistics on children and their families, including income, health, and education.
www.childstats.gov/

Coombsweb Social Sciences Server. Maintained by the Australian National University, this is a searchable repository for social sciences, humanities, and Asian studies research and related bibliographies.
http://coombs.anu.edu.au/

H-Net Humanities and Social Sciences Online. "An interdisciplinary organization of scholars dedicated to developing the enormous educational potential of the Internet."
http://h-net2.msu.edu/

National Center for Charitable Statistics. Lots of data on U.S. nonprofit organizations. Includes the Center on Nonprofits and Philanthropy.
http://nccs.urban.org/

Research Resources for the Social Sciences. Very thorough set of links to social science sources. Includes many links to Canadian sources and to news, journalism, and statistical sites.
www.socsciresearch.com/

Social Sciences Directories. From Western Connecticut University, Internet directories for anthropology, geography, economics, political science, sociology, etc.
www.wcsu.ctstateu.edu/socialsci/homepage.html

18. Sports

My Virtual Reference Desk — Sports Sites. Links to sports information and news.
www.refdesk.com/sports.html

SearchSport. Search engine and subject tree for sites devoted to professional and amateur sports.
www.oldsport.com/search/main.htm

Sportsdogs.com. The latest sports headlines grace this search engine for pro sports.
www.sportsdogs.com/

Sport Quest. "The Virtual Resource Centre for Sport Information." Includes resources on professional and amateur sports and fitness, and many Canadian links.
www.sportquest.com/

19. Travel

Excite Travel. Includes guides to more than 5,000 travel destinations worldwide.
www.excite.com/travel/

Fine Travel Magazine. Online e-zine with free full-text articles on selected destinations around the world. Aimed at appealing to travelers, not tourists.
www.finetravel.com/finetrav/

Fodor's. The perennial travel experts provide a personalized mini-guide, giving tips and information on cities and countries worldwide.
www.fodors.com/

Lonely Planet. Online source for off-the-beaten-track travel news and information.
www.lonelyplanet.com.au/lp.htm

Passport Services. For U.S. travelers, this is a source for obtaining downloadable forms for passports and birth certificates.
http://travel.state.gov/passport_services.html

U.S. State Department Travel Warnings and Consular Information Sheets. Find out what documents you need to visit foreign countries, and what to watch out for when you're there.
http://travel.state.gov/travel_warnings.html

World Travel Guide. Search for world travel information, by country or city, all within the site itself.
www.wtgonline.com/

20. Women

Canadian Women's Internet Association. Motherhood, sisterhood, spirituality, and more.
www.herplace.org/

FeMiNa. Search engine and subject tree of sites for, by, and about women, from arts and humanities to society and culture.
http://femina.cybergrrl.com/explorer.htm

WebGrrls. Sites focused on technology for women.
www.webgrrls.com/wexplorer.htm

Women. Links to all kinds of resources celebrating women's achievements, including book reviews.
www.fjg.com/women/

21. Odds and Ends

The Anagram Engine. You can spend endless hours playing with this program, which jumbles words and phrases into other combinations. It's "snuff tool" (that is, "lots of fun").
www.easypeasy.com/anagrams/

ARThur. Access a database of more than 30,000 images from selected Web sites.
www.isi.edu/cct/arthur/

Consumer World. Thousands of consumer resources on the Internet. Includes free e-mail newsletter.
www.consumerworld.org/

Consumer's Resource Handbook. This publication from the U.S. Office of Consumer Affairs includes advice to consumers and contact information for consumer protection.
www.pueblo.gsa.gov/

DisInformation. An alternative look at the news.
www.disinfo.com/

ImageFinder. Locate images from classic image collections, including Smithsonian Institution Photographs.
http://sunsite.berkeley.edu/ImageFinder/

Kelley Blue Book Used Car Guide. Tips on buying and selling cars, with average prices for new and used vehicles.
www.kbb.com/

Knowledge Hound. How to do almost anything for free — make a pizza, fix a zipper, you name it!
www.knowledgehound.com/

National Fraud Information Center. Alerts consumers to scams, including Internet fraud.
www.fraud.org/

Robin Garr's Wine Lovers' Page. All you need to know about wine, including the basics for beginning oenophiles.
www.wine-lovers-page.com/

SearchMil.com. Search engine for more than one million military-related pages, ranked according to popularity.
www.searchmil.com/

SOAR: Searchable Online Recipe Archive. More than 67,000 free recipes to tempt your tastebuds.
http://soar.berkeley.edu/recipes/

Weathernet. Bills itself as "the most comprehensive and up-to-date source of weather data on the Web."
http://cirrus.sprl.umich.edu/wxnet/

Citing online sources

"Journalists are accustomed to trusting that the people they interview by telephone are who they say they are, but online communication presents much more serious challenges to identity. E-mail is unique as a medium because it is faceless and voiceless but seems very personal, sometimes more personal than a phone conversation. At the same time, it is easy to forge and alter. All the textual artifacts that give e-mail its distinctive look — its memo format, its time and date stamp — can be falsified from any computer keyboard with a simple text editor, and transmitted with little effort or skill on the part of the sender."
— DENISE CARUSO, *COLUMBIA JOURNALISM REVIEW*, MAY/JUNE 1998

Writers, researchers, and journalists have been struggling for the last few years with questions about whether and how to use information they receive online through e-mail messages, newsgroup postings, or Web sites. Slowly, some guidelines have begun to emerge.

For journalists and writers

In the early days of the Internet, when asked how they cited online resources, journalists described a variety of approaches. Some reported that they quoted from e-mail messages freely without identifying that the quotes were obtained electronically. After all, they pointed out, journalists rarely specify whether quotes were obtained over the telephone or in a personal interview, and they didn't believe they should treat e-mail any differently. Others said they quoted from e-mail messages and newsgroup postings, but only by adding qualifiers such as "said someone who identified herself as Jane Doe in a message posted to the Internet newsgroup misc.kids." They admitted such qualifiers made their prose less than graceful.

Still others were forbidden by their editors from treating e-mail messages as anything other than leads. They were instructed that all direct quotes were obtained the old-fashioned way, by telephone, or in face-to-face interviews. Now, that approach seems to be standard at most news organizations. In the last few years, people have come to realize how easy it is to hide one's identity online. So, writers, journalists, and editors believe they have to take steps to verify what they read online before using it in their published work.

There is still a debate over whether postings to newsgroups should be considered public information and therefore open to publication by news professionals. Some argue that newsgroup postings cannot be considered private because millions of people around the world can read them, so journalists are free to quote from them in their stories. Others argue that people should not find themselves quoted in a news story unless they have been asked for, and have given, permission.

News organizations across North America have now developed policies that essentially instruct their own staff to treat newsgroups as public places when it comes to their own postings — i.e., never post something using your real identity that you would not be prepared to have published. At the same time, they have instructed their reporters to treat the postings of others as private and not to be published without the express permission of the poster.

For researchers

There is also growing consensus among researchers about how to cite online references in formal footnotes and bibliographies. There are now several resources online where such guidelines are outlined.

One of the most popular sites is **Bibliographic Formats for Citing Electronic Information** located at:

    www.uvm.edu/~ncrane/estyles/

The site provides citation formats based on Xia Li and Nancy Crane's book, *Electronic Styles: A Handbook for Citing Electronic Information*, published by Information Today, Inc. (1996). It offers guidelines for two common citation styles, that of the American Psychological Association (APA) and that of the Modern Language Association (MLA). It also adds embellishments to represent the unique features of electronic information.

Another site entitled the **Web Extension to American Psychological Association Style (WEAPAS)** offers modifications to the APA style to accommodate Web resources. Look for this site at:

    www.beadsland.com/weapas/

For those interested in the University of Chicago style as well as the APA and MLA styles, the University of Minnesota's **Online Writing Centre** has produced an easy-to-use Web site with guidelines to all three. You will find it at:

    www.rhetoric.umn.edu/Rhetoric/Student/Graduate/MStewart/ECD/modmain.htm

Another site with guidelines for citing sources using a variety of different styles is the **English Pages Online Citation Guide** at:

    http://longman.awl.com/englishpages/citation.htm

Copyright issues

"Nearly all of the information you find via electronic sources has copyright protection. Electronic journals, news wires and electronic versions of print material have the same copyright protection as material that has been traditionally published. You should work under the assumption that information posted to news groups and discussion lists is copyrighted ... The best alternative is to secure the permission of the creator of the work you wish to quote."
— RANDY REDDICK AND ELLIOT KING, *THE ONLINE JOURNALIST* (2ND ED.).
ORLANDO, FL: HARCOURT BRACE, 1997, P. 211.

Copyright, once considered a boring topic for seminars and conferences, is now attracting widespread attention, thanks to the Internet. The dissemination of information and programs over the Net has raised many questions about how copyright applies to online material. While many of the copyright violations on the Net have to do with pirating software or music, there are other problems, too, of more concern to writers, researchers, and journalists.

Essentially, copyright is the exclusive right, protected by law, of any author of a creative work to control the copying of that work, whether it includes a copyright notice or not. While the details of copyright laws vary from jurisdiction to jurisdiction, most allow for some limited use of short excerpts of copyrighted material for what is called "fair use" in the United States and "fair dealing" in Canada. They also allow use of material considered "in the public domain." It's how those two exceptions are interpreted regarding online material that causes confusion and debate.

The first question is how much of an online publication can be excerpted and quoted verbatim without permission under the rules about fair use. Downloading or printing material for personal use is allowed under the fair-use provisions of copyright laws. But if you want to distribute something to someone else online or off, only short excerpts of some else's work can be reproduced for such purposes as criticism, commentary, news reporting, scholarship, or research.

The second question is whether any information online can be considered in the public domain. Brad Templeton, former publisher and editor of the electronic newspaper *ClariNetNews* maintains a Web site called "Ten Big Myths about Copyright Explained" in which he writes:

> Nothing modern is in the public domain anymore unless the owner explicitly puts it in the public domain. Explicitly, as in you have a note from the

author/owner saying, "I grant this to the public domain." Those exact words or words very much like them.

Some argue that posting to Usenet implicitly grants permission to everybody to copy the posting within fairly wide bounds, and others feel that Usenet is an automatic store and forward network where all the thousands of copies made are done at the command (rather than the consent) of the poster. This is a matter of some debate, but even if the former is true (and in this writer's opinion we should all pray it isn't true) it simply would suggest posters are implicitly granting permissions "for the sort of copying one might expect when one posts to Usenet" and in no case is this a placement of material into the public domain.

It is also clear that people cannot post copyrighted information on their Web pages without permission. They can, however, include links on their pages to the original source of the copyrighted material, making it easy for their readers to access the material.

One of the more extensive sites for information about copyright and fair use is at **Stanford University**. It includes information and links related to the use of copyrighted material by individuals, libraries, and educational institutions. It can be found at:
http://fairuse.standford.edu/

One other aspect of copyright that should concern writers and journalists is who owns the copyright to their work. If they do not sign over the electronic rights to their work, they maintain copyright. But these days, many publishers include clauses in their contracts with writers demanding that those rights be turned over to the publisher.

Associated Press policy for using electronic services

These rules apply to the Internet, commercial online services, and other electronic resources used by staff of The Associated Press.

The 1997 guidelines are intended as guardrails against careless use of the new electronic vehicles.

Some of the points should seem obvious, because our old values of accuracy and responsibility remain the same. Other rules will seem new, as the technologies are new.

But no rules can protect us entirely. Use common sense, be cautious, and think before you act. If you're not sure, ask for guidance. What you do on a computer can be awfully hard to take back.

1. Accounts on AP's electronic services are intended to aid the business and professional activities of AP staff. The accounts are for business use only, the same as AP portable computers and cellular phones. If you have private business to conduct, use a private account. Although you can access the AP accounts from home, this is not a license to connect for personal use.

    Remember that connecting to electronic services uses a limited resource that costs the AP money. The same Internet connections and dial-up ports are needed to file and distribute AP text, photos, graphics, audio, video, and data.

2. Each account is assigned for use only by the AP staffer. Sharing accounts is not permitted. No generic or departmental accounts will be assigned. Choose a password that would be difficult to guess (not any form of a family name or birthdate, not a word in any dictionary). The system will require you to include two characters not in the English alphabet, and to change your password frequently.

3. Conduct business on electronic services as if you are appearing at a public meeting representing the AP, or writing a letter on company letterhead. After all, every message sent with an AP account is stamped "ap.org." What you write, even in private e-mail but especially in posts to lists and Usenet newsgroups, could be forwarded to millions of people, and no doubt will be saved somewhere by somebody. Many mailing lists that are erroneously thought of as private are routinely archived on Usenet newsgroups or the World Wide Web, which are public. Even World Wide Web servers collect at least part of the addresses of all users visiting them. And any user of AP's Internet server can see generally what activity any other user is

doing. In short, if you wouldn't want your online activity to be shown on CNN or in Times Square, don't do it on the Internet or America Online.

4. AP has longstanding rules against News employees participating in political activities or taking sides on matters of public debate. These rules apply to electronic communication as well. Do not express opinions about products, companies or individuals. Non-news employees, who may be unaccustomed to these rules, should remember that Internet readers won't know whether a user from ap.org is a newsperson. Even what a non-News employee does can reflect on AP's newsgathering.

5. To do their work, AP staff need to participate in electronic discussion groups on professional or technical topics. Posting to other groups of general interest should be limited to seeking information. For example, a reporter doing a story on prostate cancer may post to a medical group, or a group for older men. Or a technician may seek help on a software discussion group.

6. When participating in discussion groups, be sure the reader knows that you are not stating AP policy. Someone reading a message from you@ap.org won't know AP's organizational structure. If complaints or questions come to you because you are identified as an AP employee, refer them to the appropriate supervisor.

7. Act as if the laws on libel and privacy apply to electronic communications. Remember that the laws of other jurisdictions may be more restrictive than your own. Respect the privacy of individuals, who may not be aware that their comments in electronic forums could be distributed by journalists. Do not quote private individuals or public figures from online communications unless you verify the identity of the author and assure yourself that the author meant to speak publicly. Often, if you contact someone online, it's best to conduct an interview by telephone or in person. If you have online discussions to gather information, make sure the other party knows you are a working journalist. Although some Web pages and browsers allow sending of what's called anonymous e-mail, send only mail with your name and AP affiliation attached.

8. Apply the strictest standards of accuracy to anything you find on electronic services. The Internet is not an authority; authorities may use it, but so do quacks. Make certain a communication is genuine before relying on it as a source for a news story. More than one person may share an e-mail address, and e-mail addresses and Web page sponsorship can easily be faked. Ask yourself, "Could this be a hoax?" Do not publish on the wire any electronic address without testing to see that it's a working address, and satisfying yourself that it is genuine. Apply, in other words, your usual news judgment.

9. Respect the copyrights of individuals and organizations, including the AP. Do not forward or post anyone's material without permission. Do not post or send to individuals any proprietary AP material, including news stories, photos, graphics, audio, video, data, or any internal communication.

10. Abide by the courtesies of the electronic community. Courtesy requires basic technical competence. For example, be careful not to send a message to a mailing list that was intended for only one user. If you subscribe to a mailing list, keep a copy of the message telling you how to unsubscribe. Don't type in all caps; people will think you're shouting. Avoid the "flame wars" that easily erupt when conversations are conducted online. And, because AP's Internet server has limited capacity, clean out your mailbox and home directory routinely, and log off when you're not using the system.

The Internet Handbook for Writers, Researchers, and Journalists

Glossary

Anonymous FTP   One of the Internet's main attractions is its openness and freedom. FTP (*file transfer protocol*) Internet sites let you access their data without registering or paying a fee.

Applet   A small program written in a computer language called Java. Applets can be embedded in HTML pages to produce animations, calculations, and other dynamic elements.

Archie   A search tool that helps you locate information stored at hundreds of anonymous FTP sites around the Internet.

ASCII (Ask-ee)   American Standard Code for Information Interchange, plain text without formatting that's easily transferred over networks. (Got a question? Just ASCII.)

Backbone   The main communication line that ties computers at one location with those at another. Analogous to the human nervous system, many smaller connections, called nodes or remote sites, branch off from the backbone network. (Don't slip a disk!)

Bandwidth   An indication of how fast information flows through a computer network in a set time. Bandwidth is usually stated in thousands or millions of bits per second. See Ethernet.

Baud   Unit of speed in data transmission; maximum channel speed for data transmission.

BinHex   A method for converting non-text files into ASCII. BinHex is one of the ways of coding a file (such a word processed file) for transfer through electronic mail. MIME and Uuencode are two other ways of coding messages for e-mail transfer.

Bit   A single-digit number in base-2, specifically, either a 1 or a zero. The smallest unit of data that can be handled by a computer. It takes eight bits (a byte) to represent one character (e.g., a letter or number) of text.

BITNet   One of the precursers of the Internet, BITNet stands for Because It's Time Network. BITNet involved a network of educational sites, and many listserver discussion groups originated on BITNet.

Bounce   Return of e-mail that contained a delivery error.

Bozo filter   A program that screens out unwanted and irritating incoming messages. (Both messages and filter can be breaches of netiquette.)

bps   Bits per second: a measure of how fast data are moved from one place to another. For example, a 28.8 modem can move 28,800 bits per second.

Browser   A software program that is used to access various kinds of Internet resources. Netscape and Internet Explorer are examples of Web browsers.

Bulletin board   A computerized "meeting space" where individuals log onto a (usually) quite small computer and exchange messages and computer programs.

Byte   A set of bits that represent a single character. There are eight bits in a byte.

kilobyte (KB) = 1,024 bytes of data
megabyte (MB) = 1,048,576 bytes
gigabyte (GB) = 1,000 megabytes
terabyte (TB)= 1,024 gigabytes

CCITT   The Consultative Committee for International Telegraph and Telephone makes technical recommendations concerning data and telephone communications systems.

CD-ROM   Compact Disk Read-Only Memory. CD-ROM can hold the equivalent of 1,500 floppy disks. It is the most popular carrier of interactive multimedia programs that feature audio, video, graphics, and text.

Chat and talk   A chat program lets you electronically "converse" online with many people simultaneously. A talk program is like a personal telephone call to a specific cybernaut — only in text. See IRC (Internet Relay Chat).

CIX   Commercial Internet eXchange, a group of companies providing a range of specialized services, such as financial data, for a fee.

Client   A desktop personal computer that communicates with other PCs and larger computers, called servers or hosts.

Client/server computing   Combining large and small computers in a network so data are readily available when and where they are needed. For example, in a retail store, information is collected from customers at point-of-sale terminals. Then it is directed to a server in the store and forwarded to a larger enterprise server for inventory management and other functions.

The Internet Handbook for Writers, Researchers, and Journalists

CNRI Corporation for National Research Initiatives, an organization that is exploring different ways to use a national information highway.

Computerphobe Someone who is afraid of using computers. (Now, who could that be?)

Cookie A piece of information sent by a Web server to a Web browser as a kind of memory device. A cookie enables the server to tell where you left off in a previous interaction, or what set of preferences you might have chosen. Cookies allow the computer to "remember" login or registration information, and they allow customized information to be sent to the user.

Copyright The legal right granted to a copyright owner to exclude others from copying, preparing derivative works, distributing, performing, or displaying original works of authorship of the owner. Copyrighted works on the Internet are protected under national and international laws. Examples of copyrighted works include literature, music, drama, pictures, graphics, sculpture, and audio-visual presentations.

Cybernaut Someone who explores the vast world of cyberspace where only the brave dare venture.

Cybernetics In 1948, Norbert Wiener coined this term to describe the "entire field of control and communication theory, whether in the machine or in the animal." *Cyber-* has become a popular prefix for many Internet terms: cyberlingo, cyberwonk, cybercast. (What hath Norbert wrought!)

Cyberspace Word coined by William Gibson in his 1984 sci-fi novel, *Neuromancer*. Refers to all the sites that you can access electronically. If your computer is connected to the Internet or a similar network, then it exists in cyberspace. Gibson's style of fiction is now called *cyberpunk*.

Daemon Web software on a UNIX server; a program running all the time in background, providing special services when required.

Dedicated line A telephone line that is leased from the telephone company and used for one purpose. In cyberspace, dedicated lines connect desktop systems to servers.

DES The Data Encryption Standard represents a set of criteria for providing security for transmitted messages. Standards like this lay the groundwork for electronic commerce over the Internet.

Dial-in connection A way to access a computer on the Internet using a PC, telephone line, and modem. Slower than connecting directly to the Internet backbone, but provides accessibility from many sites and does not require specialized equipment.

Domain   The system of organizing the Internet according to country or type of organization, such as educational or commercial. For instance, an educational institution such as The Franklin Institute Science Museum in Philadelphia, USA would have ".edu" as a suffix to its domain name (*sln.fi.edu*). Other typical suffixes include ".com" for commercial organizations and ".org" for non-profit groups.

Domain Name System (DNS)   The scheme used to define individual Internet hosts.

Download   When you transfer software or other information from the Internet to your PC. *Upload* refers to transferring content to a server from a smaller computer or a PC.

E-mail   Electronic mail. The term has several meanings: the network for sending messages; the act of sending a message electronically; and the message itself. It all comes down to using a computer network to send electronic messages from one computer user to another. Fortunately, all the electronic junk mail you receive is environmentally friendly since it generates no paper — unless you print it.

Electronic commerce, e-commerce   Buying and selling products and services over the Internet.

Ethernet   (Not an illegal fishing device.) A common type of network used in corporations. Originally limited to 10 million bits of information per second, technical improvements have raised Ethernet bandwidth (how fast information flows through a computer network in a set time) to 100 million bits of information per second — in concept, enough speed to transfer the entire contents of the *Encyclopaedia Britannica* in one second.

E-zine   A Web-based electronic publication.

FAQ   List of Frequently Asked Questions (and answers) about a particular topic. FAQs can usually be found within Internet discussion groups that focus on specific topics. Read FAQs before asking a question of your own — the answer may already be waiting.

Finger   A program that provides information about someone connected to a host computer, such as that person's e-mail address.

Firewall   A mechanism to keep unauthorized users from accessing parts of a network or host computer. For example, anonymous users would be able to read documents a company makes public but could not read proprietary information without special clearance.

Flame   Rude or ludicrous e-mail. Advice: Don't reply to flames, just extinguish them by deleting.

Freenet   A community computer network, often based on a local library, that provides Internet access to citizens from the library or sometimes from their home computers.

FTP   File transfer protocol; a program that lets you transfer data from an Internet server to your computer.

Gateway   A system that connects two incompatible networks. Gateways permit different e-mail systems to pass messages between them.

Gigabyte   A unit of data storage that equals about 1,000 megabytes. A CD-ROM holds about two-thirds of a gigabyte (650 million bytes). That's enough space to hold a full-length motion picture. (Don't forget the popcorn.)

Gopher   A old Internet system that used menus and special software on host computers for easy navigate around the Internet. (The area of navigation was referred to as *GopherSpace*.)

GUI   Graphical User Interface, software that simplifies the use of computers by letting you interact with the system through graphical symbols or icons on the screen rather than coded commands typed on the keyboard. Microsoft Windows and the Apple Macintosh operating systems are the two most popular GUIs.

Hacker   The best reason of all to put up a firewall. Originally, some of these pranksters breached computer security systems for fun. Computer criminals have created chaos on computer networks, stealing valuable data and bringing networks down for hours or days. See DES (Data Encryption Standard).

Home page   The main page for a site on the Internet. Businesses, organizations, and individuals may post home pages to the World Wide Web. Also can be the first page that appears when you call up your browser.

Host   A server computer linked directly to the Internet that individual users can access.

Hotlists   Frequently accessed URLs (*uniform resource locators*) that point to Web sites. Usually organized around a topic or for a purpose, e.g., a hotlist of search engines on the Web.

HTML   *HyperText Markup Language*; the codes and formatting instructions for interactive online Internet documents. These documents can contain hypertext, graphics, and multimedia elements, including sound and video.

Hypermedia   Multimedia and hypertext combined in a document.

Hypertext   An electronic document that contains links to other documents offering additional information about a topic. You can activate the link by clicking on the highlighted area with a mouse or other pointing device.

Information Highway   Also referred to as I-Way, Internet, Infobahn, Autostrada, National Information Infrastructure (NII), Global Information Infrastructure (GII). The network is currently "under construction" to make existing computer systems more efficient at communicating and to add new services, such as electronic commerce, health information, education, polling — just use your imagination.

Infrastructure   The base on which an organization is built. It includes the required facilities, equipment, communications networks, and software for the operation of the organization or system. But most important, it includes the people and the relationships that result.

Internet   An interconnection of thousands of separate networks worldwide, originally developed by the U.S. federal government to link government agencies with colleges and universities. Internet's real expansion started recently with the addition of thousands of companies and millions of individuals who use graphical browsers to access information and exchange messages.

InterNIC   The *Inter*net Network Information Center. The NIC is run by the U.S. National Science Foundation and provides various administrative services for the Internet.

Intranet   A private, internal network for a company or organization that uses the same kind of software that is used on the Internet. A company intranet, for example, could be used as the basis for an internal electronic mail network and for posting company procedures and announcements in the form of Web pages.

IP   Internet Protocol, the communications language used by computers connected to the Internet.

The Internet Handbook for Writers, Researchers, and Journalists

IP number   A unique address assigned to a computer on the Internet. Individual domain names (such as *nasa.gov/*) are all associated with an IP number that designates the location of the computer. IP numbers are made up of four parts separated by dots, e.g., 145.122.241.2.

IRC   Internet Relay Chat, a software tool that lets you hold keyboard conversations. See Chat and talk.

ISDN   The Integrated Services Digital Network defines a new technology that delivers both voice and digital network services over one "wire." More important, ISDN's high speed enables multimedia and high-end interactive functions over the Internet, such as video-conferencing.

ISP   Internet Service Provider: a company or institution that provides access to the Internet. Most often, an ISP will sell dial-in access to a computer that is connected to the Internet.

Java   A programming language invented by Sun Microsystems that is specifically designed for writing programs that can be quickly downloaded to your computer and run. It is possible to write a Java program to do many of the things we currently use a personal computer for, such as word processing.

Knowbots   An intelligent program or "agent" that you can instruct to search the Internet for information about a particular subject. While still in their infancy, these agents are the focus of intense software research and development.

LAN   *Local area network*, a collection of computers in proximity, such as an office building, that are connected via cable. These computers can share data and peripherals such as printers. LANs are necessary to implement client/server computing since the LAN allows communication to the server.

Listserv, listserver   An electronic mailing list used to deliver messages directly to the e-mail addresses of people interested in a particular topic, such as journalism.

Luddite   Person who believes that the use of technology will diminish employment.

Lurking   The practice of reading about a newsgroup in order to understand its topics and tone before offering your own input.

Mbone   Multicast backbone, an experimental system that sends video over the Internet.

MIME (Not Marcel Marceau.) Multipurpose Internet Mail Extensions, an enhancement to Internet e-mail that lets you include non-text data, such as video and audio, with your messages.

Modem (*Modulator-dem*odulator) A device that allows your computer to connect to another computer over telephone lines.

Mosaic This sophisticated, graphical browser application lets you access the Internet World Wide Web. After the introduction of Mosaic in 1993, the use of Internet began to expand rapidly.

Multimedia Multiple forms of communication including sound, video, video-conferencing, graphics, and text delivered via a multimedia-ready PC.

Net surfing The practice of accessing various Internet sites to see what's happening. (A whole new world for the Beach Boys!)

Netiquette Standards of behavior and manners to be used while working on the Internet. For example, a message in ALL CAPS can mean the sender is shouting.

Network People connected via computers to share information.

Newbies Newcomers to the Internet.

Newsgroup The Internet version of an electronic discussion group, where people can leave messages or post questions.

Newsreader A program that helps you find your way through a newsgroup's messages.

Newsserver A computer that collects newsgroup data and makes it available to newsreaders.

NFS The Network File System lets you work with files on a remote host as if you were working on your own host.

NNTP Network News Transport Protocol, an extension of TCP/IP protocol; describes how newsgroup messages are transported between compatible servers.

NSFNet Large network run by the U.S. National Science Foundation. It is the backbone of the Internet.

Packet A collection of data. Packet switching is a system that breaks data into small packets and transmits each packet independently. The packets are combined by the receiving computer. (Danger! We may have crossed over into geekspace.)

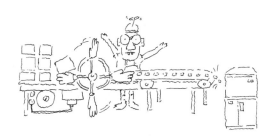

Point of presence (POP)   A method of connecting to an Internet service locally. If a service company has a POP in your area, then you can connect to the service provider by making a local call. POP is also used for *post office protocol*.

Postmaster   The person at a host who is responsible for managing the mail system.

PPP   *Point-to-point protocol* connects computers to the Internet using telephone lines; similar to SLIP.

Protocol   Rules or standards that describe ways to operate to achieve compatibility.

Public domain software   Computer programs you may use and distribute without paying a fee. Shareware is distributed at no cost, but you are expected to pay the author a fee if you decide to keep and use it.

Resource hog   A program that eats up a large amount of network bandwidth.

Router   A device that acts as a traffic signal to direct data among different networks. Routers often have enhanced processing capabilities that enable them to send data on an alternative path if one part of the network is busy.

Server   Equivalent to a host, a machine that works with client systems. Servers can be anything from PCs to mainframes that share information with many users.

Service provider   A company that provides a connection to the Internet.

SIG   Special Interest Group. (Also nickname of Wagnerian opera hero.)

sig   Signature file. A combination of characters that can be automatically appended to any outgoing electronic message — e.g., the sender's name, address, phone/fax numbers, or a humorous or thought-provoking quotation.

SLIP   Single Line Internet Protocol, a technique for connecting a computer to the Internet using a telephone line and modem. Also called *Serial Line Internet Protocol*. See PPP.

Smiley   Manipulating the limited potential of keyboard characters to show goodwill, irony, or other emotions with a "smiley face." There are a number of text-based effects, for example, (–: and ;–).

SMTP   Simple Mail Transport Protocol, the Internet standard for transmitting electronic mail messages.

Sneakernet   The 1980s way of moving data among computers that are not networked, by storing data on floppy diskette and running the disks from one computer to another. (Very good for the cardiovascular but not the information system.)

SNMP   Simple Network Management Protocol is a standard of communication of information between reporting devices and data collection programs. It can be used to gather information about hosts on the Internet.

Spamming   Indiscriminately sending a message to hundreds or thousands of people on the Internet, e.g., unsolicited junk mail. Not good netiquette.

Streaming   Audio, video, and text available for viewing on your computer even as it is in the process of downloading to your system from a Web site.

T1   Telecommunications lingo for digital carrier facility used to transmit information at high speed. (T1 is to the Web what passing gear was to the '64 Cadillac.) If you want to turbocharge your network backbone, many companies are expanding to the even faster T3 service.

TCP/IP   Transmission control protocol/Internet protocol; communication rules that specify how data are transferred among computers on the Internet.

Technogeek   A person who is so involved with computers and the so-called "virtual world" as to have only a tenuous hold on the real world. (But then again, what is reality?). Similar terms: nerd, propeller head, techie.

Telnet   Software that lets users log on to computers connected to the Internet.

Token ring   Featured on LANs (local area networks) to keep control messages (tokens) moving quickly among the users.

UNIX   Software operating system that provides the underlying intelligence to Internet servers. Browser programs have helped increase Internet usage by hiding the complexities of UNIX from the average cybernaut.

URL Abbreviation for *uniform resource locator*, the Internet addressing system. (What's your URL?)

Usenet *User Network*, an array of computer discussion groups, or forums, that can be visited by anyone with Internet access.

Virus Destructive computer program that invades by means of a normal program and damages the system.

WAIS Wide Area Information Servers search through the Internet's public databases for specific information. For instance, you could locate information about a particular medical break-through by searching through the research libraries of teaching hospitals connected to the Internet. (WAIS and means!)

Web site A sequence of related Web pages normally created by a single company or organization.

Webster Habitué of Web sites and other cyberplaces.

White Pages Because they remind people of the old telephone book, services that list user e-mail addresses, telephone numbers, and postal addresses.

Winsock *Windows Sock*et, an extension program designed to let Windows applications run on a TCP/IP network.

Worm This computer program replicates itself on other systems on the Internet. Unlike a destructive virus, a worm passes on useful information. (Maybe we're fishing too deeply!)

WWW The World Wide Web is a hypertext-based collection of computers on the Internet that lets you travel from one linked document to another, even if those documents reside on many different servers.

Index

Reddick, Randy 94, 256
Reuters 8, 87
reverse directories 101, 102–103
robots 53
Rolling Stones 8
Rose, Marshall T. 116
RTVJ-L 111

S
Salon 9, 39
Schaadt, Nancy 117
Scout Report 32, 132
search assistant software 61, 127
Search Engine Watch 47, 171
search engines 47, 52–63, 69,
    114, 122
    advanced search 49, 55, 57,
    58, 59, 60, 68, 71
    concept search 58
    links search 120
    news search services 87
    specialized 62
    See also metasearch tools
search strategies 46–47, 70–71,
    121
search tools 44–71, 121
    comparison of 68, 69–70
    tutorials 48, 75
Search.com 83
Seeing Ear Theater 12
Seltzer, Richard 155, 190
Shareware.com 185
shell account 177
Sher, Julian 44, 116
Sherlock 2 175
SLiRP 177
Snap 27, 32, 51, 61
software
    downloading 15, 184–186
    online resources 207
Sotheby's 4
Sources Online 106
spiders 53
Spire Project 81
SPJ-Ethics 112
SPJ-L 112
starting pages (for journalists)
    65–67
Stoll, Clifford 3
Stone, Barbara 133
streaming media 33–35
Strom, David 116
studioNEXT 12
StuffIt 187
subject directories 47, 48–51, 69

subject guides 73–75
subject trees See subject directories
Submit It! 170
Switchboard 104
Sympatico 32, 39, 177
SyncIt 126
Syracuse University (Newhouse
    School) 109

T
Tango 21
Tate, Marsha 133
Teaching Journalism Online 67
telnet 25, 78–79, 85, 270
Templeton, Brad 256–257
Terkel, Studs 1
Thomas Legislative Information
    92
Time Daily 89
Times, The 89
Tomlinson, Ray 13
toolbar 20–21, 23–24
Tucows 35, 41, 61, 78, 159, 183,
    188

U
Ultimate Collection of Newslinks
    90
Ultimate E-Mail Directory 101
Ultimate Yellow Pages 75
UnCover 52
United Nations Web Site Locator
    92
URLs 23, 24–26, 271
USA Today 89
Usenet 106, 107, 271
    See also newsgroups

V
video 8, 11–12, 14, 33–34,
    35–38, 58, 59
videoconferencing 41–42
viruses 188–189
Visible Human Project 6
Voice of the Shuttle 75

W
Walsh, Nancy 129
Washington Post 87, 89, 90–91
    Federal Internet Guide 90–91
Web accelerators 179
Web browsers 10, 11, 18, 19–30,
    135, 136, 138, 142, 144, 147,
    157–158
    features 26

History feature 24, 26, 29
    navigating 23–24
    Netscape vs. Internet Explorer
    19–21
    offline 183–184
    preferences 26–28
    tips 29–30
    See also Internet Explorer,
    Netscape, Opera
Webcam 42
WebCATS 77
Web conferencing 38–39
WebCrawler 62
WebData 83
Web Devil 194
Web fax 16
WebFerret Pro 127
Web page development 134–173
    design 160–162
    file formats 155–156
    graphics 153–158, 162–163
    home pages 161
    links 144–145, 147, 148,
    162, 169
    navigation 162
    online resources 207–208
    registering sites 170–171
    tags 138–149, 153
    writing style 164–168
Web phone 15
WebRings 171–172
Web Sleuth 127
Web walks 42
WebStripper 184
WebTabs 126
WebTV 42
WebWhacker 184
WebZip 184
Weinman, Lynda 157, 173
West's Legal Directory 106
White House, The 92, 93
White Pages 100
Whois 119
Whowhere 101
wildcards 57, 59
Will-Harris, Daniel 172
Williams, Margo 48
Windows information 185
WinStar Telebase 85
WinZip 187
Wiseman, Ken 72
WIW-L 112
wizards 27
World Fact Book See CIA World
    Fact Book